WHIRLW

The Whirlwind's cockpit was extremely compact: just 32-inches (81-cm) wide at its widest point. During the aircraft's life, the layout was subject to several changes, most significantly the relocation of the undercarriage and flap controls from the starboard sidewall to the left side of the instrument panel as seen here. To the right of the instrument panel are the pairs of engine instruments. Most RAF fighters used a simple rudder bar, but the Whirlwind was fitted with the Lysander's 'footplate' style rudder pedals, even though these were much disliked by A&AEE's test pilots. (*Niall Corduroy*)

WHIRLWIND
WESTLAND'S ENIGMATIC FIGHTER

NIALL CORDUROY

FONTHILL

L6844 went to Farnborough in early 1940 for testing in the RAE's full-size wind tunnel. The propellers were replaced by dummy spinners and the undercarriage was removed to allow the attachment of pylons used to support the aircraft in the tunnel. (*Niall Corduroy*)

FONTHILL MEDIA
www.fonthillmedia.com

A CIP catalogue record for this book is available from the British Library

Typeset in 10pt on 12pt Sabon LT Std
Typesetting by Fonthill Media
Printed and bound by CPI Group (UK) Ltd, Croydon, CR0 4YY

ISBN 978-1-78155-430-2

Contents

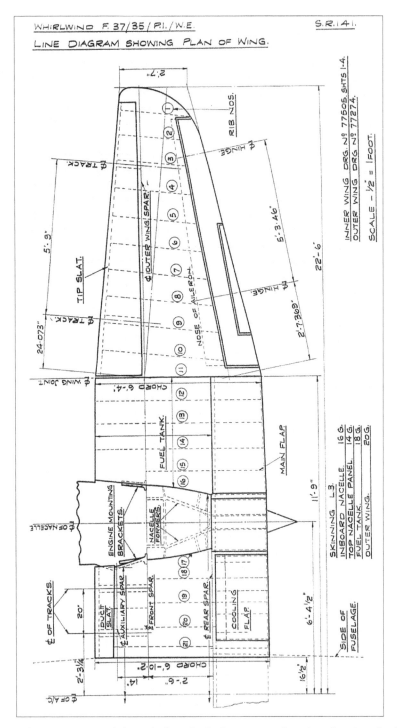

General arrangement of the Whirlwind's high-aspect ratio wing showing the large automatic slats on the outer panels (locked shut early in the Whirlwind's career) and the placement of the three wing spars in the centre section. (*Agusta Westland*)

Acknowledgements

My sincere thanks for their assistance in researching this book go to the staff of the Public Records Office of the National Archives, Kew, England; Peter Davies, Peter Deverett and their colleagues at the RAF Museum Department of Research and Information Services, Hendon; David Gibbings and the late Fred Ballam of AgustaWestland; Dave Birch of the Rolls-Royce Heritage Trust and Dr Francesca di Florio of the Martin-Baker Aircraft Company. I would also like to thank a number of individuals who have provided information or leads to new sources of information, photographs or simple encouragement and stimulating discussion: Robert Bowater, Jerry Brewer, the late Regis Decobreck, Paul Fitzgerald, Stuart Hawkins, Paul McMillan, James and John Munro, Ian le Seur and the late Ray Wood. Finally, I must thank my lovely wife Karen for her patience, support and encouragement over the years that this book has been in preparation.

The second Whirlwind prototype, L6845, seen at Yeovil soon after completion in March 1939, fitted with engines rotating in the same direction and driving magnesium-bladed Rotol propellers rather than the de Havilland units fitted to all other Whirlwinds. Other differences from the first prototype are visible: the enlarged rudder with horn balance and the small 'bullet' fairing between the fin and horizontal tail plane. (*AgustaWestland*)

The Hydran magazine, conceived by Sqn Ldr John Munro of the Air Ministry Armament Directorate, was an unusual device. The unbelted rounds were stored in a series of vertical hoppers, beneath which ran a worm drive operated by a pneumatic stepper motor to drive the rounds towards the gun. (*Niall Corduroy*)

The worm drive of the Hydran magazine fed ammunition sideways towards the cannon, requiring the gun to be mounted on its side rather than upright as Hispano intended. (*Niall Corduroy*)

CHAPTER 1

Origins

The basic feature of the Whirlwind was its concentration of firepower: its four closely-grouped heavy cannon in the nose had a rate of fire of 600 lbs/ minute – which, until the introduction of the Beaufighter, placed it ahead of any fighter in the world. Hand in hand with this dense firepower went a first-rate speed and climb performance, excellent manoeuvrability and a fighting view hitherto unsurpassed. The Whirlwind was, in its day, faster than the Spitfire down low and, with lighter lateral control, was considered to be one of the nicest "twins" ever built... From the flying viewpoint, the Whirlwind was considered magnificent.

Philip J. R. Moyes, *Aircraft Profile No. 191: The Westland Whirlwind*
(1967)

RAF single-seat fighter design in the two decades before the Second World War was influenced by a single overwhelming concern: the defence of London. London was a highly valuable target and, the Air Ministry thought, a uniquely vulnerable one. At a time when sound location was in its infancy and radar some way in the future, the first warning of attacking bombers would come when they approached the east coast of Britain, but by then they would be within twenty to thirty minutes flying time of the capital. The RAF saw the challenge of intercepting enemy aircraft with almost no warning as its own unique problem. As one officer put it: 'As is well known, the main problem of the defence of London is time.'[1] The initial solution was a system of three defensive zones through which the enemy would have to fly in turn: nearest the coast a gun-defended zone, further inland an 'Aircraft Fighting Zone' and then another gun-defended zone close to London. The 'Zone' fighters – Siskins, Bulldogs and Gauntlets – would fly standing patrols and be guided via radio to the attackers using information supplied by observers on the ground, tactics that required fighters with considerable endurance. The RAF assumed that its enemies would bomb by day and night so the Zone fighters, aided by searchlights, would also have to be able to fight at night.

In the late 1920s, the system was expanded when a few fighter squadrons were placed near the coast, the intention being that they would not fly standing patrols, but only take off when the enemy was first seen and then make a visual pursuit. Radio would not be needed and clearly these tactics would be unworkable at night. This role was initially filled by standard zone fighters, but in 1927, the RAF issued a requirement for a dedicated 'Interceptor' aircraft, a requirement eventually met by the Hawker Fury.[2] The Fury's performance sharply illuminated the compromises inherent in the Zone fighters. It no longer needed a heavy fuel load or radio and freed of the need to operate safely at night, the aircraft could have a higher landing speed (which allowed greater wing loading). Unsurprisingly, the Fury was nearly 40 mph (64 kph) faster than its Zone fighter contemporary, the Bulldog.

Thus, during these critical years there were two distinct, but converging, strands of RAF single-seat fighter development: Zone and Interceptor fighters. In 1934, the RAF adopted an eight-gun armament for a new Interceptor to replace the Fury. The following year, for a new Zone fighter to replace the Gauntlet and Gladiator, it accepted greatly reduced endurance in search of increased performance. These were the two defining steps in the evolution of a uniquely British style of single-seat fighter, one in which speed and firepower were emphasised at the expense of endurance and manoeuvrability.

The Eight-Gun Fighter

Heavier armament was central to the 'Interceptor' concept and, in order to gain practical experience with it, the Air Member for Supply and Research (AMSR), AVM Sir John Higgins, asked in 1927 for a purely experimental six-gun fighter. Subsequent tests of the two prototypes concluded that each was the equivalent of any two two-gun Zone fighter.[3] The first production application of increased armament came in 1930 when the Deputy Chief of the Air Staff, Sir Cyril Newall, strongly criticised the two-gun armament of a proposed new Zone fighter: 'We are not making any advance at all in the armament of our fighters if we allow ... the same armament that was carried in 1917.'[4] In addition to four guns, Newall also wanted progress in other areas. Gun interrupter gear, he noted, weighed as much as a gun, reduced the rate of fire and had 'not developed a bit since it was first invented'. He got his way when the F.7/30 requirement was issued in October 1931. It called for four guns, two of which were to be mounted outside the propeller arc, unimpeded by interrupter gear.

It had been realised during the First World War that aircraft were largely immune to rifle calibre bullets unless they hit the crew, fuel tanks or engine either through good shooting or good luck. Clearly the Air Ministry believed in neither and began to take an increasingly abstract and statistical approach to fighter armament. The approach was not of aiming fire at a vulnerable part of the target, but creating what AVM Hugh Dowding (who succeeded Higgins as AMSR in 1930) referred to as a 'Beaten Zone', a cloud of bullets sufficiently dense to ensure, statistically, that a vulnerable part of the target would be hit. This approach reached its zenith in the brief debate on the armament of the Fury replacement, F.5/34, for which the Ministry's Armament Directorate analysed the bullet densities produced by various gun installations in a given period of time and concluded that six guns would achieve the required density at 240 yards range and eight guns would do so at 280 yards. The two additional guns were forecast to reduce maximum speed by just 1 mph and with little further debate the eight-gun armament was incorporated into the F.5/34 requirements.[5] Prototypes were later ordered from Gloster and Bristol. The RAF's eight-gun fighter was born.

The Stillborn F.10/35

By October 1934, the F.7/30 Zone fighter programme had yet to produce a useable aircraft, the designs submitted were seen as being out of date and the Ministry turned its attention to a replacement for it under the number F.10/35.[6] The first draft of the requirements called for a 300 mph maximum speed and, following the standard set a year earlier for the F.5/34 Interceptor, an eight-gun armament.[7] Therefore, the new aircraft was to be 40 per cent faster and carry twice the armament yet offer roughly the same endurance as its F.7/30 predecessor.

At a conference to review the specification, Fighting Area (the predecessor of Fighter Command) expressed its needs in terms of a hypothetical fighter sortie and asked for enough fuel for thirty minutes for climb and reserves, sixty minutes at economical speed for patrol, plus fifteen minutes at maximum power for combat. This was accepted and the requirement amended to reflect the new, reduced, fuel load.[8] This was a significant decision: endurance had now been almost halved, substantially eroding one of the main distinctions between the Zone and Interception classes.

The Ministry issued the revised outline requirements to the industry in April 1935 and began work on the detailed specification that would normally follow. The majority of the RAF's single-seat fighter squadrons had always been equipped with Zone fighters and the timing of F.10/35 was such that it should have produced the RAF's standard single-seat fighter of the early years of the Second World War. Indirectly it did, although no new aircraft was ever built to fulfil it.

Dowding's Experimentals

In addition to specifying and ordering prototypes of replacements for the RAF's regular service aircraft, AMSR also ordered prototypes which met no specific operational need but served purely technical purposes. Some, such as the 1927 six-gun fighters, explored new armament concepts. Others, including the Schneider seaplanes and Hawker's High Speed Fury, were experiments in achieving the highest possible speeds, a tradition Dowding continued in 1934 by ordering two prototypes as part of the High Speed Research Programme. Originally intended as one-off aircraft, they ultimately became the best known of the RAF's wartime single seat fighters.

The first was one of a series of Hawker proposals for a high-speed fighter monoplane powered by the Rolls-Royce PV12 (later named Merlin) and with the same armament and endurance as the Fury. Dowding's team quickly agreed to order the aircraft for the High Speed Development Programme.[9] It was given the type number F.36/34 and later named Hurricane. The second originated with Supermarine's much delayed F.7/30 prototype. Supermarine's designer, R. J. Mitchell, appears to have lost interest in the aircraft in its original form and proposed a Merlin-powered 'update' representing, in effect, a completely new aircraft. Unsurprisingly, the Ministry rejected such extensive changes to a prototype that was already late. Instead, it ordered the aircraft as a new prototype and issued a brief specification for it: F.37/34, an 'Experimental High Speed, Single-Seater Fighter' to 'conform to all the requirements stated in Specification F7/30' including the four-gun armament and the endurance of a Zone fighter. It was later christened the Spitfire.[10]

In April 1935 when the Ministry issued the reduced-endurance eight-gun F.10/35 requirements, Hawker's F.36/34 prototype was under construction, but the Supermarine F.37/34 was still being designed. Mitchell quickly realised that the reduced endurance specified for F.10/35 allowed his F.37/34 experimental aircraft to be adapted to meet it: 200 lbs less fuel would offset the weight of the four additional guns required by F.10/35. Commercially, the appeal of doing so was obvious. F.37/34 provided for a single experimental aircraft, but F.10/35 might be ordered in large numbers. Mitchell discussed his ideas with Ralph Sorley of the Operational Requirements Branch who not only supported the proposal, but suggested that Hawker's F.36/34 also be brought in line with F.10/35.[11] Both aircraft were in the hands of talented designers, Sorley thought, and would be available long before any all new F.10/35 prototype. Despite the reservations of some within the Ministry's technical directorates, Hawker and Supermarine were asked to make the necessary changes in early June. The wings of the Supermarine were to be redesigned to carry eight rather than four guns and a new set of eight-gun wings for the Hawker made in parallel so as not to delay its first flight.[12]

The Director of Technical Development (Air Cdre Verney) subsequently questioned the value of continuing with F.10/35 as a new project if the Hawker and Supermarine aircraft were already being modified to meet it. There were also the two F.5/34 Interceptors (subsequently also brought in line with F.10/35) and three private venture fighters from Vickers, Bristol and Martin Baker. With seven fighters under construction it seemed pointless to ask for yet another. Verney suggested that F.10/35 should either be withdrawn or reworked to call for something even more advanced. Dowding agreed that as 'his' experimental aircraft had now been 'roped into' the F.10/35 programme, it had limited value and on 21 June, the Ministry suspended the requirement.[13] Although largely unnoticed at the time, the merging of Dowding's prototypes and the two 'Interceptors' with the F.10/35 'Zone' fighter requirement ended the distinction between the 'Zone' and 'Interception' fighter classes. The Ministry had long expected them to converge and had blurred the distinction between them by specifying eight guns for both and then accepting greatly reduced endurance for the F.10/35 Zone fighter.

'A fighter superior to anything we know of elsewhere'

A little later, Sorley gave his analysis of the cannon gun's potential in a paper for the Air Ministry's Air Fighting Committee. 'The decisive effect of one 20 mm or larger calibre projectile on a modern aircraft is, I think, indisputable ... The basis for discussion, however, is not of the result which is obtained, but rather one of the chances of obtaining the result in the minimum of time.'[14] Sorley rejected the currently popular (especially in France) practice of using a single engine-mounted cannon because in a short burst the gun fired so few rounds that it was unlikely that any would hit a vital part of the target. 'The single cannon mounted on the engine can be regarded as only a first step ... If the problem of rigid wing mountings for 20 mm guns can be solved we should be able to fit four 20 mm each with sixty rounds for approximately the same weight as eight machine guns ... If we can tackle this new problem quickly and successfully we should have a fighter superior to anything we know of elsewhere.'

He proposed that to obtain his suggested four-cannon fighter the Ministry could convert the suspended F.10/35 requirement to carry four cannon (a suggestion that led directly to the Whirlwind) or the wings of the existing F.36/34 and F.37/34 designs could be adapted to carry the guns (which later led to the cannon-armed variants of the Hurricane and Spitfire). Courtney and Ellington endorsed Sorley's proposals[15] and the Ministry issued the revised version of the F.10/35 requirement, now renumbered F.37/35 (The full text of which appears in Appendix 1: Operational Requirement F.37/35) on 1

February. Armstrong-Whitworth, Fairey, Hawker, Vickers and Westland were asked to submit designs to meet it.[16]

The Air Ministry adopted the eight machine gun fighter armament in careful stages over several years and carried out extensive trials before selecting the Browning gun. In contrast when it accepted Sorley's proposed four cannon armament, no particular gun had been formally selected (although the Hispano was clearly preferred), no real gun trials had been performed and there was no plan to manufacture the weapon in the UK. Nonetheless, this armament became the standard for the RAF's fighters and remained so until well into the jet age.

The Air Ministry judged Westland's design for an alternative twelve machine gun nose to be 'unsatisfactory and unsafe'. Martin Baker Aircraft mocked up a greatly improved installation; however, no photographs or drawings survive. The project was dropped shortly afterwards. (*AgustaWestland*)

CHAPTER 2

Contenders and Prototypes

The Ministry followed up the brief Operational Requirements document by issuing the detailed F.37/35 Specification on 30 March 1936 and invited Armstrong-Whitworth, Fairey, Hawker, Vickers and Westland to submit their proposals by 1 May. At this time, the Air Ministry and many designers doubted the practicality of mounting large calibre weapons or even multiple machine guns in unbraced monoplane aircraft wings. Mindful of these concerns and aware that at least one design team was already considering a twin-engine submission, Verney modified the specification to now allow twin-engine designs. In order to obtain early firing experiments with the 20-mm cannon, the Ministry also ordered a Dewoitine 510 fighter from Lioré et Olivier in March 1936 and made separate arrangements for the supply of the engine and nine Hispano cannon. It also ordered four Oerlikon cannon even though it had largely discounted that weapon due to its low muzzle velocity and poor rate of fire.

There were substantial changes in the structure of the RAF during the two months between the issue of the specification and the evaluation of the designs submitted for it. In order to decentralise control and to align its peacetime structure with that expected in time of war, ADGB was replaced by separate functional commands, each subdivided into groups. After five and a half years leading the Air Ministry's research and development effort, Dowding left the Ministry in April 1936 to lead the newly created Fighter Command and was replaced at the Ministry by AVM Wilfrid Freeman. Dowding and his team oversaw the birth of the first generation of aircraft with which the RAF would fight the Second World War. Freeman and his colleagues would now drive the development and production of those aircraft and their replacement by a new generation.

The Contenders

Of those invited to tender only Hawker and Westland submitted proposals. Armstrong-Whitworth and Vickers formally declined to tender, and although Fairey carried out some design work, it too did not submit a design. In addition to Hawker and Westland Bristol, Boulton Paul and Supermarine also asked if they could participate, the five companies submitting eight designs for consideration.[17]

Boulton Paul offered two single-engine monoplanes with wing-mounted cannon. The P.88 Scheme A was powered by a two-speed supercharged 18-cylinder Bristol Hercules radial engine to give an estimated top speed of 337 mph. Scheme B was forecast to achieve 358 mph using a 1,750-hp Rolls-Royce Vulture. Although the two proposals were of similar configurations, the 44-foot-span Scheme B aircraft was very large by British single-engine fighter standards, its weight and size being close to that of the Republic P-47 Thunderbolt. Hawker submitted a version of the Hurricane featuring two Oerlikon cannon in each wing even though the Ministry had indicated a clear preference for the Hispano weapon. Bristol submitted single and twin-engine proposals. Type 153 was powered by a single Hercules while Type 153A was a twin-engine design with a truncated nose blended into the leading edge of the wing and holding the cannon. Bristol specified a pair of 15.6-litre 9-cylinder Aquilas, the smallest of its new family of sleeve-valve engines.

Like Bristol and in search of the most compact design for their twin-engine submissions, both Supermarine and Westland specified the smallest possible engines consistent with achieving the required performance. Supermarine's twin-engine Type 313 used the 21-litre Rolls-Royce Goshawk B, an evaporatively-cooled derivative of the Kestrel. Westland worked on a single-engine Hercules-powered proposal, but eventually submitted the twin-engine P9 also powered by a pair of Kestrel engines. Supermarine also submitted a single-engine proposal with wing-mounted cannon. The Type 312 was recognisably a Spitfire, but with numerous aerodynamic refinements including the relocation of the radiator and oil cooler from the wings to a long duct under the fuselage. Hawker and Boulton Paul promised delivery within fifteen months, Bristol eighteen months and Westland eighteen to twenty-four months. Supermarine estimated twenty-seven months for its twin-engine design and twenty months for the cannon-armed Spitfire. At the tender design conference in May 1936, the Vulture-engine Boulton Paul P88B was selected as the preferred single-engine design followed by the Bristol and then the Supermarine and Hawker designs. The Supermarine Type 313 was the preferred twin-engine proposal, largely because of Mitchell's reputation for designing fast aircraft, but Verney thought that Westland's P.9 was the more advanced design of the two.

To insure against delays caused by accidents and to accelerate the development process, the RAF generally ordered two prototypes of new designs. Despite his personal preference for the Westland P.9, Verney recommended that the Air Ministry should order two Supermarine Type 313 and two Boulton Paul P.88B prototypes, provided that Supermarine could deliver more quickly than the twenty-seven months originally quoted.[18] He noted that although building new wings for the Hurricane and Spitfire might appear the easiest way of acquiring an experimental cannon-armed fighter, Hawker and Supermarine's design workload was so high that neither could produce such a prototype any more quickly than a less busy company could deliver a completely new aircraft.

Freeman felt that the best way of encouraging Supermarine to deliver faster was to introduce some competition by also ordering a single prototype from Westland.[19] Had Freeman not made this suggestion the Westland P.9 would probably have remained an intriguing, but unbuilt project. Ellington agreed and on 10 August, Verney was told to order the prototypes – two each from Supermarine and Boulton Paul and one from Westland. At this point, Supermarine advised the Ministry that the company's experimental department was so busy it would be better to build one prototype and a large quantity of spares rather than two complete aircraft. Accordingly, the Ministry agreed to order just a single prototype from Supermarine and two from Westland.[20]

Boulton Paul quoted £38,000 for its two prototypes, Westland £45,500 and Supermarine £23,361 for a single prototype with spares. The total cost of over £105,000 far exceeded the £20,000 originally set aside for the F.10/35 programme and required the Ministry to seek Treasury approval for the expenditure.[21] It presented its somewhat disingenuous case to the Treasury in November. 'After a full and careful investigation of the potentialities of the cannon gun aircraft, the Air Staff has decided that action shall be taken to build experimental prototype machines embodying the special features necessary for incorporation of the guns. In view of the considerable attention being given to this type of aircraft abroad it is deemed essential that construction of the experimental machines now proposed should be regarded as a matter of urgency.'[22] The Treasury approved and on 7 December, the Ministry ordered the two Boulton Paul P.88Bs (L6591 and L6592) and the single Supermarine Type 313 (L6593) with its package of spares.[23] But not the Westland prototypes.

'The design is all in his head'

The Westland P.9 order was not placed because disquieting news had reached the Ministry of a plan for Westland to increase its share capital in order to acquire four other British aircraft companies. The Ministry was suspicious of the motives of the financiers promoting the scheme and were worried that Westland might become financially overstretched and unable to fulfil its existing military contracts. More alarming was that the Westland Board, with the exception of Sir Ernest Petter, opposed the proposal and Teddy Petter told Freeman that he, factory manager John Fearn and the other directors, would resign if the acquisitions proceeded. The Ministry regarded the loss of Teddy Petter and John Fearn as a potential disaster. Without Fern, production Lysanders would 'probably be delayed by 6-9 months' and there would be no point in ordering the F.37/35 prototype if Petter left because, as Newall put it, 'the Westland design for a cannon gun fighter is all in his head'.[24]

Sir Ernest was summoned to the Air Ministry and told that unless Westland kept its existing design and production staff it could expect no further Ministry orders. Subsequently, the proposed mergers were dropped and Teddy Petter and John Fearn remained in their positions. Nonetheless, the contract for the prototypes, eventually issued on 19 January and agreed three weeks later, allowed the Ministry to cancel the order without penalty should Petter or Fearn leave the company. Westland's P.9 proposal specified counter-rotating engines, but, wary of the complexity of having two completely

L6844 was the first Whirlwind prototype, seen here in late 1938. She flew briefly with No. 263 Squadron before being retired to No. 4 School of Technical Training at St Athan. (*Robert Bowater*)

different engines and propellers for a single aircraft type, Verney instructed that while the first aircraft (L6844) could have counter-rotating engines, the second (L6845) should be fitted with a pair of identical right-hand rotation Peregrines. Comparative trials between the two prototypes would then show whether the expected improvements in handling and stability justified the complication of the counter-rotating engines.

Two-Horse Race

By the time the Air Ministry ordered the Westland prototypes it had already cancelled one of its competitors. While it was evaluating the F.37/35 proposals in the summer of 1936, the Ministry also issued a requirement (B.12/36) for a new heavy bomber that would form the cornerstone of the RAF's future bomber force. Supermarine's proposal was overwhelmingly preferred to the competing designs including Short's Stirling. This, however, was a large and very complex aircraft and Supermarine was already heavily occupied with other design work and finalising the Spitfire for production. The company indicated that it could produce the B.12/36 prototype within eighteen months, but only if work on its F.37/35 cannon fighter and R.1/36 flying boat were postponed. Ellington agreed that irrespective of where the company's super-bomber might be mass produced, if Supermarine were to build even a prototype of it in addition to the cannon fighter and flying boat '…they would have a design and production programme which would be completely beyond their capacity'.[25] The Ministry ordered two prototypes of Supermarine's super bomber and duly cancelled the company's F.37/35 contract on 28 January on the condition that Supermarine communicated 'certain features' of its design to Westland. The Westland P.9 and the single-engine Boulton Paul P.88 were now the only contenders for the F.37/35 requirement.

Building the Prototypes

Despite the delay in ordering the Westland prototypes, work on the aircraft progressed quickly. By April 1937, the mock-up was complete and some manufacturing drawings had been released. Progress at Boulton Paul was less impressive: the mock-up was still being built and the design team was completing strength calculations.[26] The mock-up conference for the Westland prototype in May focused, as usual, on cockpit instrumentation and control positioning, but also introduced a new requirement when Westland was also told that all future production aircraft (not just Whirlwinds) would have to offer adequate cooling in tropical conditions.[27] By mid-summer, the first two prototype Peregrine engines were nearly complete and Rolls-Royce successfully completed a 100-hour development test with a modified Kestrel engine incorporating some Peregrine features and running at its intended output of 840 bhp. The company also completed a 100-hour test with a standard Kestrel V using 100 octane fuel.[28]

There was progress with the Hispano gun, the new fighter's raison d'être. The RAF's Dewoitine had arrived at A&AEE Martlesham Heath in August 1936 followed by its cannon in October. However, earlier firing trials in France revealed that the breech of the gun tended to rebound as it closed and, for safety reasons, A&AEE was told not to fire the example it had received. Hispano made further modifications to cure the problem and also changed the rifling of the barrel from five degrees to seven degrees to improve accuracy. In January 1937, A&AEE received a modified gun and ground firing trials with it mounted on a Hispano crankcase began on 22 January. Subsequently, the gun was installed in the aircraft and further ground firing trials carried out with the engine stopped and running. Air-to-ground firing trials began in early February, but revealed consistently poor accuracy even though the gun and gunsight had been correctly harmonised. Eventually, it was discovered that the French Levallois reflector sight, mounted ahead of the windscreen, was being deflected back by the airflow, resulting in the mean point of impact on the target being well below the point of aim. Therefore, the windscreen was moved forwards of the sight and the reflector screen mounting reinforced. Tests continued at Orfordness later in February, this time with a balloon-hoisted target, but this was damaged by high winds. A smaller thirty-foot target was then used, but this too was 'destroyed' by high winds rather than by cannon fire.[29] The tests were not completed until the end of the summer, but by then arrangements were being made for mass production of the gun in the UK. Freeman and others met Count Poniatowski, Hispano-Suiza's president, on several occasions, but efforts to broker an agreement between Hispano and Bristol, EMI (Electrical and Musical Industries) or BSA (British Small Arms) all failed in turn. In October, Poniatowski suggested that Hispano might set up a British company and appeared well prepared to do so. He assured Freeman that the company had been duplicating its tooling for some time and that 80 per cent of the machine tools required were already available to be shipped to England from France as soon as they were needed. Some in the Ministry speculated that Poniatowski's enthusiasm for such a project was due to his desire to put at least some of Hispano's activities beyond the reach of the French government that was at that time engaged in the wholesale nationalisation of the country's aircraft and armament industries.[30]

One-Horse Race

The two Whirlwind prototypes continued to make good progress during the summer of 1937, but many changes were made to the design. The most visible of these was the replacement of the twin-finned tailplane by a single fin with the horizontal tail mounted high up on the fin clear of the turbulent wake generated by the large Fowler flap when it was lowered. Meanwhile at Boulton Paul, progress on the P88 remained slow and by the end of the summer, even the wooden mock-up was incomplete.[31]

The rapid progress at Westland prompted the Air Ministry in October 1937 to question the value of continuing with Boulton Paul's competing P88. In May, the Ministry had issued requirement F.11/37 for a two-seat, cannon turret fighter and Boulton Paul's P92 appeared to be the most promising proposal. The Ministry was worried that if it ordered prototypes of the new fighter from Boulton Paul, the company's design workload would then, as had been the case with Supermarine ten months earlier, be greater than it could cope with. Boulton Paul's Defiant programme was running behind schedule, progress on its F.37/35 prototype had been slow and the company's small design team was also engaged on a variety of armament projects. The Air Ministry duly decided to cancel the P88 on 19 October and ordered two P.92 turret fighter prototypes.[32] The Westland P9 Whirlwind was now the only remaining contender for the F.37/35 project.

Over the winter, Westland began final assembly of the first prototype. Meanwhile at Rolls-Royce, a Peregrine I completed a 100-hour development test. The first Peregrine II, a left-hand rotation engine, was ready to start its 100-hour service type test and two pairs of engines were being built for the Whirlwind and the second Gloster F.9/37 prototypes.[33] By March, work on the first prototype slowed because Westland had still not received its engines, undercarriage, radiators and oil coolers, and it seemed clear that the first flight would not take place in July as originally hoped. Nonetheless in mid-May, although the Whirlwind had neither flown nor been ordered into production, the Ministry provided £12,500 to Westland for the manufacture of production jigs and tooling.[34]

The flight-ready engines and other components eventually arrived during late April and May. Meanwhile, Rolls-Royce began the 100-hour type testing of the Peregrine II engine and received the special left-hand ten-foot de Havilland propeller for bench-testing. By July, the Peregrine II had completed its full type test without incident and a Peregrine II was installed in Rolls-Royce's Heinkel He 70 for endurance tests. The wings of the first Whirlwind prototype were by now complete and the engines, fuel tanks and radiators were installed, but during July and August, further delays began to creep in.[35] The first of these came in late July when it was decided to replace the aircraft's mechanical engine controls with hydraulic Exactor units.[36] These were bi-directional remote controls comprising a pair of hydraulic cylinders, one at the cockpit end and the other at the engine, connected by a single small bore pipe. Springs acting on the cylinders' pistons maintained a constant fluid pressure in the system and as the two cylinders were of the same diameter, a movement at one end produced an identical, but opposite movement at the other, in theory, if not always in practice. Such controls were a popular choice for large multi-engine aircraft, including the Sunderland, Stirling and Whitley where the design and maintenance of mechanical controls consisting of push-pull rods and bellcranks were difficult and flexing in flight of a large airframe might prevent accurate control. Petter's reasons for adopting them for the compact and stiff Whirlwind are less clear, but they remained a weakness of the aircraft for its entire career.

A cause for further delay arose in August with the discovery of a crack in a casting forming the inboard wall of one of the fuel tanks. On the first prototype, the pair of tanks in each wing was manufactured as a single unit that was then slid over the main spar like a sleeve. To replace it required a great deal of dismantling, including removal of the outer wing. Only at the end of August was the tank removed, rebuilt with a new casting, pressure tested and reinstalled.[37]

'...an unnecessarily long time to produce aircraft designed early in 1936'

While construction of the Whirlwind prototypes progressed through the summer of 1938, some within the Air Ministry became concerned that if production orders were not placed Westland would be unable to deliver the aircraft quickly. In June 1938, Wilfrid Freeman's Research and Development directorate assumed responsibility for aircraft production and two new Director-Generals were appointed to assist him in this expanded task: Ernest Lemon for Production and AVM Arthur Tedder for Research and Development. A month later, AVM William Sholto Douglas (Assistant Chief of the Air Staff) told Freeman that current forecasts indicated that Whirlwind deliveries might begin in June 1940, which seemed to him to be '...an unnecessarily long time to produce aircraft designed early in 1936'[38] and suggested that the Ministry should either help Westland to expand its own capacity or bring another company such as Fairey into the Whirlwind programme.

The rationale behind the original 1936 cannon fighter requirement had been that explosive cannon shells would do fatal structural damage to an enemy aircraft and none of the early discussions touched on the use of armour-piercing ammunition should the enemy armour its bombers. However, development of new armour steels made it possible to provide protection against rifle-calibre bullets using relatively thin and light plates and, as early as November 1936, Dowding told Ellington (then CAS): 'If the enemy adopts this practice, our eight gun fighters will be comparatively ineffective.' Now, eighteen months later, Douglas saw the need for cannon-armed fighters as urgent, both to defeat the enemy's armour plating and to allow the fighter to open fire from longer ranges if the enemy fitted cannon as defensive armament. He explained to Freeman: 'The reason why I am so keen to get into production on this type as quickly as possible is that I am certain that, before long, we shall require S[ingle] S[eat] Fighter mounting guns of greater calibre than .303. The answer nearest in time appears to be this F.37/35.'[39]

Douglas' proposal that another aircraft company should be brought into the Whirlwind programme to accelerate production divided opinions within the Ministry. Verney (DTD) argued that the initial subcontracting programme for the Spitfire had failed because subcontractors had started to build wings long before Supermarine had managed to build production units. The many design changes that Supermarine subsequently found necessary had then caused damaging delays. To avoid repetition of this mistake Verney recommended that the Ministry should wait until Westland was producing the aircraft and could issue final production-proved drawings before involving another company. Conversely, Ernest Lemon felt that another company would have to be brought into the programme. 'If the F.37/35 is required in any quantity, it would be beyond the capacity of Westlands. Their shops are poorly equipped and there is insufficient labour in the district.'[40]

Attracting and training workers was a limiting factor in increasing airframe production and one of the reasons the Air Ministry encouraged the industry to sub-contract as much component manufacturing as possible. Westland's location in the small town of Yeovil, set in a sparsely populated county better known for fruit growing and dairy farming than engineering, only made these problems worse. Contemporary figures show that in August 1938, Westland had a productive workforce of just 726 – around a fifth of that employed by Bristol – and was subcontracting only 13 per cent of the man hours involved in Lysander production, compared with 35 per cent for the Hurricane and 60 per cent for the Spitfire.

However, during the last half of 1938, there were substantial changes in the ownership of Westland and the resources available to it to expand production. In September, the shipbuilders and steelmakers John Brown acquired a controlling interest in the company and a new board of directors was appointed with Lord Aberconway of John Brown as chairman. At the same time, Petters sold its engine-building business and Westland acquired the old Petters factory, thereby doubling the floor area available for aircraft manufacture. Subsequently, the Associated Electrical Industries group also acquired a substantial shareholding in Westland Aircraft Ltd.

Eleven Whirlwinds are visible in this picture of Westland's production line at Yeovil. (*Niall Corduroy*)

New Rivals

Quite how the aircraft industry heard of the Ministry's concerns about Whirlwind production is uncertain, but it soon received several unsolicited proposals for new cannon fighters that, their designers claimed, could be produced quickly. Among these was a Supermarine proposal for a six-cannon derivative of its earlier twin-engine Type 324 submission for F.18/37, which had been rejected at the time in favour of simpler single-engine proposals such as the Hawker Typhoon. With a pair of 1,150-hp Merlin engines, Supermarine predicted a maximum speed of 465 mph (750 kph).[41] Unsurprisingly, Douglas enthusiastically urged Freeman to order prototypes. He was '...disturbed at the prospect of having no fighters available capable of carrying 20 mm guns other than the Westland F.37/35 and the Boulton & Paul F.11/37, both of which have a number of features which may give rise to teething troubles. I cannot help but feel therefore that it would be wise to develop this Supermarine design as a fixed cannon fighter in order to give us another string to our bow.'[42]

In his view, progress on both Westland's F.37/35 and Boulton Paul's turret-equipped F.11/37 had been slow and ordering the Supermarine might encourage both companies to accelerate their prototypes. The Ministry's technical staffs were less impressed. The armament arrangement was 'impracticable' and Liptrot dismissed the design as 'essentially a rehash of a tender design which has already been considered and found to be unacceptable'.[43] Most importantly, Supermarine could not realistically be expected to get this all-new design into production until perhaps eighteen to twenty-four months after the Whirlwind. The Ministry rejected the proposal in November 1938, but by then more attractive alternatives were available.

In October 1938, Bristol suggested a conversion of its Beaufort maritime bomber into a cannon fighter with either a two-gun turret or four fixed cannon in the fuselage. The 'Beaufort Fighter' married the Beaufort's wings, undercarriage and tail with a new and smaller fuselage. To obtain increased performance, Hercules engines replaced the Taurus units of the Beaufort. To provide clearance for larger propellers, the engine nacelles were moved up to the wing centreline and a slimmer and shorter nose was fitted. Where Beaufort components required reinforcement, the gauge of material used was increased or steel was substituted for aluminium so that the new parts could still be made using the existing jigs and templates. Many of the controls and systems within the new fuselage were also taken directly from the Beaufort. Bristol predicted a maximum speed of 361 mph (581 kph) and a range of 760 miles (1,200 km).[44]

This proposal for a cannon fighter based on an existing design for which production tooling had already been built met the Ministry's needs more closely than an all-new design could. Bristol forecast that it could fly the first prototype within six to eight months and begin production deliveries in September 1939.[45] Douglas pressed for the aircraft to be ordered, Newall approved on 1 February 1939 and the Ministry ordered 300 aircraft soon afterwards.[46] The formal operational requirements for the new aircraft clearly outlined its place in the Ministry's (and particularly Douglas') thinking: 'It is important that this type of fighter should be introduced into service as early as possible to meet the development of defensive armament and armour protection in enemy bomber aircraft. It is considered that this requirement can most rapidly be met by development of a suitable existing type as an interim type to precede the normal replacement for the F.37/35 design.'[47] The prototype Beaufighter flew in July 1939 and the first production aircraft a year later. For an 'interim type', the Beaufighter enjoyed a long and varied career. Nearly 6,000 were built, it established a formidable reputation as a night fighter and maritime strike aircraft, and the RAF did not retire its last Beaufighters until 1960.

While the Ministry debated these proposals, final assembly of the first Whirlwind prototype continued and undercarriage, flap and wing stiffness tests took place in September. Later that month, the Ministry told Westland that Lorenz blind landing equipment would be required for production aircraft and that the flap and undercarriage controls should be moved to the same side of the cockpit as the throttles.[48] The latter was a result of experience with the Hurricane and reflected a desire to place these controls so that the pilot could take off and land without having to change hands on the control column.

First Flight

Harald Penrose, Westland's chief test pilot, began taxiing trials at Yeovil on the afternoon of 5 October and three days later the aircraft was dismantled and taken by road to RAF Boscombe Down for its first flight.[49] Boscombe Down, the home of two Fairey Battle squadrons, was chosen because it was more suitable for testing a high-speed prototype aircraft than the cramped airfield at Yeovil. During fast taxiing on 11 October, Penrose ran out of runway and decided to take off. He later recalled:

A No. 263 Squadron Whirlwind at dispersal in Knighton Wood, RAF Warmwell, in the summer of 1943. (*Robert Bowater*)

...in the course of half an hour it was obvious there were various imperfections of control. Thus the side-hinged rudder was ineffective over the first five degrees and too heavy at big angles; there was a directional oscillation with the rudder free; the tip slats extended with an unacceptable jerk; as speed increased there was a suspicious nose down tendency; in tight turns the machine shuddered, suggesting interference between the fin and tailplane despite the latter's high position to overcome downwash when the flaps were lowered. As for the engines, performance was satisfactory except that they were running too hot – and I still did not like the smoke and flames exiting at the trailing edge.[50]

After another flight three days later, the aircraft returned to Yeovil to continue development flying and undergo a lengthy series of modifications to its flying controls. It was already clear that the cooling system was marginal and in November, the coolant was changed from water to 100 per cent ethylene glycol, a change that would disguise the symptoms of overheating if not address the cause. After just four hours total flight time, the starboard engine failed on 10 November and Penrose was obliged to make a precautionary landing at RAF Warmwell.[51]

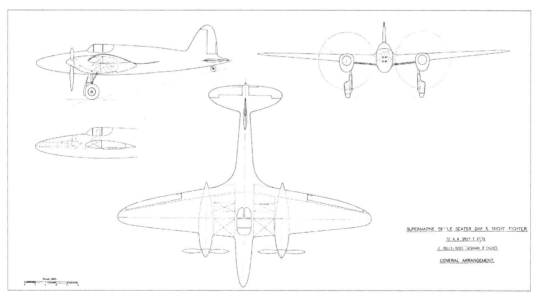

Supermarine's Type 313 was the Air Ministry's preferred twin-engined proposal for the F.37/35 requirement. Slightly larger than Westland's P9, it was also powered by a variant of the Rolls-Royce Kestrel, in this case the Goshawk B, an engine that combined the evaporative cooling of the Goshawk family with the separate pent-roof cylinder heads of the very earliest Rolls-Royce Merlins. (*Niall Corduroy*)

CHAPTER 3

Perfecting the Whirlwind

Even before the Whirlwind had been ordered, Westland informed the Air Ministry that if 500 aircraft were ordered by 1 January, deliveries could begin in September 1939.[52] This was far in advance of the June 1940 date given earlier by the company. At the same time, the Ministry began planning new 'Group' production schemes for the key new aircraft types being considered for production in which established aircraft manufacturers were paired with new 'Shadow' factories run by companies from outside of the aircraft industry and supported by a network of subcontractors making components and assemblies. In this programme, Westland was partnered with the Castle Bromwich Aircraft Factory (CBAF) then under construction under the aegis of Lord Nuffield of Morris Motors, Britain's largest carmaker. CBAF had been promised an initial order for 1,000 Spitfires, but at a planned output of thirty aircraft per week, this would occupy the factory for just eight months and the Supply Committee suggested that in addition to any Westland order a further 800 Whirlwinds should be ordered from CBAF.[53]

However, before placing any production order, the Air Ministry needed its own assessment of the Whirlwind's flying characteristics and asked Petter to allow it to be evaluated by pilots from the Aeroplane and Armament Experimental Establishment (A&AEE). Although the prototype had flown fewer than fifteen hours in total and was still being modified, Petter agreed to the tests, but poor weather delayed them until 30 December. Normally a prototype would be thoroughly tested at A&AEE Martlesham Heath for a period of weeks or months, but in the case of the Whirlwind, four A&AEE pilots went to Boscombe Down where each flew the aircraft for just forty minutes. Their opinion was that the aircraft was 'exceptionally easy to fly' and 'likely to make an exceptional fighter after some modification to its controls'.[54] Their conclusions agreed with those of Penrose: the ailerons were heavy, the rudder was overbalanced for small deflections and the elevators lacked authority at low speeds. In general they liked the Whirlwind's handling and stability, but criticised the poorly-synchronised throttles, ineffective brakes and the Lysander-type rudder pedals. No performance tests were carried out and, although A&AEE had heard that engine cooling was inadequate, no problems arose during the flights due to the exceptionally cold weather conditions. The following day, Penrose flew L6844 to RAE Farnborough for resonance tests on the rear fuselage and tail which had displayed significant vibration at speed in early flights. Delayed by persistent bad weather the aircraft returned to Westland on 24 January.[55]

On the basis of A&AEE's positive report Tedder and Freeman felt that the Whirlwind should be ordered into production immediately and, just days after the brief flight trials, the Air Ministry ordered 200 aircraft on 11 January 1939. Westland was asked to deliver the first two production aircraft in March 1940 and told to plan for a potential wartime output of sixty Whirlwinds per month.[56] At the same time, DGP recommended that more Lysanders should be ordered to enable Westland to attract and keep the workforce needed to maximise Whirlwind output as soon as possible after production had started: 215 Lysanders were ordered soon afterwards.[57] Rolls-Royce was told to plan for an output of 440 Peregrine engines, but no firm order could be placed until the second prototype had been tested to determine whether the Whirlwind required counter-rotating engines.

Westland's Chief Test Pilot Harald Penrose puts P7110 through her paces in this beautiful photograph of the graceful and iconic Whirlwind. (*Niall Corduroy*)

Petter was adamant that the counter-rotating engines would be necessary and was unswayed by the results of tests in which the pilots had detected no subjective handling differences between a standard Bristol Blenheim and one fitted with counter-rotating engines. Petter believed that these findings would not apply to the much more compact and heavily-loaded Whirlwind. Above all, he was concerned that the engines needed to be ordered immediately if Westland was to begin Whirlwind deliveries in September 1939.[58] The Ministry was more pragmatic. It believed that Whirlwind production was unlikely to start until March 1940 and the decision regarding the engines could therefore wait until the second prototype had flown without introducing any delay into the programme.[59]

The second Whirlwind prototype, L6845, first flew on 29 March and on 15 April, two A&AEE pilots again visited Boscombe Down to compare the aircraft's handling with that of the first prototype. The pilots reported no major difference between the aircraft, although the lack of elevator authority noticed on the first prototype was now even more apparent and needed to be addressed urgently. The counter-rotating engines were duly abandoned. Rolls-Royce was given a firm order for 440 Peregrine Is and told to plan for a total output of 2,200 engines by June 1941 to power 1,000 Whirlwinds from Westland and CBAF with a 10 per cent provision for spare engines.[60] Long before placing the production order, the Ministry had discussed with Westland the additional items of equipment that any production aircraft would need to carry in the light both of rapid technological progress and the evolution of the Ministry's conception of the war it would soon have to fight: provision of oil and water cooling for tropical conditions, rear armour and an armoured windscreen, propeller de-icing, provision for a VHF radio transceiver as an alternative to the HF unit currently specified, and Lorenz blind landing equipment were all to be included in the production specification. Somehow all these changes would have to be accommodated not just by the Whirlwind but also by its near contemporaries: the Hurricane, Spitfire and Defiant.[61]

Petter attended a meeting at the Air Ministry on 23 February to settle the remaining technical queries affecting the aircraft. The Ministry began by making concessions. The Whirlwind had failed its undercarriage drop tests, its tyre pressures were excessively high, incurring the risk of damaging grass airfields, and while the specification required three inches propeller to ground clearance with the undercarriage compressed there was in fact none, but the Ministry accepted the design as it stood as to do otherwise would require substantial redesign of the nacelles. It was less willing to compromise on the cockpit layout and specifically the location of the flap and undercarriage controls in the cockpit, an issue raised fifteen months earlier, but apparently ignored by Westland. Petter repeatedly told the Ministry that these changes would delay the issue of production drawings by as much as two or three months and, although it was standard ministry practice to approve changes on the basis of a mock-up in order to avoid delays, he insisted on making trial installations of each of the new features on one of the prototypes.[62] His inflexibility prompted a forceful note from Freeman:

> The Service is in the position of the customer and must reserve and insist on the right to obtain an article which will meet its operational requirements. We realise that compromises have to be made between the desire to meet new requirements (which are inevitably in a continual state of development owing to technical and operational progress) and the requirements of early and rapid production. We try to give firms information of new requirements as early as possible ... In the past it has been our experience that firms welcome such advance information and make provision accordingly. If such provision is not made at an early stage there is a grave risk of either delay in the incorporation of equipment which the service vitally needs or delay in aircraft production. I cannot help feeling that some of the trouble which is now being experienced over the Westland fighter is due to the fact that no action was taken at Yeovil when these preliminary warnings were given.

Despite the firm tone of this note Freeman conceded that, in the interest of production, the required changes need only be incorporated from the twenty-fifth aircraft onwards. Eventually, it was agreed that the cockpit layout changes would appear on the tenth production aircraft and propeller de-icing, Lorenz blind landing equipment and provision for VHF radio (including relocation of the radio mast from the canopy to the forward fuselage) would feature from the twenty-fifth airframe.[63] The largest challenge was presented by the additional equipment to be installed in the rear fuselage. Originally, it had been intended that the TR9D radio would sit on the shelf under the cockpit canopy behind the pilot and access to other equipment in the rear fuselage would be by removing the upholstered cover from the tubular frame of the pilot's seat. That route was barred when armour behind the seat was introduced and the new rack to hold the TR1133 VHF radio and desert ration packs required a large access door to be introduced in the starboard side of the fuselage. This in turn necessitated substantial strengthening of the fuselage structure and it seemed unlikely that such major structural changes could be applied retrospectively to the first twenty-four aircraft. The Ministry thus had to accept that the first nine Whirlwinds would be so non-standard that they would have to be regarded effectively as prototypes and used 'on experimental duties of one sort or another', the tenth to twenty-fourth aircraft would still be short of some operational equipment and only the twenty-fifth and subsequent aircraft would fully meet the Ministry's requirements.[64]

During May 1939, concerns resurfaced that the Whirlwind's advanced features might make it difficult to maintain and service. Fred Rowarth, Chief Engineer at A&AEE, visited Westland to inspect the first prototype and concluded that 'for an aircraft of such advanced design, maintenance requirements are generally well covered'. There were some criticisms. The ducted exhausts, each assembled with over sixty nuts and bolts, would make regular inspection of the exhaust manifolds impossible; checking the hydraulic fluid level required removal of the entire nose cone; bleeding the tailwheel hydraulics required a mechanic to crawl down the inside of the fuselage; and it was impossible to reach the rearmost pairs of the Peregrine's spark plugs without first removing the coolant header tank.[65]

While Rowarth and his colleagues were inspecting the first prototype, Penrose demonstrated the second aircraft to an audience of high-ranking government officials, senior officers and the press at an event at RAF Northolt. Although prevented from naming the aircraft, *Flight* magazine noted that 'the' fastest time of the day 'was not put up by the Spitfire, but by a secret twin-engine machine which streaked over from the west'.[66] Meanwhile, development flying continued with the two prototypes with the first aircraft being used primarily for cooling trials and the second on handling development. The aircraft's handling, of which Penrose, the company's own test pilot, seems to have been more critical than the RAF's test pilots, had now been greatly improved by fitting a rudder featuring a large horn balance and an unusual concave profile on one side to compensate for the rudder's offset hinges and the asymmetric responses they produced.[67]

A Narrow Escape

On the afternoon of 10 June, Penrose was flying L6844 on a routine test flight from Boscombe Down when the aircraft suddenly rolled to starboard. Realising that the port aileron was no longer under his control, he levelled the aircraft using just the starboard aileron and landed safely despite a strong crosswind. The cooling duct of the port outboard exhaust system had failed, allowing escaping hot air to play on a forked joint in the aileron control rod, which subsequently failed. Many at the Ministry felt that the ducted system was insufficiently developed to be used on production aircraft and that as an interim measure, a conventional external manifold should be used.[68] In order to get the first prototype flying again quickly, Westland improvised a shortened duct exiting the wing behind the main spar and worked with Rolls-Royce on an external system for the second aircraft, subsequently adopted for production aircraft.[69]

In December 1938, the Supply Committee had recommended that a large order for Whirlwinds should be placed with the Castle Bromwich Aircraft Factory (CBAF). At the time, CBAF was struggling to get the Spitfire into production as its management claimed that Supermarine's production drawings had been repeatedly changed. On 15 June 1939, Lord Nuffield and Oliver Boden (Nuffield's senior production advisor) met with Kingsley Wood and Freeman. They were 'alarmed that if they were to turn over to Whirlwind production, similar difficulties would be experienced with drawings and modifications with the result that production would be delayed,' and doubted whether they could switch from Spitfire to Whirlwind production without a substantial loss of total output.[70] Accordingly on 4 July, the Supply Committee reported that 'the provisional order for 600 Whirlwinds from the Castle Bromwich factory should be cancelled, together with related orders for Peregrine engines'.[71] The factory eventually built nearly 12,000 Spitfires before its closure in 1945. It now builds Jaguar cars.

The Westland orders for Whirlwinds remained in place, but even these were affected by the cancellation of the CBAF aircraft. The intention had been that Westland and CBAF would share an extensive network of subcontractors supplying Whirlwind components. These subcontractors would now continue to make Spitfire parts for CBAF and Westland would need to look elsewhere.[72] In July, Penrose was incapacitated by a recurrence of the dysentery he had contracted during an earlier Westland sales mission to Greece. To stand in for him the Air Ministry loaned RAE test pilot Arthur Clouston to Westland. Clouston, famous for his earlier record-breaking flights to South Africa, Australia and New Zealand, arrived at Yeovil on 4 August and continued the test programme until 27 August when he delivered L6845 to A&AEE at Martlesham Heath for its first formal trials.

This rear view of a pre-production Peregrine shows the downdraught carburettor and central-entry supercharger that were the principal differences between the Peregrine and earlier Kestrel variants. The piping at the rear of the carburettor routes hot oil to the throttles to prevent carburettor icing. To the right of the carburettor is the automatic boost control and to the left the electrical generator (only installed on the port engine in the Whirlwind). (*Rolls-Royce Heritage Trust*)

CHAPTER 4

Trials, Cancellation and Reprieve

Early in the afternoon of 27 August, Clouston delivered L6845 to A&AEE at Martlesham Heath for full performance and handling trials, but returned to Boscombe Down the following day due to the deteriorating international situation. In doing so it preceded the wholesale move of A&AEE and its fleet of seventy aircraft from its exposed position on the east coast to its designated war station at Boscombe Down where the establishment formally reopened on 20 September. Westland used this interval to camouflage the second prototype and to extend the inboard exhaust manifolds to direct the exhaust stream away from the leading edge duct feeding the radiators and carburettor air intake.[73]

Freeman's Axe

Many miles away from A&AEE, in the collection of requisitioned hotels in Harrogate to which it had been evacuated on the outbreak of war, Freeman and his staff were considering the shape of the aircraft production programme in what was now a war economy. Inevitably, there would be casualties of the new programme and the Whirlwind would be one, but the impetus for its cancellation came from an unexpected quarter.

Early British planning had envisaged only a small British Army commitment in France, but in April 1939, the Cabinet set the Army the goal of creating a field force for deployment overseas of no less than thirty-two divisions (500,000 men) and in May instituted limited conscription measures to achieve it. The RAF's agreement with the Army was that it would provide army support aircraft for the field force divisions on a pro-rata basis and the aircraft production implications of the consequent need for many more Army Co-operation units to support the new force were realised as early as June 1939.[74] The Air Ministry was highly sensitive to the Army's needs as it had already lost control of naval aviation to the Admiralty and now faced similar pressure to relinquish control of Army aviation.[75]

The RAF's last peacetime expansion plan called for the number of Army Co-operation units to remain stable at nine squadrons over the period between March 1939 and March 1941, but subsequent estimates concluded that the expanded field force would require thirteen additional single-engine Army Co-operation squadrons. Initially these would require 234 aircraft and it was predicted that they might lose as many as 163 aircraft per month in intensive operations, losses that would have to be replaced. The Westland Lysander was the only modern aircraft for this role, but the RAF had only 232 Lysanders and Westland, which had resisted previous pressure to have the aircraft built elsewhere, was building just forty per month.[76] The Director of Aeronautical Production noted that increased Lysander production to meet this need could only be achieved at the expense of Whirlwind output. Freeman went further and suggested 'that in order to accelerate Lysander production, Westland should stop work on the Whirlwind'.[77]

Freeman also wrote to Sir Charles Bruce-Gardner, Chairman of the Society of British Aircraft Constructors, and, like Freeman, a member of the Expansion Progress Committee. Freeman's wide-ranging analysis outlined how the production programme might evolve in the face of expected material shortages. For example, he proposed to limit Stirling production, not because it was a bad bomber, but because each Stirling absorbed twice as much labour and 50 per cent more material than a Halifax. For the fighter programme, Freeman suggested that the Hurricane and Spitfire should continue until replaced by the Beaufighter, Tornado and Typhoon. The only other fighter remaining in production would be an updated Defiant. He continued:

> It is strongly recommended, and I have no doubt will be approved, that the Whirlwind should be stopped forthwith, thus enabling us to replace it at Westlands with the Lysander, which is required in large quantities to meet the needs of an expanding Expeditionary Force and of our Dominion forces. Further it will enable us to stop the production of the Peregrine engine, thus allowing Rolls-Royce to concentrate on the Merlin and Vulture, and at a later date the Griffon.[78]

Newall approved Freeman's proposal and, in mid October, the Supply Committee reported: 'orders for Whirlwind aircraft, Peregrine engines and allied equipment should be cancelled at once and all work on them stopped. Jigs and tools and semi-manufactured material should be put in store pending further instructions.'[79] A few days later, Freeman advised Ernest Hives of Rolls-Royce that 'Peregrine production for Westland Whirlwind fighters should be stopped at the earliest practical point.'[80] It had originally been intended that a version of the Peregrine, detuned to give less power, but offer longer service intervals, would replace the Kestrel XXX engine used in the Miles Master trainer, but it was now decided that this was not practicable and the Master was redesigned to accommodate the Bristol Mercury radial engine. Lord Aberconway, Westland's chairman, promptly wrote to Kingsley Wood, challenging the decision to cancel the Whirlwind. Wood responded:

> The decisions that have been reached as regards individual firms have been determined in the light of the programme as a whole. As you will realise the large increase in the size of the Army has meant a corresponding increase in the requirements of Army Co-operation aircraft and, while we have several fighter types in production or nearing the production stage, the only really satisfactory Army Co-operation type is the Lysander designed by the Westland Company. We are, therefore, anxious for Westlands to concentrate their undivided energies on the production of this aircraft and there is no doubt that the demands to be placed upon them and the firms associated with them in Lysander production will require their full attention. It is clear that this can only be achieved by curtailing the Whirlwind contract.

Wood also noted the aircraft and engine programmes were interdependent and that total Rolls-Royce production would be greater if the Peregrine was eliminated and the company focussed on those engines for which demand was highest.[81]

A Limited Reprieve

This was not quite the end of the road for the Whirlwind. Although Newall approved the cancellation of the production programme, he asked for eight, essentially hand-built, Whirlwinds for a new role.[82] This requirement arose out of the early photoreconnaissance experiments carried out by the highly secretive Secret Intelligence Service Flight at Heston.[83] In peacetime, the Flight had achieved considerable success using a few civilian-registered Lockheeds and FO Maurice 'Shorty' Longbottom of the Heston Flight summarised its experiences to date in a memorandum to the Air Ministry in August 1939. He suggested that fighters, with their radio and armament replaced by fuel, would be the best method of performing photo-reconnaissance over enemy territory in wartime, the aircraft relying on speed and height to elude fighters and flak.

Longbottom suggested the Spitfire, but noted: 'There is a new fighter, of which the prototype has been made, which would be an improvement on the Spitfire. This is the Westland Whirlwind, with two Rolls-Royce Peregrine engines, which has top speed of 370 mph.'[84] Longbottom suggested that if its fuel capacity was increased to 408 gallons the aircraft would offer a safe range of 1,400 miles at 300 mph. Although he suggested that a twin-engine type might offer added safety during long, over-sea flights, Longbottom's primary interest in the Whirlwind was because of its speed and presumed ability to be modified to carry more fuel than the Spitfire.

Although Newall asked for just eight Whirlwinds to meet this requirement,[85] the Supply Committee decided in late October to order eighteen: ten as complete aircraft, four more without engines and a further four in component form for spares. Westland was told to finish and store the production tooling and jigs for the aircraft 'until such time as it was necessary to stop this work in order to speed up Lysander production'.[86] Despite this limited reprieve, Aberconway continued his campaign to save the Whirlwind and told Freeman that components had already been made to build around 100 Whirlwinds at little additional cost. Freeman's view was that Westland could restart Whirlwind production in the future provided it did not interfere with Lysander production.[87]

Later in November, Eric Mensforth, joint Managing Director of Westland, also reported to the Supply Committee that a significant number of Whirlwind components had already been manufactured. In the light of this, and the availability of a substantial number of part-finished Peregrine castings and forgings, the committee reinstated an order for 114 Whirlwinds to use up the material and avoid waste. Westland was asked to provide spares for the life of the aircraft and to complete and store the production jigs and tooling. Twenty-six of the 114 Whirlwinds were to be unarmed reconnaissance aircraft and the remainder fighters.[88]

Full Trials and Farnborough

On 20 September, A&AEE re-opened at Boscombe Down and Whirlwind testing resumed with the first air-firing tests.[89] In mid-October, both engines were returned to Rolls-Royce where new ignition harnesses, induction pipes and flame traps were fitted. During October, Rolls-Royce carried out 100-hour type testing of redesigned supercharger impellors featuring a thickened hub and circular arc rotating guide vanes. These redesigned impellors were also fitted to L6845's Peregrines, which were proof run in January 1940 before being returned to A&AEE to be refitted to the aircraft.[90]

While awaiting the return of its engines, L6845 was further modified. It had been delivered with carburettor air intakes comprising convoluted alloy ducts fed from the radiator duct in the wing leading edge. While the engines were away these were replaced by conventional external intakes above the cowlings and leading directly into the downdraft carburettor. To cater for a change from pure glycol cooling to pressure cooling using a mixture of water and ethylene glycol, the coolant header tanks were enlarged requiring changes to the profile of the upper nacelle panels, which were more bulged. Finally, cooling ducts were added to cool the fuel pumps and prevent vapour locks in the fuel system. Less visible changes modifications included reinforcement of the cannon mountings and a change from hydraulic to pneumatic cannon operation.[91] The engines were returned and the aircraft flew again on 22 January. Performance testing continued through February during which time a further 90 lbs of ballast weight was fitted into the radio bay.

In early March, the engines were again removed and returned to Rolls-Royce for inspection following excessive coolant pressures in the port engine. Rolls-Royce also replaced the boost controls and throttle linkages with production parts. While the engines were away more changes were made to L6845. The elevator servo was modified to improve elevator authority and the cannon mounting was modified again.[92] The aircraft flew at the beginning of April and on 25 April. With the tests completed, L6845 left A&AEE to return to Yeovil for preparation for delivery to the RAF.

When A&AEE eventually published its findings, it reported a maximum speed of 354 mph at 15,800 feet, rather less than the 370-390 mph expected by both the Air Ministry and Petter. The Whirlwind climbed to 15,000 feet in 5.7 minutes, but at 24,000 feet, the rate of climb fell to less than 1,000 feet per minute and it took nearly twenty-five minutes to reach 30,000 feet. The A&AEE pilots liked the Whirlwind's handling although they felt that the rudder and the ailerons were heavy for a fighter. Take off and landing were straightforward and the aircraft's behaviour on one engine was excellent. The test pilots liked the cockpit layout although they found the seat uncomfortable and the only other criticisms were of erratic operation of the Exactor controls and poor brakes.[93]

While L6845 underwent its much delayed trials at Boscombe Down, L6844 went by road to the Royal Aircraft Establishment at Farnborough in early February 1940 for full-scale wind tunnel tests to discover if any simple modifications to the aircraft would reduce its drag. For these tests the undercarriage and tailwheel were removed and replaced by a mounting pylon and tail strut covered by dummy undercarriage doors. The propellers were also replaced with dummy spinners with no apertures for the blades.

The biggest reduction in drag was achieved by sealing gaps around the cowlings, exhaust ducts, flap and cooling cavities, tail and canopy. Tests using wool tufts also revealed turbulence where the radiator inlet met the fuselage and nacelle and the addition of fairings blending the ends of the radiator intake into these surfaces produced significant improvements. RAE estimated that these changes would increase the Whirlwind's top speed by 15 mph.[94] The RAE also carried out vibration tests on the second prototype to establish the effect of the stiffening of the fin and its attachment to the fuselage, and the introduction of a small 'acorn' fairing between the fin and horizontal tailplane. The RAE's measurements showed reduced vibration in the vertical plane, but that the horizontal vibration was not much better than before, although it appeared at higher speeds than previously. At 360 mph, the amplitude of this very low frequency vibration (7.3 Hz) was as great at 0.05 inches (1.27 mm).[95]

Photoreconnaissance Whirlwinds

Little detailed data for the proposed reconnaissance variants of the Whirlwind has survived. The key Air Ministry file covering these developments was not chosen for preservation and was destroyed post-war. From the information that does remain it is clear that Westland proposed two different versions. For the first the cameras and a new 150-gallon fuel tank replaced the guns in the nose. At a weight of 10,700 lbs, maximum speed was forecast to be 373 mph, service ceiling 30,000 feet and range at 300 mph was 1,000 miles. In the more radical second proposal the undercarriage was fixed down freeing up space for additional fuel tankage in the nacelles to give a range of 1,500 miles. The weight of the aircraft was expected to be 12,000 lbs and service ceiling and maximum speed would be reduced to 28,000 feet and 345 mph respectively.[96] The Typhoon, Wellington V, de Havilland B.1/40 (not yet named Mosquito), the Spitfire with a Merlin XX engine and a Merlin-powered Lockheed P-38 Lightning were also considered, but the Ministry's preferred option was the Whirlwind and Westland was told to proceed with its first, less-radical proposal with the expectation that it would fly in July 1940.

The forecast performance of the reconnaissance Whirlwind was based on Westland's estimates of the standard aircraft's performance adjusted to reflect the increased weight of the reconnaissance version. When the A&AEE tests showed that the Whirlwind's service ceiling at its normal weight was just 30,300 feet rather than the expected 31-33,000 feet, it was concluded that the ceiling for the heavier PRU version could be as low as 28,000 feet. Until late March, the first two production Whirlwinds (P6966 and 6967) were being assembled as reconnaissance aircraft and P6968 as the first production fighter[97], but on 30 March 1930, Peck wrote to Sholto Douglas (ACAS(T)):

> We understood the Whirlwind would be an improvement in all respects upon the present Spitfire. It would have two engines and higher performance. It is therefore very disappointing indeed after what we had been told to learn that the Whirlwind has a ceiling of only 28,000 ft. I regret that this ceiling renders the aircraft unsuitable for the requirement and, in that event, the

only thing to do is to renounce the 26 aircraft which I believe have been earmarked for this work and to look around for something else unless we can use the Whirlwind for bad weather reconnaissance.[98]

Although Tedder and Sholto Douglas continued to discuss the project until May, Peck's decision marked the end of the Whirlwind as a reconnaissance aircraft. All 114 production aircraft were delivered as fighters.

Petter's 'Whirlwind Mk II'

Despite the cancellation of the Whirlwind programme, Petter met with Tedder and others in February 1940 to discuss proposals for the further development of the aircraft. His proposed changes[99] included the use of a developed Peregrine engine running at 12 lbs boost and offering a rated altitude of 20,000 feet that Petter felt would increase the Whirlwind's top speed by 40 mph. He also proposed using new Rotol propellers with a pitch range of thirty-five degrees in place of the de Havilland twenty degrees units currently fitted. These would reduce the tendency of the engines to overspeed during high speed dives, shorten the take-off run and make better use of a more powerful Peregrine.

The Whirlwind's cooling system was clearly of marginal capacity with the existing Peregrine and if the engine were uprated, the cooling system would need to be improved. Petter suggested the use of a new fin and tube radiator type made by Morris Radiators. These were far more efficient than the honeycomb radiators currently used, offered less drag and could also be made in a rectangular shape, thereby making full use of the area within the duct of the Whirlwind compared with the three drum-shaped radiators fitted as standard. The increase in both area and efficiency was expected to improve heat dissipation by 26 per cent. Petter also suggested the inclusion of any small changes recommended by RAE Farnborough as a result of the wind tunnel tests being carried out there.

From the start of the RAF's interest in the Hispano cannon, the limited capacity of the sixty-round magazine had been seen as the gun's main weakness and by early 1940, numerous companies were working with varying degrees of enthusiasm and success on continuous ammunition feeds. For the improved Whirlwind, Petter suggested the Bristol-designed feed because it required relatively few changes to the nose and gun mounting structure. After meeting with representatives of the Ministry's Armament Directorate, Petter substituted the Hydran ammunition feed for the Bristol one. The unusual Hydran or 'M-Type' feed seems to have had considerable support within the Air Ministry, partly perhaps because Sqn Ldr John Munro of the Armament

Directorate had conceived it. The feed comprised a box of vertical cells each holding unbelted rounds underneath which was a worm drive driven by a pneumatic stepper motor, which fed the rounds towards the gun. British Thomson Houston (then owned by United Electrical Industries, a major Westland shareholder) built prototypes of the feed in a variety of capacities: left- and right-hand versions capable of holding 121 rounds for the Whirlwind and the inner guns of the Typhoon, 114-round versions for the outer guns of the Typhoon and a 300-round version for the Beaufighter.[100] To accommodate the bulk of the feed, Westland designed a new, longer nose with the guns in a horizontal row with the inner guns further back than the outer ones, a layout that released considerable space in the upper part of the nose. Petter proposed to fill this space with an additional 27-gallon fuel tank in order to maintain endurance with the thirstier uprated Peregrine.[101]

Petter forecasted an increase in service ceiling to 39,000 feet and a maximum speed of 400 mph at 15,000 feet and no less than 422 mph at 20,000 feet compared with his optimistic estimate of 390 mph at 15,000 feet for the standard aircraft. As we have already seen, when A&AEE eventually released its report on the Whirlwind, the maximum speed of the second prototype was found to be just 354 mph. Petter submitted a third proposal in early May 1940 that not only included the nose fuel tank (now of thirty gallons capacity) but also three Browning machine guns with 400 rounds of ammunition each.[102] Petter's proposals would undoubtedly have resulted in an improved aircraft, but posed a problem for the Air Ministry in determining an appropriate development policy for an aircraft that had been cancelled.

Westland was instructed to proceed with trial installations of the new radiators, the Hydran feed for the guns and nose fuel tank. Although Petter had envisaged this package as representing a Whirlwind 'Mk II', Farren made it clear that what the Air Ministry required was not a new version of the aircraft, but urgent testing of the Hydran feed in the hope that it could be incorporated in at least some of the Whirlwinds already ordered and, later, a fully interchangeable new nose containing the guns and additional fuel.[103]

The engine and propeller proposals posed different problems, however. The Rotol propellers suggested by Petter were designed to fit the No. 5 size propeller shaft used by the Rolls-Royce Merlin and other engines, not the smaller No. 4 size shaft of the Peregrine. There was no other application for a high performance propeller in this size and the effort of designing and testing it would only benefit the 114 Whirlwinds on order. The proposals for engine development raised similar questions. Rolls-Royce was developing the Peregrine to run at 12 lbs boost on 100 octane fuel for short periods, in much the same way it had cleared the Merlin for emergency, short term use at higher boost pressures at the expense of reduced overhaul intervals. To raise the Peregrine's full throttle height to 20,000 feet as proposed by Petter, it would require at least a change in supercharger gearing and probably a redesigned supercharger. To use the higher boost continuously rather than just for short periods would require changes to the cooling system and a great deal of testing. Again, the Whirlwind would be the only aircraft to benefit from this work.

Although the engine and propeller developments could not be justified for the 114 aircraft being built, they might have been if more Whirlwinds were ordered. Opinions within the Air Ministry were divided. Rowe thought it unlikely: 'It is difficult at this stage to foresee the possibility of further production of the Whirlwind, which would justify the consideration of a Mark II version of the aeroplane; it is probable that developments of the Beaufighter, the Tornado and Typhoon are likely to outweigh any advantages the Whirlwind may possess at the moment.'[104] He felt that the Ministry should make the most of the Whirlwinds on order, but order no more. Farren and Tedder agreed that it was unlikely that the propeller and engine developments could be completed in time to be applied to any of the existing order, but thought that 'if started now they might be well advanced, and if a proposal for a further order was seriously considered we should be in a better position ... I do not like the idea of one of our latest types equipped only with engines rated for 87-octane fuel. Unless we conclude that the engine is unlikely to stand up to a full 100 octane rating without serious changes I think we should be well advised to go ahead with it.'[105]

Bulman stressed the impact on Rolls-Royce production that would be caused by making significant modifications to the Peregrine or ordering further Whirlwinds. He warned that 'to produce further Whirlwinds even of the current type will necessitate a curtailment of some other Rolls-Royce programme' and that more Peregrines could only be produced at Rolls-Royce's Derby factory 'with more than a 2 to 1 reduction of Merlin, or by postponing the Griffon'.[106]

No New Whirlwinds

Freeman ended any further debate about additional Whirlwind orders with a terse memo: 'No new Whirlwinds.'[107] Bulman promptly advised Rolls-Royce that work on developing the Peregrine for a full 100 octane rating should be suspended. A few weeks later, Westland submitted a fourth proposal for Whirlwind development, this time directly to Fighter Command. In addition to the new nose with a twenty-five-gallon fuel tank, Westland proposed a thirty-five-gallon tank in the rear fuselage, replacing the ballast weight and taking total fuel capacity from 134 to 194 gallons.[108]

The Hydran ammunition feed underwent low temperature tests at the RAE at Farnborough in May 1940 and ground firing trials at Hydran in early June. These were generally successful and in July, L6844 was fitted with a redesigned nose containing a single Hispano and feed. A single gun and hand-built magazine was used initially in order to accelerate the trials. The aircraft then went to A&AEE for ground and air trials. The air firing trials were also promising, but the feed did not work reliably under conditions of negative gravity and suffered stoppages when firing very short bursts. Hydran modified the magazine and firing trials continued, but the problems remained.[109]

Nonetheless in early August 1940, the aircraft was fitted with a full set of four cannon and Hydran magazines for further testing.[110] During tests with the full four-gun armament the same problems presented themselves, together with two new ones. The ammunition boxes were thought to be too fragile to survive the rough handling they would be subjected to in the field. The problem was made worse by their weight when full. The magazine and its accessories weighed nearly 35 lbs (15.8 kg). Filled with 121 rounds of ammunition it weighed over 100 lbs (45.6 kg) – nearly twice the weight of a loaded drum magazine. One can imagine the difficulty in loading such a heavy magazine into the high nose of the Whirlwind. The only alternative would be to load each individual round laboriously into the magazines in situ. More seriously, the magazine consumed pneumatic pressure so quickly that after a single long burst the pressure had dropped below that needed for it to function. This problem was made worse by the absence of a pneumatic pump in the Whirlwind, in which the sole source of compressed air was the fixed bottle in the nose. In view of these difficulties no air firing was carried out with all four guns installed.

The French had also realised the limitations of the drum-fed Hispano and fortunately Manufacture National d'armes de Châtellerault (MAC) had produced a far more effective belt feed than any of the British projects. This was first demonstrated to the French authorities in April 1940 and in May, Captain Adams of the Air Ministry's Armament Directorate brought a model of the feed and a set of drawings to England. At a conference (attended by Petter and Davenport) held at A&AEE on 8 October, it was decided to abandon the Hydran feed and accelerate development and production of the Châtellerault installation. Westland had already been instructed to prepare a trial installation of the feed and was constructing a new nose for the aircraft.

L6844 duly reappeared at A&AEE in September 1940 for trials with the Châtellerault feed before being returned to Westland in April 1941. In May, it was sent to the Aircraft Gunmounting Establishment (AGME) at Duxford for further testing of the installation which was, at that time, also intended to be used in the Westland Welkin. Subsequently, the Welkin cannon installation was changed to a ventral one and bore no resemblance to that of the Whirlwind.

The Whirlwind belt-feed installation was technically cleared, but it was decided not to introduce it into production as this would only be possible for the last few aircraft of the Whirlwind's short production run. While at AGME, L6844 underwent gun maintenance trials and a considerable amount of air firing at up to +4 g and -1.5 g. During one such flight the tailplane was badly damaged by ejected belt links. When AGME was disbanded in January 1942, the unserviceable aircraft was left behind and allocated, but not used by the Air Fighting Development Unit.[111]

The Merlin Whirlwind?

Westland continued to press for the reinstatement of the Whirlwind and in January 1941, Mensforth proposed directly to Fighter Command rather than the Air Ministry a new version of the Whirlwind powered by Rolls-Royce Merlin XX engines.[112] Although the Merlin was only slightly heavier and longer than the Peregrine, several challenges needed to be overcome to install it in the Whirlwind. The Merlin used an updraught carburettor that occupied much of the space at the lower rear end the engine normally occupied by the Whirlwind's main undercarriage mountings. The Whirlwind's engine nacelles were too close to the fuselage to allow the use of the larger diameter propeller needed to make efficient use of the Merlin's power. Petter's proposed solution, which also overcame ground clearance problems, was to use a smaller diameter, four-bladed propeller.

In February, Sir Henry Tizard, chairman of the newly-created Joint Development and Production Committee, reviewed the case for continuing Whirlwind production. Westland argued that the aircraft was popular with the squadron, had powerful armament, was almost as fast as the Spitfire and could be made faster and that to stop production would dislocate Westland production and lead to the loss of skilled labour. It is hard to sympathise with this last argument since 300 Spitfires had been ordered from Westland in August 1940 and the factory was busier than at any stage in its history.

Tizard noted that the current Whirlwind required two engines that had no other use and consumed 50 per cent more material than a Spitfire to do the same job less efficiently. In reality, the position was somewhat worse: contemporary figures record that the manufacture of a complete Whirlwind consumed nearly three times as much alloy as a Spitfire.[113] The Beaufighter used even more material, but fulfilled roles that the Whirlwind could not. It offered greater range than the Whirlwind and its spacious fuselage could accommodate airborne radar for night fighting or the bulky non-voice radio equipment needed for long-range operation and a second crewman to operate it. For Tizard there were only two options: cease production as planned or increase it to cover losses in intensive operations. Tizard let the cancellation stand and ended any chance of a further order for Whirlwinds.[114]

The 114 production aircraft that were built had an unusually long and eventful career. There were minor changes to the Whirlwind during its life, but the aircraft retired in December 1943 were essentially the same as those that had entered service in 1940. There was, however, a further short-lived proposal that would have led to a very different looking aircraft – the proposal to fit one or more 40-mm cannon.

Big Gun

During the inter-war years, RAF doctrine was that, apart from artillery spotting, using aircraft in direct, tactical support of the Army's ground operations was not a proper use of air power. However, the brief campaign in France in 1940, during which the British Army had appeared powerless to stop the German panzers, prompted the Air Ministry to investigate methods of attacking tanks from the air. These investigations acquired further momentum during late 1940 with the threat of invasion of Britain. Although the 20-mm cannon had some potential for attacking tanks,[115] future work on anti-tank weapons focussed on developing armour-piercing ammunition for the Vickers and Rolls-Royce 40-mm cannon originally commissioned in 1938 as air-to-air weapons. This work eventually led to the Vickers-equipped Hurricane IID.

Early in 1941, a Beaufighter was experimentally fitted with a single Vickers 40-mm gun at the Aircraft Gun Mounting Establishment (AGME) at Duxford. It was chosen for these trials simply because its large gun bays and robust construction allowed the experimental installation to be made quickly and easily. However, when Sholto Douglas heard about it he assumed that the intention was to produce anti-tank Beaufighters. He had fought hard to expand the night fighter force in the face of competing demands for Beaufighters from Coastal Command and the idea of tank-busting Beaufighters represented a further diversion from the aircraft's vital role as night fighters. He hoped 'that no large numbers will be converted'. Ever helpful, he suggested that an effective anti-tank aircraft should be a small, manoeuvrable and fast aircraft that could evade light flak and short-range fighters. The Beaufighter was none of those things, but he offered the Whirlwind as an alternative. It was he said, 'about 30 mph faster near the ground and very much more manoeuvrable'. He understood that a 40-mm gun would fit into the Whirlwind and was prepared to release the aircraft to be converted.[116]

Douglas' comment that he believed the gun would fit, implying that some preliminary study had already taken place, caused some surprise in that neither the Air Ministry, Westland nor MAP were aware that any such work had been done.[117] The Air Ministry politely rejected Douglas' suggestion because there were too few Whirlwinds to make it worthwhile and it did not want to distract Westland from the high priority Welkin high-altitude fighter. Despite this the idea resurfaced in December 1941 when Sir Archibald Sinclair (Secretary of State for Air) formally asked for a renewed investigation into a 40-mm-armed Whirlwind.[118]

Two possibilities for mounting one or two 40-mm guns were reviewed with Westland: either mounted beneath the fuselage inboard of the propeller arcs or replacing the existing nose cannon.[119] The first option would allow the Hispanos to be retained in the nose and would not significantly shift the aircraft centre of gravity. However, there were no suitable mounting points on the structure under the fuselage, there was a risk of blast damage to the lower centre-section skinning, and to clear the bulky ammunition hopper, the guns would need to be mounted well below the lower surface that might cause pitching problems when the guns were fired. Mounting the cannon in the nose was felt to be the better possibility. Two guns would require more ballast weight in the tail to restore the centre of gravity and a longer nose that would impair directional stability and the pilot's view. Mounting one cannon in the nose would be easier and Westland estimated that a prototype could be built in about three months.

Early in January 1942, representatives of MAP, Westland and Vickers met with Captain Frazer Nash of Nash and Thompson, which had been selected to carry out the design work in order not to distract Westland from the Welkin.[120] The chosen configuration was for a single Vickers cannon mounted in the nose together with two Browning .303 guns for sighting, but the meeting also noted that there were only seventy to eighty Whirlwinds in existence and no more would be built. Nevertheless on 26 January, Westland and Nash and Thompson were told to proceed with the project.[121] However, Sinclair finally conceded on 30 January that because so few Whirlwinds were available the project should be dropped.[122] In the short time available it seems unlikely that any detailed design had been carried out and certainly no work was started on the construction of a prototype.

CHAPTER 5

'An infinity of trouble' – Early Days with Fighter Command

The first production Whirlwind (P6966) flew on 22 May 1940 and was delivered to the RAF on 4 June. Many previous accounts of the aircraft have claimed that Whirlwind deliveries were delayed by ever-changing Air Ministry requirements or late delivery of engines, but the seventeen-month interval between the issue of the contract and the delivery of the first production Whirlwind compares favourably with those for the Hurricane (eighteen months), Spitfire (twenty-five months) or Defiant (twenty-nine months).

Fighter Command chose Blenheim-equipped 25 Squadron to carry out service trials of the Whirlwind. The six Blenheim squadrons were the only ones in which all of the pilots were qualified to fly twin-engine aircraft and 25 Squadron was one of the most experienced. The squadron's commanding officer, Sqn Ldr Ken MacEwen, visited Yeovil on 23 May to be briefed on the Whirlwind. Three of the squadron's senior NCO ground crew underwent training at the factory and MacEwen delivered L6845 to the squadron at North Weald on 30 May. Four squadron pilots flew it the next day, one describing it as 'absolutely lovely'. On 1 June, four more pilots flew the aircraft including Station Commander Wg Cdr Francis 'Victor' Beamish who offered a more measured verdict of 'as ordered'.[123]

On 3 June, the cockpit canopy of L6845 partially collapsed in flight, but the squadron gained a second Whirlwind the following day when MacEwen delivered P6966. The day after its canopy had been repaired, the tailwheel leg of L6845 collapsed on landing.[124] This was the first of an epidemic of tailwheel failures caused by loss of pressure in the Dowty oleo leg or mechanical failure of the leg spigot. These failures persisted until 1942 and were by far the most important cause of Whirlwind unserviceability: over 150 instances were recorded. At best, the resulting damage was confined to the leg, the tailwheel doors and the wooden fairing at the base of the rudder. At worst, the sudden impact caused by the leg's collapse fractured the bulkhead casting at the base of the fin spar to which the tailwheel was mounted and sometimes the rudder hinge casting higher up the fin. During the Whirlwind's life, the tail oleo was modified three times in an attempt to cure the problem and the aluminium alloy bulkhead was replaced by a steel one.

On 19 June, the squadron, which had now also taken delivery of P6967, moved to Martlesham Heath. A week later, Winston Churchill, Britain's new Prime Minister, visited the squadron and was shown the Whirlwind.[125] The aircraft flew very little during this period as Westland, Rolls-Royce and de Havilland engineers made minor modifications to them. Westland reinforced the cockpit canopies and made changes to the outer slats, and modified the fuel breathers. De Havilland technicians replaced L6845's Rotol propellers with de Havilland units and, to cure the tendency of the engines to reach excessive speeds when diving, the pitch range of the propellers of all the aircraft was reset from twenty-five/forty-five degrees to twenty-eight/forty-eight degrees. Rolls-Royce technicians adjusted the engines of L6845 to give 9 lbs boost and those on P6966 12 lbs. During bench tests of the engine at 12 lbs boost in March 1940, the company had recorded an output of 1,000 hp at 3,000 rpm. Therefore, for a short period, P6966 was probably the most potent Whirlwind of them all.[126] P6967 also needed repair after an undercarriage mudguard detached in flight and damaged the nacelle and propeller. The mudguards were removed from all three aircraft and deleted from future production. They had been rendered superfluous when the Whirlwind's horizontal tailplane was moved to its final location high on the fin where it was no longer vulnerable to debris thrown up by the wheels.

P6967 flew with both Whirlwind squadrons before ending her days as an instructional airframe at No. 6 School of Technical Training. She was scrapped on 4 November 1944. (*Robert Bowater*)

Enter Beaverbrook

One of Churchill's first actions as Prime Minister was to create a Ministry of Aircraft Production (MAP) to take over the Air Ministry's production responsibilities. He chose newspaper owner and businessman Lord Beaverbrook to lead the new Ministry and, a few weeks later, Beaverbrook asked for Dowding's opinion of the Whirlwind in view of the short production run currently planned.[127] Dowding felt that the question was premature as only three aircraft had been delivered and serviceability had been low. Nonetheless he gave his first impressions:

> The pilots like them (though this may be largely due to their relief in getting away from the Blenheim); and they may be worth their weight in gold in the near future as being almost the only fighter aircraft capable of attacking tanks from the air. Against them there is their very high approach and landing speed. Pilots tell me that they have to bring them in at 110 mph and, even then, the controls are 'sloppy'. This means that they can probably never be used at night. Then again, if the Lysander is any criterion, we must expect an infinity of trouble with cowlings, fittings etc., unless the firm has learned wisdom from past experience. Further, I think that it is a very extravagant design. By this I mean that it takes two engines to lift four cannon guns, whereas the new Hawker fighter should be able to lift six with one engine and give a similar performance with a lower landing speed. Altogether, I feel we may be very glad indeed to have as many Whirlwinds as we can get in the near future both as anti-tank weapons and in order to attack bombers as they become less and less vulnerable to rifle-calibre machine gun fire, but we shall be glad enough to drop them when the Hawker fighter comes into heavy production.[128]

Although the Hawker Typhoon prototype had flown, Dowding could not know how long Fighter Command would have to wait for it to appear in quantity or that it would fail in its intended role as a Hurricane and Spitfire replacement.

263 Squadron Reformed

In mid-June, when asked if 25 Squadron should continue service trials on the first few Whirlwinds or completely re-equip with the aircraft, Dowding ruled that the unit should become the first Beaufighter squadron as and when Beaufighter production allowed. He recommended to the Air Ministry that the Whirlwinds should go to 263 Squadron and on 3 July, Fighter Command ordered the transfer of the aircraft as soon as they were serviceable, including the second prototype which was to be used for training.[129] 263 Squadron was regrouping after the two brief campaigns it had fought in Norway with Gladiators and the loss of its commanding officer and many of its pilots aboard HMS *Glorious*, sunk on 8 June by *Scharnhorst* and *Gneisenau*.

For the second Norwegian expedition the squadron had twenty-eight pilots on strength. Three were killed in Norway, another was posted during the campaign and a further ten were lost with HMS *Glorious*. The fourteen surviving pilots were Flt Lts Caesar Hull and Randolph Mills, FOs Harry Olivier and Bill Riley, POs Alan Britton, Joe Hughes, Irving McDermott, Stuart Parnall and Peter Wyatt-Smith and Sgts Herbert Kitchener, Dennis Mason, George Milligan, Patrick Watson-Parker and Basil Whall. Hull, Mills and Wyatt-Smith had all returned to England with injuries before the end of the campaign in Norway while the others returned with the ground crews by ship. The squadron was ordered to reassemble, re-equipped with a full complement of Hurricanes under the temporary command of A Flight commander Mills at Drem, east of Edinburgh on the southern shore of the Firth of Forth. On 18 June, before many of the pilots had arrived at their new station, nine new Hurricanes were delivered to Drem.[130]

New pilots arrived during the following weeks to bring the squadron back up to full strength. Some stayed only briefly, but others including Flt Lt Wynford Smith, POs Eric Bell, Alan Downer, Roy Ferdinand, Tom Pugh and

In 1940, No. 263 Squadron was part of the Air Component of the Expeditionary Force in Norway. The Norwegians used log-lined dispersals and on their return to RAF Drem in Scotland, the squadron used the idea. They proved to be located too far from the dispersal hut, however, and they were not used, except, as in this instance, for photo opportunities. (*Robert Bowater*)

Patrick Thornton-Brown and Sgt Frank Morton, will reappear in the story. Among the new arrivals were two pilots from the RAE Experimental Section. James Tobin and Alan Moffet spent three weeks at 6OTU before joining 263 Squadron and returned to the RAE four weeks later, the purpose of their attachment to the unit being unknown.

On 6 July, Sqn Ldr Harry Eeles, 263 Squadron's newly-appointed commanding officer, delivered Whirlwind P6966 to his squadron, now based at Grangemouth. At Fighter Command's request L6845 remained at Martlesham Heath for a short time for cannon adjustment trials, but both it and P6967 were flown north to 263 Squadron over the next few days. 263 Squadron spent the rest of July in training and flying some operational patrols on Hurricanes while a third flight, led by Wynford Smith, was created to perform development flying with the Whirlwind. Three more Whirlwinds were delivered to the squadron during July and work continued on fitting rear armour to the aircraft and further engine modifications by Rolls-Royce. The month was not without incident: three Hurricanes were lost in accidents and two pilots were killed. Smith and Eeles walked away from their accidents in Hurricanes P2991 and P2990, but Alan Downer died of his injuries after force landing Hurricane P2917 on the night of 20 July. Eric Bell was killed on 23 July when his Blenheim crashed on approach at Aston Down while on a twin-engine conversion course at 5OTU.

'An infinity of trouble'

Dowding had forecast 'an infinity of trouble' with the Whirlwind. In July, he got it and late in the month the Whirlwinds were grounded. Rivets in the outer slat shells were failing and the slats were jumping off their sprockets; welds were failing in the convoluted carburettor intake ducts and the wingtip fairings were cracking after as little as ten flying hours. After the tailwheel oleo of P6967 collapsed during a landing on 23 July, the impact again cracking the rear bulkhead casting and even causing one of the slats to jump from its sprockets, Eeles ordered that the tailwheel oleos, which appeared to require re-pressurising weekly, should all be stripped and examined.[131] The pilots' greatest concern was the failure of the wingtips and the risk of them jamming an aileron in flight. Because of this the squadron's engineering officer, FO Bertram Grant, in consultation with Sqn Ldr William Disbrey, 13 Group Engineer Officer, grounded the aircraft until Westland supplied reinforced wingtips.[132]

At a Fighter Command conference early in July to discuss, among other things, fighter tactics in the event of a German invasion of England, Dowding ordered that his few cannon fighters 'should not be thrown into air combat since, in the event of enemy tanks being introduced into this country ... they would be invaluable'. Dowding also ruled that pilots should practice attacking ground targets. Accordingly, once modified wingtips arrived from Westland, the squadron focussed on making the cannon installation reliable and practicing firing at ground and air targets.

There were more personnel changes during August. Both flight commanders were posted out to command Hurricane units in the south, but new pilots FO David Crooks, DFC, POs David Stein and Donald Vine and Sgt Cliff Rudland joined the squadron. Stein had an eventful introduction to the life of a fighter pilot. On a night patrol on 24 August, just three weeks after joining the squadron straight from an OTU, the oil pressure of his Hurricane's engine fell to zero, the engine caught fire and he was obliged to take to his parachute.

In August, the squadron lost its first Whirlwind when the port main wheel tyre of P6966 burst on take off at Grangemouth and the remains of the tyre and inner tube jammed the undercarriage leg. Irving McDermott circled to burn off fuel before taking to his parachute. P6966 crashed near Dunmore, burying itself deeply in the boggy ground while McDermott landed near Stenhousemuir where he was promptly arrested by the Home Guard and only released when Eeles vouched for his identity.

During August, the experiment with the third flight, C Flight, to carry out Whirlwind development was abandoned. The Whirlwinds now operated in A Flight while B Flight carried out all operational flying using Hurricanes. In testing the Hispano gun, it proved to be highly reliable; however, early British installations of the weapon were less successful, partly because they had been designed at a time when British understanding of the gun's action was somewhat incomplete. Correct tensioning of the drum magazine spring was critical and the gun was prone to ejection problems, particularly when installed in ways other than those intended by its designers. To help resolve these difficulties, Sqn Ldr John Munro was posted to the squadron from the Air Ministry's Armament Directorate. Munro had been responsible for the conception of the Hydran magazine described earlier and also played a pivotal role in the development of the first experimental cannon installations on the Hurricane and, particularly, Spitfire.

Cannon firing trials continued during August, but not without interference from the continuing tailwheel problems. Eeles took P6970 for firing at the ranges at Luce Bay only to have the tailwheel collapse and a week later suffered a similar failure when he took P6969 for firing trials at the butts at Turnhouse. Unsurprisingly for much of August none of the Whirlwinds was serviceable. Fortunately, modified Dowty tailwheel units began to arrive at the end of the month.[133] Firing trials produced not only regular shell ejection problems but also damage to the skin of the aircraft's nose cone. The squadron improvised a crude, but effective reinforcing plate for the nose, but Westland later designed a reinforced cowling that was easily detachable with a single large captive nut at the tip of the nose replacing the numerous fasteners at its rear end.[134] During August, the squadron's Hurricane Flight continued training and on five days during the month, was asked to keep one or two sections of aircraft at readiness for operations. They were, however, not called upon, even on 15 August when 13 Group was heavily committed against the Luftwaffe's first and last large scale daylight attack on north-east England when Luftflotte 5 sent a substantial force to targets in North Yorkshire and Tyneside.

On 3 September, the squadron moved from Grangemouth back to Drem and during the month, even though it continued to be shown as non-operational in the Fighter Command order of battle, the Hurricanes of B Flight flew thirty-two operational patrols totalling nearly 100 sorties. During these they intercepted Blackburn Sharks and Bothas and Supermarine Walruses, but not the enemy.

The Whirlwind's problems persisted and serviceability in September was only 55 per cent. Late in the month, representatives of 263 Squadron, RAF Maintenance Command and Westland, met at Drem to review the squadron's difficulties. Shortage of spares was identified as the greatest obstacle to serviceability, but the main technical issues were stripped teeth on the slat sprockets and the continuing wingtip failures. Hydraulic pipes had fractured because of poor workmanship and fragments of fuel tank sealant had made their way to the fuel filters causing in-flight engine failures. For many of the more minor complaints, Westland had already produced modified parts. A new canopy was designed to eliminate the tendency for the Perspex to crack along the riveted top seam of the original design. The welded alloy carburettor air intake duct was still cracking at the welds because of movement of the engine in its bearers. Westland designed a new duct with a flexible joint, but the squadron preferred the simple downdraft intake of the second prototype to the convoluted duct of the production aircraft.[135] The Peregrine engines had been reliable, but shown inconsistent boost pressures whenever climbs to higher altitudes had been attempted so P6967 was loaned to Rolls-Royce for investigation.

During October, two more Whirlwinds were delivered. P6974, the first aircraft incorporating the large 'acorn' fairing on the tailplane and various modifications prompted by the squadron's experience to date, arrived on 8 October. Hughes and Morton subjected the next aircraft, P6975, to ten hours of intensive aerobatics at Yeovil before it was delivered to the squadron on 22 October. In the middle of the month, the second prototype, which had been persistently unserviceable because of corrosion in its cooling system, was returned to Westland to be brought up to current production standard.[136]

In October and November, Westland, MAP and the Air Ministry all suggested that the Whirlwind's technical problems might be more easily addressed if 263

F/O Joe Hughes tucks No. 263 Squadron Whirlwind HE-B into formation. (*Robert Bowater*)

Squadron were moved to 10 Group in the south west of England and nearer the Westland factory at Yeovil, but Dowding was reluctant to do so. He told the Air Ministry that 'the squadrons in 10 Group have a considerable amount of fighting to do and must be in a fully operational condition'.[137] His response to Beaverbrook was even more blunt: 'I purposely put 263 Squadron well out of the way because I know Westlands and I know what a packet of trouble the squadron would be in for. I cannot put them anywhere in the South because I cannot carry any "passengers" in that part of the world.'[138] To ease some of the squadron's problems, MAP loaned a de Havilland Rapide to Westland to transport urgently needed Whirlwind spares to Scotland.

In a note to Beaverbrook at the end of October, Dowding expanded upon his earlier preliminary opinion of the Whirlwind. He noted the aircraft's ongoing 'teething' troubles and that Westland was unlikely to produce more than one aircraft per week under the existing arrangement: 'It therefore becomes necessary to give careful consideration to the question of whether it is worth while persevering with the type at all.'

As the Battle of Britain developed, there had been a tendency for combat be joined at ever greater heights. With increasing frequency, the RAF's fighter pilots were directed to intercept raids only to find the enemy 5,000 or 10,000 feet above them and the Germans began flying fighter sweeps at up to 30,000 feet, at which heights the inferiority of the Hurricane to the Messerschmitt Bf

109E (and even the heavy twin-engine Bf 110) had become all too apparent. Dowding was concerned about the Whirlwind's apparently poor performance at altitude and in his note quoted a report by Sqn Ldr Eeles: '...the performance of the Whirlwind above 20,000 feet falls off quite rapidly and it is considered that above 25,000 feet its fighting qualities are very poor'. In the context of the altitudes at which combats were now taking place, Dowding felt it was 'quite wrong to introduce at the present time a fighter whose effective ceiling is 25,000 ft'. He also felt that the aircraft's rate of glide and high-landing speed precluded its use as a night fighter, although Eeles felt otherwise. Referring to an earlier proposal to re-engine the Whirlwind with Allison engines, Dowding concluded: 'It is, of course, possible that the introduction of American engines might completely alter the performance and characteristics of the type; but, failing that, I recommend that we cut our losses and do not persevere with the Whirlwind as a service fighter type.'[139]

'...not every Hun comes over above 20,000 feet'

Dowding's indifference to the aircraft prompted the Air Ministry to review the curtailed Whirlwind programme. After being reassured by MAP that 'no useful purpose would be served by attempting to cut down the number of aeroplanes at this stage', Jo Andrews (Assistant Chief of the Air Staff (Tactics)) recommended that the Whirlwind programme should continue because, as he told Arthur Harris (then Deputy Chief of the Air Staff): 'We want early operational experience of the 20 mm cannon and not every Hun comes over above 20,000 feet.' Harris agreed and also did not share Dowding's adherence to the RAF's pre-war conviction that aircraft with low landing speeds were required for safe fighter operations at night. Harris thought that the Whirlwind might even be a useful 'stop gap' night fighter. 'It is within my humble experience that nearly all types are regarded as difficult or impossible to fly at night ... I have never yet met an aircraft that can be safely flown by day which cannot safely and easily be flown by night, once the pilots can night fly properly on any type. Conversely nearly all new aircraft are at first regarded as dangerous or difficult at night.'[140] The order for 114 Whirlwinds remained in place.

During November, 263 Squadron flew forty-eight uneventful operational sorties with its Hurricanes and received four more Whirlwinds (P6976-P6979).[141] Redesigned shell case ejector chutes made of steel rather than aluminium alloy were fitted and the earlier aircraft were retro-fitted with the new, large 'acorn' tailplane fairing, Wynford Smith diving P6975 successfully to 430 mph after it had been so fitted. Other problems, however, continued with no less than five cases of slat sprocket failure.

'...producing large numbers of Lysanders, which nobody wants...'

By November, the Battle of Britain had been won and AVM Sholto Douglas replaced Dowding as C-in-C Fighter Command. Petter wrote to Douglas on 26 November explaining that some initial difficulties were inevitable with what he described as 'probably the most radically new aeroplane that has ever gone into service'[142] and that resolving these difficulties had been made more difficult because the aircraft had been based 400 miles away from the factory. On 26 November, Fighter Command issued orders for 263 Squadron to relinquish its Hurricanes and move south to Exeter as a Whirlwind-only unit.[143] Douglas implored Petter to bring the squadron up to full strength of sixteen aircraft as soon as possible. He added that Westland was 'concentrating on producing large numbers of Lysanders, which nobody wants and which are doing no good in the war, instead of concentrating on producing Whirlwinds, which are wanted badly'.[144] Ironically, Douglas appears to have been unaware – or had forgotten – that the earlier need to accelerate Lysander production had prompted the Whirlwind's cancellation in the first place.

263 Squadron was not wholly enthusiastic that it was to operate exclusively on Whirlwinds and 'It was with great regret that leave was taken of the

No. 263 Squadron Whirlwind P6971 with Australian F/O Robert Tuff. The aircraft was first delivered on 31 August 1940 and following an eventful life was scrapped on 14 July 1944. Tuff made the ultimate sacrifice in possibly the most selfless act of the war. On 22 February 1944 after No. 263 Squadron had converted to Hawker Typhoons, Squadron Leader Geoff Warnes was forced to ditch off Guernsey due to engine failure. Tuff saw that Warnes was in difficulties in the rough sea, so abandoned his own aircraft in an effort to help him. Neither man was seen again. (*Robert Bowater*)

Hurricanes.'[145] Nonetheless, on 28 November, its ten serviceable Whirlwinds left Drem for Exeter via Sealand, leaving P6968 and 6974 behind at Drem under repair. On the flight south, Wyatt-Smith left P6979 at Sealand after suffering engine control problems on the first leg of the flight while Munro landed P7971 at Exeter on one engine after the other developed an internal glycol leak.[146]

Douglas visited Exeter on 4 December to meet the squadron, but fortunately was not there the following day to witness a further series of minor accidents. P6972 swung off the runway and hit a pile of timber, damaging a propeller. P6977 required a new outer wing after Ferdinand swung off the runway and collided with the unserviceable P6971. Finally, Thornton-Brown had to make a single-engine landing in P6970 after a throttle jammed fully open.[147]

Training flying continued and by 7 December the squadron had a full complement of sixteen Whirlwinds. Only six of these were serviceable. P6968 was still at Drem and P6979 at Sealand, five more were unserviceable at Exeter and three newly delivered aircraft were being fitted with cannon and radio equipment. Despite this, Eeles, Smith and Hughes flew the Whirlwind's first operational patrol on the morning of 7 December although the unit remained 'non operational' in the Fighter Command order of battle for two more weeks. Only on 22 December, over five months after taking delivery of its first Whirlwind, was one section of the squadron formally declared operational with the aircraft.[148]

Whirlwinds and Lysanders move down the production lines at Yeovil. In the last six months of 1940, Westland built an average of nearly seventy aircraft per month, an output it would not better at any point in the war, but very few of the aircraft produced were Whirlwinds. The average monthly Whirlwind output was less than three aircraft. (*Agusta Westland*)

CHAPTER 6

Operational at Last

The Whirlwind's operational career started uneventfully enough at Exeter with routine patrols, convoy escort sorties and training flights by non-operational pilots. Unfortunately, during one of these training sorties the squadron suffered its first fatality. On 12 December, during firing practice against sea markers at Sand Bay near Weston-Super-Mare, the pilots all made a successful first attack and Britton then dived down to carry out a second pass, but was not seen again by his fellow pilots. Sea and land searches were ordered and two days later P6980, but not the body of the pilot, was found in the sea some distance away from the firing range.[149]

Sqn Ldr Eeles was posted out on 16 December and John Munro assumed command of the unit while a few days later B Flight commander Olivier was posted to North Africa. Training flying was hindered by the unsatisfactory state of the airfield at Exeter, but was then halted entirely when 263 Squadron was told on 18 December to prepare to move to another airfield. As was the normal practice, the aircraft were grounded other than for operational flying in order to ensure that as many as possible would be serviceable and able to move at short notice. The routine patrols continued and on 23 December while on an interception patrol, Wynford Smith spotted a Ju 88 near Start Point, but it escaped into cloud before he could close to firing range. During this period, the ground crew and Westland technicians continued modifying the squadron's aircraft to bring them up to current production standard including fitting the large 'acorn' fairing to the tails of the last few aircraft not already so fitted.

Aware that during the short winter days aircraft would have to return from patrol at dusk, Munro decided that at least some of the pilots should learn to land the Whirlwind at night. In the late afternoon of 26 December, he carried out seven or eight landings over a period of half an hour. As a result of heavy use of the brakes with little opportunity between landings for them to cool, the brakes overheated and both tyre tubes burst when he was taxiing back in, but Munro concluded that the Whirlwind was quite capable of being used at night.[150]

On 29 December, the squadron was ordered to detach six Whirlwinds to St Eval in order to escort a pair of the RAF's first Consolidated Catalinas on the last leg of their 3,000-mile delivery flights from Darrell's Island, Bermuda, to Milford Haven. The first three Whirlwinds took off from Exeter in very poor weather shortly after midday with Smith (flying P6975) leading Vine (P6978) and Kitchener (P6981). Having quickly become lost, Smith and Vine flew into high ground while descending through the dense low cloud to ascertain their position. Kitchener saw the ground just in time, climbed and returned safely to Exeter. Later that day in better weather, Pugh, Crooks, Kitchener, Milligan, Mason and Morton successfully reached St Eval without further incident. During the earlier flight, Kitchener had briefly seen a dull red flash to his right, but was unsure of his exact position. Because of Kitchener's uncertainty, the remoteness of the area, foul weather and persistent heavy snowfall, the wreckage of the aircraft and the bodies of the pilots were not found until 9 March.[151]

Thus by the end of December, both flight commanders and three other pilots had gone: Smith, Vine and Britton killed in accidents and Olivier and Wyatt-Smith posted to the Middle East. In the words of its Intelligence Officer, 263 Squadron had 'for the second time, been reduced to a shadow

A member of the ground crew ushers a taxiing No. 263 Squadron Whirlwind at RAF Exeter in December 1940. (*Robert Bowater*)

of its former self'.[152] Early in January, David Crooks was promoted to acting Flight Lieutenant and became a flight commander while PO Bernard Howe was posted in from Beaufighter-equipped 25 Squadron.

Chameleons, Condors and other Creatures of Habit

From its monitoring of the Luftwaffe's plain language and low-grade cipher radio traffic and its meticulous analysis of radar plots of German operations, the RAF had obtained a fairly clear picture of the enemy's order of battle and operational habits, although it continued to overestimate the Luftwaffe's overall strength. The Whirlwind's early operations in 1941 were based on just such intelligence and the first would be codenamed 'Chameleon'.

From its various sources Air Intelligence had deduced that when Luftwaffe bombers were operating on moonlit nights, E-boats sailed from Cherbourg to a point just off the English coast at Start Bay in order to pick up Luftwaffe aircrew forced to ditch in the sea. 10 Group proposed that 263 Squadron's Whirlwinds should intercept and attack these vessels. In order to avoid arousing German suspicions these operations were designed to look like routine fighter patrols. The aircraft were not to search or to orbit the E-boat's rendezvous point and were to maintain radio silence until they were back over the British coast on their return journey. Take off would be as late as possible, consistent with the aircraft being able to perform their patrol and land back at Exeter just before dusk. Climbing to 15,000 feet just off the English coast, the aircraft were to fly towards Cherbourg on the same course as that believed to be taken in the opposite direction by the E-boats. They would then descend gradually to reach 3,000 feet at a point fifty miles out to sea and then return along the same route. The timing and route ought to allow the aircraft to discover the E-boats either on their way to their rendezvous off the English coast or on their way home, but would minimise the risk of them finding them at the precise rendezvous and raising German suspicions. Whether or not the operation would be ordered would depend partly on weather conditions and on the basis of intelligence as to the Luftwaffe's bombing target for the night.[153] On 9 January, Munro, Pugh and Crooks carried out the first 'Chameleon' patrol from Exeter, but did not locate the enemy in the Channel. The patrols were repeated, uneventfully, on 13 and 17 January and then appear to have been discontinued.

On the same day that 10 Group had issued instructions for the 'Chameleon' patrols, it also issued orders for the interception of lone German aircraft believed to make daily patrols passing well off the coast of Cornwall in order to attack shipping in the Atlantic Ocean or the Irish Sea. Since these aircraft were plotted more than forty miles off the coast, the task of intercepting them would again fall to the Whirlwinds and 10 Group instructed 263 Squadron to detach four Whirlwinds to St Eval for a trial period of seven days. Hughes, Stein, Kitchener and Thornton-Brown flew to St Eval on 8 January and did not have to wait long for their first combat with the enemy.

Early in the morning of 12 January, Stein and Mason were vectored onto an aircraft approaching Lands End from the south west. While climbing to 10,000 feet, Mason separated from Stein who carried on alone. Forty miles south west of the Scilly Isles, he saw a Ju 88 5,000 feet below him, just above a layer of cloud and travelling west. Stein worked his way up-sun and then dived down to attack. One cannon jammed but the remaining three fired a total of 111 rounds. The rear gunner of the Ju 88 also briefly opened fire. Stein saw his cannon rounds hitting the top of the bomber's fuselage followed by a small explosion, but his view was obscured by smoke from his guns and saw nothing more. The Ju 88 then dived down into the dense cloud layer and was not seen again. Stein claimed the Ju 88 as damaged, the first combat claim by a Whirlwind pilot.[154]

The following day, Thornton-Brown and Kitchener were on patrol well out to sea when they saw a Heinkel He 111 bomber flying eight to ten miles away. They pursued the aircraft and opened fire from extreme range as they believed, wrongly as it turned out, that they were low on fuel. The Heinkel carried out violent evasive manoeuvres and dived from over 20,000 to 3,000 feet before escaping into cloud. Neither of the Whirlwind pilots claimed to have damaged it.[155]

Back at Exeter, Pugh had a narrow escape on 19 January when both engines of P6984 suddenly stopped at 1,000 feet when he lowered the undercarriage in the circuit to land at Exeter. In a poor position to glide to the airfield, Pugh took to his parachute. The cause was later discovered to be maladjustment of the gravity switches in the Graviner fire extinguisher system, which had stuck in the 'fire' position during Pugh's earlier aerobatics leading to extinguishing fluid being sprayed into both engine nacelles as soon as the undercarriage was lowered.[156]

Later in January, the detachment at St Eval was increased from four to eight aircraft in response to a 10 Group instruction for the interception of KG40's Focke-Wulf Fw 200 Condors operating from Bordeaux. Radar plots revealed that these aircraft passed no closer than forty-five miles from Land's End so, again, the Whirlwinds were the prudent choice for operations that would inevitably take place far out to sea. Again, basic security precautions were to be taken. Radio silence was to be maintained as far as possible, the traditional call of 'Tally Ho' was not to be given when the enemy was sighted and the results of any combat were not to be reported by radio. Despite the elaborate preparations, there is no record of any encounter between 263's Whirlwinds and the Condors of KG40.[157]

F/L Tom Pugh of 263 Squadron seen in February 1941. He later commanded the squadron but was lost whilst leading 182 Squadron in August 1943. (*Niall Corduroy*)

Towards the end of January, six new pilots joined the squadron: PO Albert Tooth and Sergeants Glynn Foden, Doug Jowitt, Cecil King, Robert Skellon and Walter Waddington. On 22 January, Munro sent the less experienced pilots and four Whirlwinds to Charmy Down airfield, which was felt to be more suitable for training flying than Exeter. Poor weather delayed the start of training until 1 February. Hugh Saint reported that most of the pilots 'bounced rather a lot' and both Skellon and Jowitt damaged the tails of their aircraft during heavy landings. Both Whirlwinds were left behind for repair by Westland technicians when the detachment returned to Exeter on 7 February.[158]

Strange Victory

8 February brought what was perhaps the first Whirlwind victory. Westland sent a case of champagne to the squadron, but there was little to celebrate and the circumstances of the combat are as unclear now as they were then. Hughes and Rudland took off from Exeter at 08:40 for a local practice flight, but twenty minutes later were ordered to intercept a lone aircraft approaching from Cherbourg. Orbiting ten miles south of Start Point in light rain and dense cloud, Rudland saw and attacked a single-engine floatplane that he later

identified from photographs as an Arado Ar196, but broke away when he saw what he thought were British roundels on the fuselage. Hughes also fired at the aircraft before he too saw the markings and broke away. The 'Arado' flew north west into cloud and Hughes and Rudland returned to Exeter.

At around the same time, Crooks (flying P6968) and Graham (P6969) of the detachment at St Eval took off, also for a practice flight. They too were ordered to intercept a raid and flew to Dodman Point. After patrolling uneventfully for a few minutes, with Crooks above the cloud and Graham below, Crooks descended though the cloud and saw Graham flying in the opposite direction. Crooks turned around intending to call Graham on the radio and instruct to fly in formation with him, but there was no sign of Graham's aircraft. While searching for him Crooks suddenly saw an enemy aircraft, which he later tentatively identified as a Heinkel He 115, descend through the cloud and hit the sea about four miles south of Dodman Point at 09:55. Crooks thought he saw one of the crew in the water clinging to one of the floats of the overturned aircraft. There was no sign of Graham. Crooks returned to St Eval assuming that Graham had already done so. When it was realised that Graham was missing, boats and an ASR Lysander were sent out to search for him, but found only wreckage and a patch of oil in the area where he and the enemy floatplane had last been seen. The coastguard subsequently reported that two aircraft had crashed into the sea three miles offshore. Initially, Hughes was credited with the destruction of the enemy floatplane, but the victory was assigned to Graham even though it was not known whether he had attacked it or not. Whether the aircraft seen to crash by Crooks was the one attacked by Hughes and Rudland thirty-five minutes earlier and fifty miles away will probably never be known, but Cherbourg-based 5/Bordfliegergruppe 196 lost Ar 196A-4 WNr. 0129. The body of the observer, Lt.z.S Hans-Erich Hirtz, was later washed ashore, but Hptm Adolf Berger (the unit's Staffelkapitän) remains missing.[159]

On 18 February, Sqn Ldr Munro was posted to the newly-created Aircraft Gun Mounting Establishment (AGME) at Duxford where his considerable experience of aircraft armament would be put to good use. His replacement as commanding officer of 263 Squadron was Sqn Ldr Arthur Donaldson, the younger brother of John Donaldson who had commanded the unit in Norway. Donaldson had spent the early part of the war as an instructor and after a short refresher course was posted in January 1941 to Douglas Bader's 242 Squadron, but made only a handful of operational flights before going to command 263 Squadron. Several new pilots were also posted in, but of them only Sgt Don Tebbit would fly the Whirlwind operationally.

Maintaining the operational and training detachments at St Eval and Charmy Down while still carrying out the 'Chameleon' and other routine patrols with the aircraft left at Exeter had placed a considerable strain on the

Formation of four
No. 263 Squadron
Whirlwinds in
silhouette. (*Robert
Bowater*)

unit. They were therefore delighted when ordered on 24 February to move the
whole squadron to join the detachment at St Eval, thus reuniting the unit on a
single airfield for the first time in since late December.

On 1 March, Kitchener and Thornton-Brown were vectored onto a Ju 88
twenty miles south of the Scilly Isles. Kitchener's guns jammed after firing
just seven rounds, but Thornton-Brown fired four short bursts at the Junkers
and saw hits on its fuselage before it escaped into cloud.[160] The following
day, the Whirlwinds of 263 Squadron, Hurricanes of 247 and Spitfires of 234
flew a rather different type of convoy patrol when they maintained relays of
patrols over the battleship HMS *Resolution* that was returning to Britain for
repairs after being damaged by a Vichy submarine during an assault on Dakar.
Kitchener and Thornton-Brown were again flying together on an early morning
patrol on 5 March when they were vectored onto an enemy aircraft travelling
north west and 6,000 feet above them south of Lizard Head. The two pilots
altered course and climbed through dense cloud to 22,000 feet where they saw

a Ju 88 a mile away and 2,500 feet above them. Struggling for altitude and climbing at an indicated airspeed of just 130-140 mph, Kitchener realised that he could not make a climbing attack from below so performed a shallow dive to gain speed before climbing up to attack. During this manoeuvre, Thornton-Brown lost sight of both Kitchener and the enemy aircraft and played no further part in the combat that followed. As Kitchener came within range, the Junkers suddenly dived into cloud. Kitchener followed, fired and saw damage to the outer port wing. Both aircraft continued to dive until they emerged below the clouds. Kitchener saw the Ju 88 five miles away and diving until it levelled off just above the sea. After a five-minute chase, Kitchener was again within range and fired the rest of his ammunition in five short bursts from 550 to 300 yards range. The rear gunner of the Junkers returned fire during the first few attacks, damaging both outer slats of Kitchener's aircraft, but then ceased. The chase had taken Kitchener well out to sea, twenty-five to thirty miles south of the Scilly Isles and as the Junkers turned south east, Kitchener reported its position and course to his controller and set course for home.[161]

The squadron usually carried out patrols with pairs of aircraft, but on the afternoon of 11 March, Kitchener was alone over St Ives when he was directed towards an enemy aircraft south of the Lizard. At 23,000 feet, he saw beneath him a Ju 88 approaching from the Scilly Isles. Kitchener pursued the Junkers, which immediately accelerated and dived. Kitchener struggled to overhaul the Ju 88, but by the time the aircraft reached 10,000 feet, he had closed to within 400 yards and fired a one-second burst. Simultaneously, the rear gunner of the Junkers hit the port engine of Kitchener's Whirlwind. With glycol streaming from the damaged engine and the Junkers rapidly approaching dense cloud, Kitchener fired a further three-second burst, shut down the overheating engine and turned for home. Approaching the newly-built airfield at Predannack, Kitchener noticed that the starboard engine was now on fire and, when at a height of thirty feet, the engine cut, P6985 spun in and crashed on the site of the First World War One airfield at Mullion. Kitchener was extracted from the wreckage seriously injured before the aircraft burned out.[162]

In the evening of 12 March, a lone He 111 bombed the dispersal areas at St Eval, slightly damaging seven Whirlwinds and some of 247 Squadron's Hurricanes, three of them severely. Two days later, Patrick Thornton-Brown was badly injured and P6988 wrecked when he crashed at Portreath in poor weather after the port engine failed while returning from a routine convoy patrol. That night, the Luftwaffe returned to St Eval and damaged a further two Whirlwinds and a Hurricane. After these raids, the squadron dispersed its Whirlwinds at night to Portreath from 15 March and on 18 March, formally moved there. The airfield had officially opened just four days earlier and although the runways were finished, most of the buildings were still under construction.

Left: No. 263 Squadron Whirlwind P6985 HE-J had a short life. Delivered on 3 January 1941, she was written off in a crash at RAF Predannack on 11 March 1941. Her pilot, Pilot Officer Horatio Kitchener DFM, was severely injured and spent several months in hospital. (*Robert Bowater*)

Below: No. 263 Squadron Whirlwinds P6985 HE-J, P6987 HE-L and P6969 HE-V in tight formation. (*Robert Bowater*)

'A Succession of Tragedies'

During a routine evening patrol on 1 April, Donaldson and Crooks were vectored towards an enemy aircraft approaching overland from the north west. Five miles north of Predannack at 8,000 feet, Donaldson saw what he identified as a Dornier Do 215. He went in to attack, fired three short bursts and saw smoke from both engines and pieces flying off the Dornier that then dived for the clouds. Donaldson gave chase and saw the burning wreckage of an aircraft on the ground that he assumed was the Dornier; however, it was Crooks' aircraft. Crooks had been flying behind Donaldson when they first saw the enemy aircraft and Donaldson had not seen him again after he had gone in to attack. A bullet hole was subsequently found in one of the engine nacelles of Crooks' aircraft and, from this and the evidence of witnesses on the ground, it was concluded that he had fallen to return fire from the Dornier.[163]

On 6 April, Howe and Tooth, during their third patrol of the day, were ordered to intercept an incoming raid. Fifteen miles south east of Lizard Point, they both saw a large splash in the sea, which they assumed to have been a bomb. Shortly afterwards they found two He 111s at 400 feet. As the Whirlwinds turned in to attack, the Heinkels closed formation and descended to just above the waves. Tooth attacked first, firing two busts at the rearmost Heinkel, during which two of his guns jammed. He saw his shells hitting the rear fuselage, aft of the rear gunner, who returned fire. Howe fired a short burst at the leading aircraft before also attacking the second Heinkel. Two of his guns jammed, but he fired the rest of his ammunition and saw flashes near the rear gunner's position after which return fire ceased. On returning to Portreath, bullet holes were found in the wing and tailplane of Howe's aircraft. Neither pilot claimed to have significantly damaged the Heinkels, which were last seen heading south at sea level, but their opponents may have been from I./KG27, one of whose aircraft landed at Tours with a wounded radio operator and considerable airframe damage.[164] The following day saw 263's last contact with the enemy for some months when Ferdinand and King saw a Ju 88 bombing a ship at the far end of the convoy they were patrolling early in the morning. They closed on the enemy and Ferdinand fired two short bursts. King then attacked but his guns jammed and the Junkers escaped into cloud before Ferdinand could renew his attack.[165]

The squadron moved from Portreath to Filton on 10 April and settled into a routine of convoy patrols that lasted until mid-June and the few interception sorties that were flown found only misplotted RAF aircraft. Despite the lack of contact with the Luftwaffe, accidents continued. Howe visited his old 25 Squadron colleagues at Wittering on 20 April and performed the customary 'beat-up' of the airfield on departure. Diving from 5,000 feet, he performed two rolls as he crossed the airfield at high speed and very low level. After the second roll, a piece of the aircraft, believed to have been one of the outer slats, detached and the aircraft (P6992) crashed, killing Howe instantly. Milligan was killed ten days later near Aldermaston when P7008 broke up in the air during practice attacks on a Wellington bomber. Accident investigators concluded that the outer slats had broken away when Milligan had made a sharp turning climb after his final attack. The port wing then failed and the tailplane detached in the subsequent spin. A third incident followed on 9 May when Cliff Rudland landed safely after the starboard slat of P6974 opened and broke away during a dive.

Other aircraft also suffered such failures. Two weeks earlier, a 16 OTU Hampden crashed with the loss of its crew when a wing failed after a slat detached while recovering from a dive. Reporting on this accident, Gp Capt Vernon Brown, Chief Inspector of the Accident Investigation Branch, suggested: '...it seems desirable that slats should be rendered inoperative on Hampdens and that on all types on which they are fitted the question of providing a means for locking them in flight should be considered'.[166] The Air Ministry prohibited aerobatics in the Whirlwind while A&AEE evaluated the flying characteristics of the aircraft with the outer slats locked shut. These trials were carried out with P6997, which had been delivered to A&AEE early in April for other tests. The test pilots concluded that take off and landing were largely unaffected and the behaviour of the aircraft under conditions when the slats would normally be open was more pleasant with them locked shut. In early June, the Air Ministry ordered that the Whirlwinds' should be locked shut.[167] Aircraft from P7054 onwards were delivered from the factory with the slats locked and Westland produced modification kits for earlier Whirlwinds.

May and early June repeated the pattern of April with many patrols but no contact with the enemy. In early May, Joe Hughes was promoted to flight lieutenant and took command of A Flight and eight new pilots joined the squadron by mid-June: PO Humphrey Coghlan (from Beaufighter-equipped 600 Squadron), Flight Sergeant Robert Brackley and Sergeant Pilots Anthony Albertini (also from 600 Squadron), Geoff Buckwell, Frank Dimblebee, Thomas Hunter, Reg Pascoe and John Walker. The squadron lost another Whirlwind on 29 May when Don Tebbit crashed P7006 on the banks of the River Severn during unauthorised low flying. Tebbit was placed under open arrest pending an investigation, but was later released due to a lack of evidence. Two weeks later he was posted to 10 Group Anti-Aircraft Co-operation Flight, but returned to 263 Squadron sixteen months later.[168]

During an evening patrol on 11 June, A Flight was vectored onto what was described as an enemy aircraft being pursued by a British fighter. The 'enemy' aircraft turned out to be a Blenheim with a Defiant on its tail, a situation that should perhaps have caused the Defiant's crew more concern than that of the Blenheim. Stein recognised the aircraft as a Blenheim just in time, but King did not and fired a two-second burst. Fortunately, his aim on this occasion was no better than his aircraft recognition and the Blenheim was unharmed. The same day, Pascoe suffered an engine failure caused by an oil leak while flying the second prototype. Despite instructions to the contrary, he decided to force land immediately, chose a poor landing site, made matters worse by lowering the undercarriage and was killed when the aircraft struck a tree and broke up. He had been with the squadron for less than a month.[169] The following day a more experienced pilot was lost when Roy Ferdinand, flying P7045 (one of the first aircraft delivered with the slats locked shut), made a series of steep turns during a low and flat approach to land at Filton, after which the aircraft stalled, crashed and burst into flames.

On the Offensive

On the basis of intelligence that Bf 109s were concentrated on the Cherbourg peninsula airfields, Donaldson, Mason, Pugh and Rudland – with Holmes and Stein as reserves – flew to Ibsley in the evening of 13 June to carry out the Whirlwind's first offensive sortie over France. At dawn the following day, Donaldson and Rudland took off to attack the airfield at Querqueville while Pugh and Mason set off for Maupertus (usually referred to by the Luftwaffe as Théville). Pugh and Mason failed to locate Maupertus in thick morning mist and unable to find alternative targets, returned to Ibsley. Donaldson and Rudland had better luck. At Querqueville, they saw no aircraft on the airfield, but did see numerous tarpaulin-covered pens on the south west boundary of the airfield, which they attacked in a shallow dive down to 100 feet. Both pilots saw their shells exploding in the pens, but observed no specific results. On the way out from the attack, Donaldson also fired at a barrack block and as they left, light flak opened up, causing minor damage to one of the engine nacelles of his aircraft. By 05:50, the two Whirlwinds were safely back at Ibsley having passed underneath the Spitfires of 234 Squadron which had taken off from Warmwell to cover their withdrawal.[170]

For the rest of June and the whole of July, the squadron returned to routine patrols and spent many days operating from Exeter, Ibsley or Portreath, standing in for other units absent from their usual bases while escorting offensive operations over France. There was no contact with the Luftwaffe and, fortunately, no accidents either.

On 1 July, two new pilots – Jack Maddocks and John Meredith – were posted from 56 OTU and the month also brought news of an AFC for Donaldson, awarded for his earlier work at the Central Flying School.

In April 1941, Air Vice-Marshal Douglas had initiated a wide-ranging study into the use of 20-mm cannon-equipped fighters for anti-tank attacks.

Whirlwind HE-Q seen in her dispersal in Knighton Wood, RAF Warmwell. Her pilot is South African Flight Sergeant Roy Wright. (*Robert Bowater*)

This appears to have been prompted both by the RAF's annual springtime obsession with the possibility of invasion of Britain and the large increase in numbers of available cannon-equipped fighters as the first production Hurricane IIcs began to arrive. Douglas wanted an examination not just of ammunition types and attack tactics, but also of how tank targets would be reported and the attacking fighters controlled.[171]

During the summer, the Hurricane IIc squadrons and 263 Squadron performed regular ground-attack training and 263 Squadron detached six Whirlwinds to Warmwell on four separate days in July to practice at the nearby ranges. On 4 August, a demonstration for a high-ranking audience was held at the Bowls Barrow firing ranges on Salisbury Plain. For the demonstration, a Mk IX Cruiser tank was attacked in turn by a Browning-armed Hurricane of 317 Squadron, a Whirlwind flown by Donaldson and a Hurricane IIc of 87 Squadron flown by Sqn Ldr Ian Gleed, DFC. Examination of the target tank after each of the attacks revealed that the .303 Browning was, unsurprisingly, totally ineffective. The 20-mm high explosive and ball ammunition was found to be more effective, but deteriorating weather and strong crosswinds caused the postponement of planned trials with the new 20-mm armour-piercing ammunition.[172] One of the observers noted that 'Both the Hurricane and Whirlwind appear to be suitable aircraft for attack on tanks, the Hurricane being superior to the Whirlwind.'[173] He also noted that that Gleed in the Hurricane attacked in a thirty-degree dive, firing long bursts, whereas Donaldson in the Whirlwind attacked in a fifteen-degree dive, firing short bursts.

CHAPTER 7

The Turning Point

Mandolin

While the ground-attack training continued, the squadron also returned to the offensive over France during the afternoon of 2 August with a pair of attacks on the airfields at Querqueville and Maupertus. Donaldson and Hughes found their target at Querqueville and fired at an aircraft as well as oil tanks and barrack blocks on the airfield. Pugh and Mason made a navigational error and did not reach Maupertus. Instead, they made an inconclusive attack on an E-boat heading out to sea from Cherbourg. The two pairs of Whirlwinds then rejoined and were covered on their return journey by Spitfires of 118 Squadron.[174]

On 5 August, Donaldson and Holmes revisited Maupertus where they fired at parked Ju 87s and Bf 109s, and Hughes and Jowitt attacked a radio station near Querqueville after searching unsuccessfully for shipping off Cherbourg.[175] Early the following morning, the squadron staged another attack on Maupertus. Operating from Ibsley, Mason led Coghlan, Rudland and Brackley, but as the squadron diarist noted 'Their navigation seems to have left something to be desired and, not to put too fine a point on it, they don't know where they got to.' Mason attacked an E-boat he found off Cap de la Hague and the others, who had become separated from their leader, attacked a radio station.[176]

Just after midday, Donaldson, Rudland, Coghlan and Albertini took off in a second attempt to find and attack Maupertus. This time they found the target and observed damaged aircraft from the previous days' attack. On their way in, Rudland (flying P7002) saw a Bf 109 taking off, reporting that 'It had not left the ground, but it had got its tail up. I fired a two-second burst at it from fifty yards and it immediately burst into flames.'[177] Rudland's victim was a Bf 109E-7 of Erg./JG2 flown by Uffz Helmut Reiner who died of his injuries four days later. All four of the Whirlwind pilots attacked parked aircraft while

Albertini also fired at gun positions. On the return flight, Donaldson found two tankers about three miles off Cherbourg and attacked both with his remaining ammunition.

Later in the afternoon, Donaldson, Rudland (flying his third sortie to France in P7002 that day), Mason and Brackley escorted by thirteen Spitfires of 118 Squadron set off to find the two tankers attacked earlier by Donaldson. This time they faced fighter opposition, being met by a group of Bf 109s five miles off the French coast at Cap de la Hague. In the ensuing dogfight, Donaldson saw Brackley being chased by two Bf 109s. Donaldson recorded 'I got on the tail of one of these and fired a half-second burst at 200 yards range. The enemy aircraft did a turn, then a half roll and a dive. On the dive I fired a half-second burst at 150 yards. I saw a panel fly off the starboard wing and also a puff of white smoke. I now think that I hit the radiator in the starboard wing.' Brackley then heard Rudland call out on the radio that he was being chased by three Bf 109s. Immediately, he saw a Whirlwind to his right with three Messerschmitts on its tail. Brackley reported '...the first enemy aircraft broke away across my nose, but it was gone before I could fire. As the second broke away, also across my nose, I fired a 2.5 second barrage and I saw it go straight into the sea.' Rudland saw a Whirlwind coming towards him with a Bf 109 on its tail. He fired a one-and-a-half second burst in a head-on attack and saw his shells hit the Messerschmitt just behind the cockpit. When Rudland broke away he could still see the Whirlwind, but not the Bf 109, which he claimed as destroyed. 118 Squadron's Spitfires then arrived on the scene and in the subsequent melee two of the pilots claimed to have shot down Bf 109s while six others had inconclusive combats. Although the Whirlwind and Spitfire pilots claimed a total of four Bf 109s shot down, the only German loss was a Bf 109 of Erg.JG2, the pilot of which appears to have parachuted safely.

The Whirlwinds disentangled themselves from the fight and headed back for England, but the starboard engine of Brackley's aircraft (P6983) began to run roughly and emit white glycol smoke. Brackley shut the failing engine down and short of fuel for his remaining engine, landed at Hurn where he hit an airfield obstruction, further damaging the aircraft. The others landed at Ibsley, but Donaldson and Rudland's aircraft (P7001 and P7002) were flown directly to Westland to have a large number of bullet holes repaired.[178] At this point, 10 Group formalised arrangements for this type of offensive operation over France by issuing specific instructions for them. These were given the codename 'Mandolin' – later replaced by the more familiar codename 'Rhubarb':

In continuance of the policy in Northern France and to increase the scope of this Group's active participation in this offensive, it is proposed to carry out raids by small numbers of fighter aircraft, operating in conditions which would allow cloud cover, against selected enemy aerodromes and other German military objectives within striking range of this Group. As aircraft will be operating in small numbers, the main factor in this operation and in selecting targets is the safety of the fighters; thus particular attention must be paid to cloud cover, and the likelihood of the pilot locating the target on coming through the cloud without making himself vulnerable by prolonged search.[179]

Targets were defined as enemy aircraft in the air or on airfields, shipping, troop movements and freight trains, but attacks on passenger trains and on targets in the Channel Islands were prohibited. Initially, only long-range Spitfires were to be used for these operations for which 10 Group set a maximum radius of action of 130 miles. On 7 August, twelve Whirlwinds escorted a Hurricane to Debden and back (135 miles each way) and the fuel remaining in the aircraft tanks were measured in order to establish a prudent radius of action for the Whirlwind. Revised radius of action restrictions were set later in August: standard Spitfires could operate at 100-miles radius; Whirlwinds and standard Hurricanes at 120 miles; long-range Spitfires and Hurricanes at 130 miles or, for special targets, 150 miles.[180]

Operation 77

On 7 August, 263 Squadron moved to Charmy Down, near Bath. From there, twelve aircraft left for Wattisham in Suffolk on 11 August in preparation for a No. 2 (Bomber) Group operation the following day. Operation 77 called for fifty-four Blenheims to bomb the Knapsack and Quadrath power stations at Cologne. The Whirlwinds were tasked with escorting them on their outward journey.

Early the following morning, the Whirlwinds flew to Martlesham Heath where their fuel tanks were topped up and took off at 10:02 to meet the Blenheims over Orfordness. The Blenheims flew towards the Scheldt Estuary at fifty feet in two formations about five miles apart – too far apart for both formations to be adequately protected in Donaldson's view. Six of the Whirlwinds flew between the two Blenheim formations and the other six up-sun of them. As the formation approached the coast, the Whirlwinds climbed to 1,000 feet and weaved above the bombers until just north west of Antwerp when, at the limit of their range, they turned for home. The Blenheims would have to continue unescorted for a further 150 miles over enemy territory. On their way home, the Whirlwinds attacked barges in the Scheldt near Walcheren, claiming one as sunk and a further two damaged, but attracting considerable flak in the process although no fighters were observed. All aircraft returned to Martlesham safely at 11:35. The Blenheims flew on alone to their targets.

Ten had been lost by the time they met the six squadrons of Spitfires placed near Vlissingen to cover their withdrawal. The formation was then engaged by fighters and flak losing several Spitfires and a further two Blenheims that were acting as navigational leaders for the escorting fighters.[181]

On 17 August, Ibsley was crowded with four Whirlwinds, the Spitfires of 234, 66, 118 and 501 Squadrons and the Hurricanes of 316 and 317 Squadrons. The intention was for the four Whirlwinds, flown by Donaldson, Pugh, Coghlan and Blackshaw, to patrol over Maupertus airfield at 15,000 feet acting as bait to draw up the Luftwaffe that would then be dealt with by the three patrolling Spitfire and Hurricane wings. As usual, the Luftwaffe ignored the provocation and no enemy aircraft were sighted.[182]

On 21 August, Donaldson was promoted to Wing Commander (Flying) at Portreath and was awarded the DFC in recognition of his leadership during recent operations. Pugh took command of the squadron and Cliff Rudland replaced Pugh as B Flight commander. Despite his new rank and responsibilities, Donaldson continued to fly with the squadron and on 24 August, led Pugh, Rudland and Albertini, escorted by seven long-range Spitfires of 66 Squadron, to attack Lannion airfield. After a certain amount of navigational confusion, which the squadron attributed to bad maps, they found Lannion and were about to attack when someone called over the radio, 'Me 109s! Beat it!' A group of Messerschmitts were seen approaching, but broke off their attack, although they pursued the Whirlwinds some fifty miles back over the sea. All the Whirlwinds landed safely at Predannack.[183]

Three Whirlwinds, again escorted by 66 Squadron, returned to Lannion on 26 August. Pugh, Coghlan and Hughes crossed the Channel at fifty feet, made landfall at Les Sept Îles to the west of the target and found the airfield easily. They attacked and claimed to have severely damaged five parked Ju 88s while the escorting Spitfires claimed damage to a further four. The Whirlwinds and Spitfires all returned safely having experienced only light machine-gun fire from defences.[184] Rudland, Mason, Brackley and Meredith, with an escort of twelve Spitfires of 234 Squadron, staged a simultaneous attack on Maupertus airfield. They also found their target easily and claimed five Ju 87s destroyed or damaged on the ground, although both Rudland and Mason suspected that they were decoys. 234 Squadron also claimed two further Ju 87s and a Ju 88, but lost one of their number to flak over the airfield.[185]

Three days later, Hughes and Holmes took off to attack Lannion airfield again, but crossed the French coast too far west near Île de Batz. Absence of cloud cover made it unwise to fly on overland to Lannion so they both attacked a radio installation on the Île de Batz before turning for home.[186] Finally on the last day of the month, twelve Whirlwinds of 263 led a wing including the Spitfire IIAs of 130 and 313 Squadrons to escort a force of Blenheims on a largely uneventful attack on Lannion.

Vindicated and Justified

The squadron viewed August 1941 as a turning point in which the Whirlwind had been 'completely vindicated and justified, having shown it is an admirable machine for ground strafing and also that it is a match for Me 109s'.[187] 10 Group's assessment was more cautious: 'The Whirlwind aircraft has proved very satisfactory for hit and run ground strafing, but it is considered that its manoeuvrability compared with Spitfires and Hurricanes makes it unsuitable for close escort operations or operations when it will have to engage enemy fighters and cannot rely on its high speed at low level to make a getaway from a specific target.'[188] Despite these reservations, the Whirlwinds again escorted Blenheims on 4 September to attack the *Sonderburg* in Cherbourg Harbour. The ship, previously the Norwegian whaling fleet depot ship *Solglimt,* was captured in January 1941 in the Antarctic by the German commerce raider *Pinguin*, taken to Bordeaux, renamed and put into service as a cargo vessel.

Led by Pugh, twelve Whirlwinds took off from Warmwell, met with six Blenheims of 114 Squadron and were joined over the coast by the high-cover escort of thirty-seven Hurricane IIs of the Exeter Wing. In a cloudless sky, the formation crossed the Channel with the Blenheims at 10,000 feet, two Whirlwinds weaving above the bombers, two behind and the others on each side. The three squadrons of the Exeter Wing flew slightly behind, stepped up between 14, 16 and 20,000 feet. As they crossed the French coast at Querqueville, six Bf 109s were seen beneath them climbing fast to place themselves above and up-sun of the bombers, but no attack developed. The Blenheims' bombs fell on jetties in the Bassin Napoleon III, well away from the *Sonderburg*. More Bf 109s were seen during the attack and 302 Squadron's Hurricanes descended to join the melee. A Messerschmitt fired a short burst at Stein from 600-700 yards range before diving away and Holmes was obliged to perform violent evasive manoeuvres to shake three others off his tail. As he later wryly admitted, 'They did all the talking.' Two or three Messerschmitts then approached the bombers, but broke away when Pugh and Rudland turned towards them. Almost immediately afterwards, Mason was attacked out of the sun by three Bf 109s. He fired a half-second burst at one, took violent evasive action and dived down to sea level before turning for home. The Bf 109s followed him for a further thirty miles, firing several bursts at the Whirlwind. Mason landed unhurt, but his aircraft was found to have a large number of bullet holes in it. On the way out of the target area, Buckwell was attacked by a further two Bf 109s. With the starboard engine of his aircraft (P7042) burning fiercely, Buckwell parachuted two miles offshore and became a prisoner of war. Three pilots of JG2 claimed a total of four Whirlwinds shot down, but Buckwell's was the only one lost. The Whirlwind pilots made no claims to have damaged the enemy, but 302 Squadron claimed one Bf 109 shot down and another damaged. The Whirlwinds and the Exeter Wing then reformed around the Blenheims to escort them home. When the bombers were well clear of the French coast, the Hurricanes turned back to patrol from Cap de la Hague to Querqueville followed by a sweep by thirty-six Spitfires of the Middle Wallop Wing. None of the pilots saw any further sign of the Luftwaffe.[189]

On 8 September, 263 Squadron again operated with Blenheims, providing escort and flak suppression for an attack on shipping reported between Cap de la Hague and Jersey. Thirty-five Spitfires of the Middle Wallop Wing provided additional escort and twenty-four Hurricane IIs of 302 and 317 Squadrons covered the withdrawal of the formation from the target area. The Blenheims met with their escort over Ibsley. 234 Squadron formed the close escort, 501 Squadron flew behind and to port, and 118 and 263 Squadrons flew on the starboard side, up-sun of the bombers. Before leaving the English coast, Rudland's aircraft developed engine problems caused by loose spark plugs. Since the formation was flying in radio silence, Rudland used hand signals to indicate his intention to return to base, but these were misinterpreted by Holmes and Hunter who turned back with him.

The rest of the formation set course at sea level and, half an hour later, found two small convoys south of Guernsey, both heading north. The first, consisting of a tug and four barges, was just south of the island and the second of eight tugs and more barges was further offshore. Pugh expected the convoy that they had been briefed to attack to be larger than either of these two groups and to be ten miles further on. Anticipating that the target convoy would soon appear ahead of them, Pugh led the Whirlwinds up to 800 feet in preparation for their anti-flak attack. However, he then saw the bombers turning sharply to port clearly intending to attack the second of the convoys already seen.

Accordingly, the Whirlwinds also attacked. Pugh and Coghlan attacked the second convoy from north to south observing cannon strikes along the whole length of the largest ship. The Blenheims then bombed, crossing the convoy from the beam. The Whirlwinds then renewed their cannon attacks. Hughes and Mason attacked a tug in the first convoy, leaving it shrouded in steam and smoke, before attacking another ship. King attacked two tugs in the second convoy and Brackley, Blackshaw and Walker attacked those in the first convoy. The Whirlwinds then returned to Ibsley, Pugh and Coghlan with the bombers, the others alone and in pairs. Brackley, returning at sea level, suddenly came upon an apparently stationary E-boat, visible only when it rose on the swell. He fired a short burst of cannon fire, but saw no results. Some of the Whirlwinds and straggling Spitfires of 234 Squadron were attacked from astern by four Bf 109s on the return journey. North of Alderney, a stream of tracer passed King's aircraft. He took evasive action and saw a Bf 109 about 500 yards behind. When he landed, several bullet holes were found in his aircraft (P7004), one of which had punctured the tailwheel tyre. Hughes returned home with Mason and three Spitfires from Middle Wallop. He also saw tracer fire passing his aircraft and turned sharply, but saw no sign of the enemy.[190]

Two days later, Mason and Stein could not find their briefed target at Quinéville so attacked a gun position near Lestre instead. Mason attacked in a sixty-degree dive with Stein following behind waiting for his leader to pull up so that he could fire in turn. Mason (flying P7001) did not pull up, but flew straight into the ground, presumably having been hit by flak. Stein made four further attacks on the position and then returned home.[191]

On 15 September, the squadron lost another aircraft when Meredith overshot while landing in P6996, attempted to take off again, but hit parked Whirlwind P7039 and a Nissen hut. Meredith suffered minor injuries, but P6996 was wrecked. P7039 needed a new outer wing and rudder, and an airman in the hut was seriously hurt.[192]

Hughes, Warnes, Brackley and Hunter set off for Morlaix airfield on 19 September, but failed to find it due to an inaccurate wind forecast. They returned on the afternoon of 28 September to attack Ju 88s expected to be there. Donaldson, Pugh, Dimblebee and King, escorted by eleven Spitfires of 313 Squadron, made landfall at Plouescat and flew on to Morlaix. Climbing to 500-600 feet, they saw the airfield and a parked Bf 109 which, in the absence of any other targets, Pugh attacked with a two-second burst while crossing the airfield at twenty feet. About halfway across the airfield and preparing to attack a fuel bowser on the north side, he felt a heavy explosion in the rear fuselage of his aircraft (P7041) and found the rudder inoperative. He fired a short burst at the bowser and then flew north with the flak following him. Dimblebee and King also attacked the Bf 109 as well as gun posts. On strafing the Bf 109, Donaldson noticed that its propeller was missing. He was also met by intense light flak while crossing the airfield. His aircraft, P7044, was hit several times in the rear fuselage, damaging the flying controls and shattering the cockpit canopy. Donaldson suffered injuries to his arms and minor concussion, but landed safely at Predannack. When his aircraft was inspected, 100 shrapnel holes were found in the rear fuselage skin, eleven in the elevator control tube and a further seven in the rudder control tube. Westland personnel repaired Pugh and Donaldson's aircraft on site at Predannack.[193]

The following day, 263 Squadron sent four Whirlwinds to attack Lannion airfield after Ju 88s had again been reported there. Nine Spitfires of 313 Sqn escorted the Whirlwinds and four Hurricanes of 247 Squadron were briefed to stage a second attack twenty minutes after the Whirlwinds. Orders for the operation did not arrive until 16:00 and after the Whirlwinds had moved forward to Predannack and their fuel tanks had been topped up, Coghlan led Warnes, Maddocks and Hunter at 18:33 into a darkening, cloudy sky. Flying at sea level, they reached the French coast near Les Sept Îles and skirted around the Côte de Granit Rose before turning east up the estuary of the River Léguer. Once the airfield had been spotted, Coghlan turned north before flying a right-hand circuit to attack the airfield in a shallow dive from 500 feet from north to south. Coghlan dived towards the hangars on the southern boundary and fired a three-second burst at a Ju 88 parked in front of them. He saw his shells hitting the fuselage and starboard wing, and then turned at low level through intense flak to attack the hangars on the northern boundary. It was now too dark to see if there were aircraft in the hangars. Warnes followed Coghlan into attack and fired two short bursts at dispersal pens before exhausting his ammunition in an attack on a gun post.

The four Whirlwinds became separated in the dark and cloud, and made their way home individually. Maddocks landed safely at Portreath. Coghlan's gyro was unserviceable (probably due to the violent evasive manoeuvres he had performed to evade flak) and his compass inaccurate. He made landfall, well off course, near the Scilly Isles where he climbed to 4,000 feet and radioed for a homing, but received no reply. He turned east and eventually made contact with the homing station and was given a course for Predannack. Then his port engine failed and, with his petrol gauges reading zero, Coghlan told his controller that he was going to bale out. However, after adjustments to the Exactor controls he persuaded the port engine to run again. At 400 feet, just short of the runway at Predannack, both engines stopped simultaneously and Coghlan made a forced landing in fields. He escaped with bruises, but his aircraft, P6998, was badly damaged and returned to Westland for repair. When Warnes arrived at Predannack at 19:50, the beacon was flashing but no other lights were showing. After orbiting for twelve minutes and almost out of fuel, he radioed to say that he going to bail out, but fortunately the airfield lights were turned on and he landed safely with just three gallons of petrol remaining. Hunter also radioed that he was going to abandon the aircraft as his engines were failing, again presumably because of lack of fuel and a parachute was later observed south west of Eddystone Lighthouse. Sea and land searches found no trace of Hunter. His body was washed ashore twelve days later just a few miles from the airfield at Predannack.[194]

CHAPTER 8

Two from One

Whirlwind production peaked in mid-1941 and by August, there were forty-seven aircraft in storage – more than enough to equip a second squadron.[195] 137 Squadron duly formed on 20 September at Charmy Down alongside 263 Squadron. The Defiants of 125 Squadron moved to Fairwood Common and Charmy Down became an all-Whirlwind station with thirty Whirlwinds on the airfield by the beginning of October. 263 Squadron's maintenance flight was expanded into a servicing echelon capable of supporting both units and Joe Hughes and Douglas Jowitt, two of 263 Squadron's most experienced pilots, were posted to form a nucleus for the new unit.[196] Hughes' departure from 263 Squadron marked a break with the past for he was the last pilot remaining on the unit who had flown during the Norwegian campaign. The new squadron's first commanding officer was twenty-eight-year-old Sqn Ldr John Sample, DFC. Sample had flown with 607 Squadron during the campaign in France and commanded 504 Squadron throughout the Battle of Britain before being rested in March 1941 as a fighter controller. His time with 137 Squadron was to be tragically brief.

Many new pilots had earlier been posted to 263 Squadron so that it could act as an informal training unit for the new squadron and twelve of these joined 137 Squadron on 8 October: FO Colin Clark, POs John 'Mike' Bryan, John Lawton and George Martin, and Sgts Ralph Häggberg, John Luing, Jack Maddocks Hugh O'Neill, Maurice 'Mike' Peskett, Basil Robertson, John Sandy and Douglas Small. South African Colin Clark, a highly experienced pilot who had carried out development flying of the early radar-equipped Havocs and Beaufighters with the Fighter Interception Unit, became commander of 137 Squadron's A Flight. With fifteen pilots available and taking advantage of unusually good weather, the squadron began intensive flying training and, just one month after formation, one flight was declared operational on 20 October.[197]

Whereas 263 Squadron's initial Whirlwind operations had consisted largely of routine convoy and interception patrols, 137 Squadron's first operational sorties were to distant targets in enemy-occupied territory. On 24 October, Sample and Clark flew to Predannack and took off at 15:00 to attack fuel trains reported at Landerneau to the east of Brest. They found no fuel trains, but Sample attacked coal trucks and Clark fired at a locomotive that he left 'enveloped in steam'. Neither pilot reported flak and both returned safely.[198] Two days later, Hughes and Robertson also met no opposition on a similar operation to Landivisiau where they attacked a train and radio station.

On 27 October, the unit was further strengthened by the arrival from 263 Squadron of a further two Canadian pilots, Sgts John Brennan and John McClure. Brennan made an inauspicious start with 137 when he belly landed P7057 on 28 October after an engine failure, but far worse was to come. Later that afternoon, Sample, Peskett and Luing took off for practice flying. Luing made a practice attack on the other pair, but as he turned in to attack he saw Sample's Whirlwind spinning down with part of the tailplane falling away. Sample bailed out of P7053 too late and was killed. The other two pilots landed safely, but examination of Peskett's aircraft (P7058) suggested that its starboard propeller had hit the tail of Sample's aircraft and the undercarriage doors and central bulge of the Fowler flap also made contact. P7058 was flown undercarriage down to Filton for repair.[199]

Despite the loss of its commanding officer, 137 Squadron returned to the offensive on 30 October. Clark and Jowitt took off from Predannack to attack trains at Landerneau. Both pilots made two runs over the target and saw their fire striking the trains. Again no fighter or flak opposition was encountered. However, on the return flight, Jowitt passed Clark who was flying on one engine in P7091. Jowitt called Clark on the radio, but, unable to understand his reply, climbed and weaved around Clark until fuel shortage forced him to leave his colleague and head for Predannack. When approaching the English coast Jowitt heard Clark announce over the radio that he intended to bail out. Robertson, who was stationed at Predannack as a reserve pilot, took off in his Whirlwind to search for Clark and a Lysander dropped a dinghy close to him, but was observed not attempting to climb into it. He was eventually picked up by a destroyer, but later died.[200]

With the loss of its squadron commander and one flight commander, and a shortage of operational pilots, 137 Squadron was made non-operational. Humphrey Coghlan of 263 Squadron was posted as the unit's new commanding officer and an ex-colleague of Coghlan's from 600 Sqn, FO Robert Woodward, joined the squadron as A Flight commander to replace Clark. Woodward had already claimed three night victories and been awarded the DFC with Beaufighter-equipped 600 Squadron, but was now recovering from leg injuries received in an accident on 20 September.

To bring 137 Squadron up to full strength ten more pilots were posted from 56 OTU. POs Norman Crabtree, an American in the RCAF, and Vivian 'Les'

No. 263 Squadron Whirlwind P6991 HE-R seen on 20 March 1942 with S/L Woodward DFC in the cockpit. (*Robert Bowater*)

Currie were immediately transferred to 263 Squadron to replace Brennan and McClure. POs Paul La Gette (another American) and Alec Torrance, and six Canadian sergeant pilots, Joel Ashton, Charles De-Shane, Joe de Houx, Charles Mercer, Jim Rebbetoy and Robert Wright, had little or no experience of twin-engine aircraft and were more or less grounded until the squadron obtained a dual-control Airspeed Oxford trainer in mid-November. The two Whirlwind squadrons were separated on 8 November when 137 Squadron was moved from 10 Group to 12 Group to be based at Coltishall in Norfolk in the east of England.

A Quiet Month

For 263 Squadron, October was operationally quiet, but not incident free. During formation flying practice on 9 October, Hoskins and Coghlan collided. Coghlan parachuted from P6999, but Hoskins spun in and was killed in P6968. On the same day, ten new sergeant pilots arrived to replace those who had left for 137 Squadron: Canadians John Brennan, Edgar Brearley, Jim Coyne, Donald Gill, Irving Kennedy, John McClure, John Mitchner and Harvey Muirhead and Americans Bill Lovell and Richard Reed. Brennan and

McClure were soon transferred to 137 Squadron. Geoff Warnes replaced Coghlan as B Flight commander and Coghlan and Pugh were awarded the DFC for their parts in the operations of August and September.

263 Squadron returned to the offensive with two 'rhubarb' operations on 29-30 October. In the first of these, Brackley and King, operating from Predannack, carried out Rhubarb 33 to Morlaix airfield where they strafed hangars parked Ju 88s. Brackley saw his shells hitting a Ju 88, but King (flying P7007) hit a radio mast on the airfield with his port wing. As he left the area, King realised that his port engine was leaking glycol and shut it down, returning home on one engine.[201]

Whatever degree of surprise had been achieved on 29 October was missing the following day when Stein and Ridley attacked the same target. Struggling to locate the airfield, they stumbled over the town of Morlaix where they were engaged by heavy flak. They eventually spotted the airfield, went into attack from fifty feet and encountered intense light flak. As Ridley pulled out after his attack he saw Stein's aircraft (P7015) flying north east toward the coast in a gentle climb with the starboard engine smoking heavily. Ridley thought Stein was climbing in order to bail out, but the aircraft came down in fields near Kermouster and burned out. Stein did not survive. Ridley's aircraft had also been hit and with oil and glycol streaming from the starboard engine, climbed into cloud and returned to Predannack on one engine, but overshot on landing and came to rest in barbed wire at the perimeter of the airfield.[202] Ridley was unhurt and the aircraft (P6994) was repaired by Westland and subsequently shipped to the USA for evaluation.

The pace of operations of late October was sustained in the following month. Blackshaw and Robinson took off on 6 November to attack transport targets west of Maupertus, but found nothing and turned for home. Approaching the coast, Blackshaw observed two Bf 109s circling to his left, but the Luftwaffe pilots did not appear to have seen the Whirlwinds. Blackshaw called 'Rats to port' to Robinson who then weaved protectively behind and slightly above his leader as the pair headed out to sea. Ten miles off Barfleur, Blackshaw lost sight of Robinson. He turned back and circled the area twice, but saw no sign of his colleague and returned to Warmwell. When he reported Robinson's disappearance, Air Sea Rescue flew sorties in attempt to find him in the Channel. Albert Tooth, previously a 263 Squadron pilot, but now with an ASR squadron, searched as far as Cherbourg, but found no trace of Robinson. Since the Bf 109s seen by Blackshaw appeared not to have approached the Whirlwinds, the squadron concluded that Robinson had probably hit the sea while weaving. However, Ofw. Magnus Brunkhorst of 9/JG2 claimed a Whirlwind shot down in the area at the same time. Twenty-one-year-old John Robinson's first operational sortie had also been his last.[203]

The Distilleries

Among Fighter Command's targets in occupied France were factories distilling alcohol from sugar beet and apples. Alcohol was used by the Germans in the manufacture of explosives, synthetic fuels and rubber. These distilleries were targets that could only be productively attacked around or shortly after the harvest season. On 7 November, five Whirlwinds operated from Warmwell to reconnoitre, but not attack, distilleries in the Cherbourg peninsula. Brackley and Walker's target was at Corseulles-sur-Mer, but Brackley returned shortly after take off with an overheating engine and Walker failed to find the target.

Warnes, Blackshaw and King were briefed to find three distilleries in the west of the peninsula, south of Coutances. They crossed the Channel together and then separated at the French coast. Warnes could not find his target at Bréhal and, after firing at a camouflaged military position near St Malo-de-la-Lande, set course for home. Blackshaw also failed to identify the distillery at Cérences and found no other targets. King found his target at Hyenville and two goods trains nearby. He was about to attack these when he saw two Bf 109s nearby so turned for the coast and climbed for cloud cover. Three miles offshore he again saw two Bf 109s about 500 feet above him. When the Bf 109s approached, King turned in to meet the attack, pulled up and fired a short burst at one from 150-200 yards. King observed an explosion at the rear of the cockpit of the Bf109 that went into a steep dive towards the sea with flames and thick black smoke pouring from it. A few minutes later, Warnes – returning alone at sea level from his unsuccessful reconnaissance of Bréhal – passed through the same area and saw a conical cloud of black smoke on the water. Expecting to find a ship he went to investigate, but found nothing and concluded that an aircraft must have crashed. Immediately afterwards he was attacked by two Bf 109s which made attacking passes, but Warnes managed to evade. Two JG2 pilots each claimed a Whirlwind shot down, but King's aircraft was undamaged and Warnes' Whirlwind had just three bullet holes in its tailplane. It is probable that the Bf 109 claimed by King was a Bf 109E-7 (WNr. 5984) of JG2, the pilot of which parachuted to safety.[204]

Although only one of the four distilleries had been successfully located, an attack on them was planned for the following day. However, a weather test flight in the morning of 8 November found the Cherbourg peninsula covered in dense cloud so a fighter sweep was arranged instead. Warnes led the eight Whirlwinds to rendezvous with the Spitfires of 118, 234 and 501 Squadrons over Studland Bay before setting course for the Channel Islands. Blackshaw returned early with fuel system problems and two other Whirlwinds were slightly damaged by flak from Alderney, but the sweep was otherwise uneventful for the Whirlwinds, although 501 Squadron lost a Spitfire to JG2.

By 15 November, the weather had improved for an attack on the distilleries and eight Whirlwinds were moved to Warmwell. The targets were as before: Cérences, Bréhal, Hyenville and Corseulles. Pugh and Blackshaw found and attacked their target at Cérences before attacking a freight train parked nearby. Warnes and Harvey lost contact with each other after crossing the French coast. Harvey failed to find the distillery at Bréhal while Warnes attacked a stationary freight train and a tall building that he thought looked more like a watermill than a distillery. He then set course for home via Guernsey, feeling that the usual route out via Cap de la Hague had been dangerously overused. Five miles west of Guernsey he saw nine E-boats travelling towards Alderney, but was out of ammunition and returned to land at Exeter with just ten gallons of fuel left.

Although King had been the only pilot to find his target, a week earlier he and Ridley could not find the distillery at Hyenville and returned to Warmwell. On their outward journey, Holmes and Green ran into a lone Bf 109 fifteen miles from the French coast, but after a brief attack it climbed rapidly into cloud and disappeared. They resumed their course, but could not find their target. On attacking a flak position near Courseulles-sur-Mer, they returned to Ibsley.[205] The squadron made a final attempt to attack the distilleries on the morning of 17 November, but was recalled due to lack of cloud cover over the target and deteriorating weather at Warmwell. While landing in the

Maintenance on a No. 263 Squadron Whirlwind at a Knighton Wood dispersal at RAF Warmwell in the summer of 1943. (*Robert Bowater*)

murk, Dimblebee hit a stationary Spitfire, causing serious damage to both aircraft.[206]

During December, the maintenance section moved from Filton to join the rest of the squadron at Colerne, but there was almost no operational flying during the month because of persistent poor weather. However, the squadron did fly a few sorties to help calibrate Searchlight Control (SLC – usually referred to as 'Elsie') radars, during one of which Derrick Prior either lost control in cloud or suffered from icing and was killed instantly when P7044 dived into the ground at Coleford in Gloucestershire.

On 30 November, 263 Squadron moved twelve Whirlwinds to Exeter to stand in for other squadrons covering bombing operations on Brest, but persistent fog marooned them until the first week of January. Fog and snow impeded flying for much of January. Training continued when the weather allowed, but, with the exception of two abortive scrambles, 263 Squadron carried out no operational flying during the month. Nonetheless, another aircraft was lost during the early evening of 3 January when P7038 caught fire while parked at Charmy Down. The fire, which was believed to have been started by a flare dispenser mounted behind the cockpit, quickly spread through the cockpit and rear fuselage, damaging the aircraft beyond repair.[207]

Four new pilots joined the squadron during the month: New Zealander PO Stewart Brannigan, Australians Sgts Colin Bell and Peter Ewing and South African Peter Jardine. In response to Fighter Command's desire that all fighter squadrons should become fully operational by night, the squadron moved to Colerne on 26 January to carry out night flying training. Poor weather precluded flying on most days and the squadron moved again on 11 February to Fairwood Common in Wales.

CHAPTER 9

263 Squadron
February to September 1942

The day after the squadron moved airfields, Sqn Ldr Pugh, who had been with the unit for eighteen months and commanded it for six, was posted to the newly formed 82 Group and replaced by 137 Squadron flight commander Robert Woodward. 263 Squadron's move to Fairwood Common introduced a six-month period occupied almost entirely by convoy patrols. The squadron put in 7,000 hours of such patrols and intercepted Liberators, Wellingtons, Beaufighters and Spitfires, but never the enemy. Frequently they found nothing at all. The airfield's undulating runways were also 'bad medicine' for the Whirlwinds and caused several spectacular accidents. Another squadron based there noted that 'at night, the runways were liable to be impeded by wild ponies, sheep and cattle roaming over the common'.[208] The first accident occurred on 13 February when Coyne, landing at dusk, swung off the runway onto uneven ground and his aircraft overturned. Coyne was only slightly hurt and P7108 was returned to Westland for repair.[209]

Thus far in the Whirlwind's career the Peregrine engines had proved to be highly reliable, even if the Exactor controls had not, but on 12 February, the first of a series of engine failures occurred. Fortunately, Bill Lovell was not far offshore and landed P7017 safely on the good engine. Seven days later, Holmes was on a convoy patrol far out to sea at low altitude and in poor visibility when P7110's starboard engine failed violently with no prior warning from his instruments. Holmes kept the Whirlwind low level over the sea, but was unable to climb or bail out. Using the flaps, he climbed over the coastal cliffs and landed at a small airfield at Carew Cheriton. When the cowlings were removed '...two buckets full of engine parts, still smoking, fell out'.[210]

Following further failures over the next few days, the squadron was grounded while Rolls-Royce investigated. The cause was mundane enough. Like most Rolls-Royce engines of the era, the Peregrine had a certain amount of external oil pipe work and a small T-piece in this was failing. The T-piece fed lubricating oil from the pressure pump to the camshaft drives and the supercharger bearings at the rear of the engine. Loss of oil pressure in either of these areas would quickly lead to engine failure. Rolls-Royce quickly produced a modified aluminium bronze T-piece and a set of piping designed to be less vulnerable to vibration. By 4 March, thirteen of the squadron's Whirlwinds had been fitted with the new parts and the unit resumed its patrols.[211]

Although the engine problems may have been solved, the Fairwood Common runways continued to claim their victims. On 7 March, Jardine landed heavily in P7039, the tyres burst and the aircraft overturned. Jardine suffered back injuries, but recovered and returned to the squadron. A week later, Currie's aircraft (P7004) burst a tyre while taking off on a scramble. On landing, his aircraft swung off the runway, hit a pile of wood and the undercarriage collapsed. Currie was unhurt, but both aircraft were beyond repair.[212]

Breaking Cover

By March 1942, the Whirlwind had been in service for nearly two years, taken part in several highly-publicised operations and featured in British and German aircraft recognition guides. Despite this, the Air Ministry had managed to keep the aircraft a 'secret' in Britain at least. The American and French press had speculated, rather wildly, about the aircraft's performance and Lord Beaverbrook had twice mentioned it in BBC radio broadcasts; however, the British media had been obliged to keep silent and publish no photographs of the aircraft. This changed on 20 March when a press party arrived at Fairwood Common to photograph the aircraft and interview pilots following which pictures and accounts of the squadron's activities appeared in the press in Britain and further afield.

During March, the squadron continued its overseas patrols including a series known as 'Pigstick' operations in which two or three pairs of Whirlwinds flew in a wide formation, with several miles between the pairs, searching for a lone Luftwaffe aircraft known from their intercepted radio transmissions to be operating regularly in the area. Although the squadron patrolled out as far as the Saltee Islands, well within the territorial waters of neutral Eire, no contact was made with the enemy.

April opened with more accidents and the loss of a further two Whirlwinds. On 1 April, Harvey escaped with bruises when P7112 swung off the runway while landing in a strong crosswind and overturned. The following day, P7041 suffered brake failure caused by low hydraulic pressure due to prolonged taxiing at low engine revs and taxied into an obstruction. Neither aircraft was repairable.[213] Landing from a patrol on 15 April, Harvey again swung off the runway in a strong crosswind. P7100 was repaired at Westland, retained

Refuelling a No. 263 Squadron Whirlwind at RAF Exeter in December 1940. (*Robert Bowater*)

by the company for various trials and eventually returned to the squadron in November 1943.

On 18 April, the squadron moved again, this time to Angle in Pembrokeshire. It flew its fourteen serviceable Whirlwinds to its new station without incident, leaving three others behind under repair at Fairwood Common while the ground crew and equipment moved by rail. Not long into the train journey it was realised that the wagon immediately behind the steam locomotive was on fire. The wagon, containing the A Flight Armoury, was moved onto a siding and the blaze extinguished before ammunition exploded. The move to Angle, forty-five miles west of Fairwood Common, placed the squadron closer to the shipping lanes it was tasked with patrolling. However, as summer arrived and the fighter pilots could sunbathe, swim and sail, they found the place remote and desolate. Worse, there were no WAAFs at Angle when the squadron moved there and the first did not arrive until mid-June.

Although most of the squadron's time at Angle was spent on convoy patrols and occasional interceptions, within a few days of its arrival, 10 Group ordered an operation that would mark the squadron's return to the offensive over France for the first time since the distillery attacks in November. The targets were the airfields at Morlaix and Lannion.[214] 263 Squadron moved its aircraft to the forward base at Predannack several times, but on each occasion the weather was unsuitable for the operation to be flown. Eventually, in the early evening of 30 April, Rudland, Harvey, Bill Lovell and Ridley set off for Lannion followed a few minutes later by Woodward, Kennedy, Holmes and Abrams to Morlaix. The Spitfires of 310 Squadron led by Sqn Ldr Frantisek Doležal and accompanied by the Portreath wing leader, Wg Cdr Mindy Blake, provided escort. However, because of another inaccurate wind forecast, they crossed the French coast too far west. Uncertain of their position and with all surprise lost, the operation was abandoned.[215]

May marked a return to the normal routine with over 300 uneventful convoy patrols being flown. Little of interest happened, but on 22 May in driving rain and dense cloud, Walker and Reed were vectored almost as far as the Irish coast in pursuit of an unidentified aircraft. They returned after two hours in the air with fuel tanks almost dry to land at the tiny satellite airfield at Hell's Mouth.

5 June marked a return to the offensive with Circus No. 7. Again, the targets were Morlaix – specifically as Ju 52 transports were believed to be located there – and Lannion. In total, eighty-one Spitfires, twelve Bostons and eight Whirlwinds were involved. Activities began with a diversionary sweep by the Ibsley Wing ten miles off the French coast across the top of the Cherbourg peninsula well to the north east of the primary target. Although British radar detected German fighters, the wing saw no sign of them. Escorted by thirty-four Spitfires of the Exeter Wing, the twelve Bostons then made the main attack on Morlaix followed by the Whirlwinds. Warnes led Crabtree, Holmes and Kennedy to Morlaix while Woodward led Blackshaw, Coyne and Muirhead to Lannion, the two formations escorted by six Spitfires of 130 Sqn and 234 Sqn respectively. Warnes' formation crossed the coast a few miles from Morlaix, but believing they were much further west, turned along the coast, missed the target and returned to base. Two of 130 Squadron's French pilots, Jacques Andrieux and Roland Leblond, did find the target and made a low-level attack, claiming one Bf 109 and a decoy aircraft destroyed, but saw no Ju 52s. 10 Group was subsequently critical of the conduct of the operation, believing that better use should have been made of the local knowledge of Andrieux (who had previously been stationed at Morlaix) in navigating the formation from the coast to its target. Woodward's formation enjoyed better luck. They crossed the French coast near Île Grande at thirty feet and snaked up the valley of the River Léguer. Having identified Lannion, they increased speed to 280-300 mph and climbed to 400 feet. The Whirlwinds attacked at once and claimed hits on one Ju 88 and five other aircraft which they subsequently suspected were decoys. Two gun posts and several hangars were also attacked. They then swept out of the target area towards the coast, reformed with their escort west of Les Sept Îles and landed at 16:50.[216]

On 1 July, many fighter squadrons were detached to airfields in the south east of Britain in preparation for Operation Rutter, the first iteration of the plan for the assault on Dieppe. Among them were Portreath's Spitfire squadrons, so A Flight of 263 Squadron moved to Portreath in their place. While there the squadron mainly carried out uneventful convoy patrols,

Above: No. 263 Squadron Whirlwind HE-X at dispersal, RAF Warmwell. (*Robert Bowater*)

Left: A No. 263 Squadron Whirlwind at dispersal in Knighton Wood, RAF Warmwell, in the summer of 1943. (*Robert Bowater*)

although two Whirlwinds were damaged on 5 July when Muirhead taxied P7013 into P7120.

Operation Rutter waited for good weather that never came and was then quietly abandoned. The Portreath squadrons returned to their base and A Flight of 263 returned to Angle on 8 July from where the routine patrols continued until 23 July when the squadron moved twelve aircraft to Predannack for 10 Group Synchronised Rhubarb 85. The Whirlwinds took off in rapid succession at around 15:30 and met their escort of twelve Spitfires of 234 Squadron at Lizard Point. Flying at sea level, they crossed the French coast west of Plouescat, headed inland and split into pairs. They found no shortage of targets between Lesneven and Landerneau. Between them they attacked rail and road transport, a radio station, gun post and distillery. While the Whirlwinds carried out their attacks, the escorting Spitfires also fired at ground targets, but lost one of their number to flak. The Whirlwinds and Spitfires then crossed out over the coast singly and in small groups. On the return flight, Woodward and Coyne saw one of their colleagues pursued by two pairs of Bf 109s, but before they could intervene the Whirlwind had been shot down into the sea. Shortly afterwards they saw another Whirlwind with its starboard engine on fire with three Bf 109s behind it. Woodward again turned back, but could not see clearly because of a dirty windscreen and radio reception was too poor for him to be able to contact other aircraft to intervene. Currie (flying P7035) and Walker (P7060) failed to return, both claimed by the Bf 109Gs of 11.(Höh.)/JG2. 234 Squadron lost three Spitfires to the Fw 190s of other elements of JG2, but 130 Squadron, patrolling between Sept Îles and Île Vierge, saw no sign of the enemy.[217]

The squadron then returned to its routine convoy patrols until 15 August when, with few regrets, most of the personnel left Angle and moved to Colerne. The squadron's Whirlwinds followed the next day and 152 Squadron's Spitfires took their place.

CHAPTER 10

The Narrow Sea – 137 Squadron at Matlaske

For 137 Squadron, the move to 12 Group opened a nine-month period, first at Coltishall and later at its satellite Matlaske, dedicated almost entirely to protecting east coast shipping. These convoys followed a narrow channel, regularly swept of mines, which threaded its way between the minefields, sandbanks and sunken wrecks littering this part of the English Channel. This route, barely a sea-mile wide in most places, split into inner and outer lanes off the Norfolk coast to allow north and southbound convoys to pass each other. For almost the whole route from the Thames estuary to the Humber, shipping was vulnerable to attack by both German light naval forces and the Luftwaffe's remaining bomber forces in the west giving 137 Squadron the opportunity to meet the enemy more often than 263 Squadron, engaged on similar duties in the west.

On 9 November 1941, the day after its arrival at Coltishall and with twelve of its twenty-six pilots operational, 137 Squadron was again made semi-operational. Flying training continued, both with the Whirlwinds and an Airspeed Oxford acquired to provide dual-control training for pilots with no experience of twin-engine aircraft, and some of the pilots practiced air firing at the Stiffkey firing range. As the weather improved, the squadron performed largely uneventful convoy patrols, interceptions and searches for E-boats until 1 December when it moved to Matlaske. The squadron's duties remained much the same with routine patrols over the shipping lanes and ports of Yarmouth and Lowestoft. Only once was the enemy seen. Maddocks observed a Ju 88 during an interception patrol, but the aircraft vanished into cloud before he could engage.

Joe Hughes had by now served continuously with a frontline fighter squadron since the formation of 263 Squadron two years earlier and was due to be rested. He made his last operational flight with 137 Squadron on 9 December and left for the Central Flying School, being replaced as B Flight Commander by FO Guy Marsland who arrived from 56 OTU. Returning from an interception patrol on 23 November, O'Neill suffered a starboard engine failure in P7094 and crashed in a field near the airfield, tearing off the aircraft's nose and propellers. O'Neill suffered slight head injuries and his aircraft was returned to Westland for repair.[218]

1942 opened with unpredictable weather, little flying and a further series of accidents in which P7105, P7062 and P7092 were damaged while being flown by Wright, Maddocks and La Gette respectively. All aircraft were repairable, but Maddocks was badly injured. There was almost no flying during the last two weeks of January as heavy snow was followed by severe frost, a thaw that waterlogged the airfield and further snow. During this period of enforced inactivity two new pilots arrived: Eddie Musgrave from Australia and Dattatreya Samant from India. Improved weather saw operational flying commence on 1 February with patrols around Great Yarmouth. On the last of these in the early evening, Martin and McClure were vectored onto an aircraft flying north about ten miles east of Winterton-on-Sea. At 17:35, they found a Do 217 just below the cloud base at 2,000 feet. Martin fired a short burst before it escaped into cloud and was not seen again.[219]

Four days later, Woodward and Robertson had a similarly inconclusive encounter over a convoy thirty miles off the Lincolnshire coast. They saw the ships' anti-aircraft guns firing but neither pilot could see the target. They

P7062 flew with both Whirlwind squadrons but was lost in a crash on 19 February 1943 with No. 263 Squadron during an Army Co-operation exercise. She clipped a tree during a low-level pass and spun into the ground near Chiseldon, Wiltshire. Her pilot, thirty-year-old Australian Flight Sergeant Frank Hicks, was killed. (*Robert Bowater*)

then observed two bomb splashes astern of the convoy and headed for this area. Robertson saw a Dornier almost directly above him flying through dense cloud and made two attacks; however, two of his cannons jammed after a few rounds. He exhausted the ammunition from the two remaining guns, but saw no results and was unable to contact ground control to vector Woodward towards the enemy.[220] This was one of Woodward's last flights with the squadron before he was posted to command 263 Squadron.

On 8 February, P/O Rebbetoy suffered an engine failure while patrolling over the sea in P7097. He returned on the remaining engine, but ran out of fuel just a mile short of the airfield and made a skilful forced landing in a field. The aircraft was dismantled and returned to Westland for repair.[221]

Fuller

In late March 1941, the German battlecruisers *Scharnhorst* and *Gneisenau* arrived at Brest after a moderately successful patrol in the Atlantic, to be joined in June by the heavy cruiser *Prinz Eugen*. The presence in an Atlantic port of this powerful force represented a severe potential threat to British convoys and the Royal Navy and RAF immediately put in place plans to neutralise it. Given the codename Operation Fuller, the plans covered attacks on the ships in port as well as if they should attempt to escape into the open sea. All three ships were damaged by bombing during 1941, but at the end of the year, photoreconnaissance and other intelligence suggested that repairs had been completed. At the beginning of February 1942, an increase in German minesweeping activity indicated that the ships' departure was imminent and hinted at the route they would take. They left Brest at 22:45 on the night of 11 February with a heavy escort of six destroyers, fourteen torpedo boats and a host of smaller vessels.

In the nine months since Fuller was developed, many resources, especially destroyers and torpedo-bombers, had been diverted to other theatres and the British reaction to the German escape was late, poorly co-ordinated and fundamentally under-resourced. Within hours of the German flotilla's departure, the British plan began to unravel. Two of the regular night air patrols monitoring the sea lanes around Brest suffered radar failures, but despite the importance of their task, were not replaced. An early morning Spitfire patrol spotted the German ships, but maintained radio silence and reported the sighting after landing. Therefore, it was almost midday before the British responded and by then the German flotilla, covered by an umbrella of fighters, was in the straits of Dover.

Among the slender naval forces available were six destroyers under the command of Captain Mark Pizey. These were exercising off Harwich when, just before midday, Pizey was informed that the German fleet was already off Boulogne travelling at 20 knots. He was instructed to follow a pre-existing plan to intercept the enemy off the Belgian coast and just before 13:00, 137 Squadron was tasked with escorting his destroyers on their outward journey. Ten aircraft were to provide the escort in relays. Pizey set course, but at 13:00, was told that the speed of the German flotilla was 27 knots rather than 20. Accordingly, he changed the course of his destroyers to intercept the Germans further north off the Maas estuaries. By this time, the Whirlwind pilots had been given their courses and at 13:10, Robertson, Mercer, Häggberg and de Houx took off. They flew just below the cloud base at 2,500 feet in box formation, but after thirty minutes failed to locate the British destroyers. Five minutes later they turned for home, but shortly afterwards Häggberg saw a group of ships about twenty miles off the Belgian coast and led the formation down to investigate. The ships were the German flotilla and as the Whirlwinds descended to 800 feet they were engaged by the Bf 109Fs of JG2.

In the dogfight that followed Robertson was attacked from behind by a Bf 109. Mercer, following close behind, had the Messerschmitt in his sights, but his cannons would not fire. Mercer was then attacked by another Bf 109 at which de Houx in turn fired inconclusively. At this point the convoy opened fire and Mercer, not wishing to fly through the flak, separated from Robertson who was not seen again, presumably falling victim to the German gunners.

Two 137 Squadron Whirlwinds beat up RAF Manston for the press on 5 March 1943. (*Niall Corduroy*)

With his guns inoperative and unable to play any further part in the combat, Mercer withdrew from the fight and turned for home, weaving at low altitude. De Houx fired inconclusively at a further three Bf 109s and saw a Whirlwind in a shallow dive and pouring glycol smoke with a Bf 109 in pursuit. With one cannon jammed and the other three out of ammunition, he also turned for home. The Whirlwind he had seen in trouble was almost certainly Häggberg's P7093. Häggberg did not return and was probably shot down by Oblt Egon Mayer of JG2 who claimed a Whirlwind at 13:38. De Houx landed safely at Matlaske, but Mercer was chased for some distance and fired at by two Bf 109s. He landed at Ipswich and subsequent inspection of his aircraft (P7055) revealed that he had a narrow escape. There were bullet holes in the starboard fuel tank, the port engine nacelle and tyre and one in the fuselage close to Mercer's shoulder. More seriously, a cannon shell had taken a 'bite' the size of an apple out of the port main wing spar.

Meanwhile, Martin, Sandy and La Gette had taken off flying the same course to relieve their colleagues. La Gette returned early with engine problems, but the other two flew on and also stumbled over the German squadron and its fighter umbrella. In the ensuing combat, Martin (P7106) and Sandy (P7050) were shot down by Fw. Hans Stolz and Uffz. Willi Reuschling of JG2. The final three pilots, Bryan, Ashton and De-Shane, took off at 14:25 flying on a new heading that reflected the altered course of the destroyers. They found

Whirlwind P7055 was a presentation aircraft as *Bellows Argentina No. 1*. Serving with No. 137 Squadron as SF-S between 1 November 1941 and 24 June 1943, she was transferred to No. 263 Squadron. *Bellows Argentina No. 1* was scrapped in July 1944. (*Robert Bowater*)

the destroyers and patrolled over them uneventfully for half an hour before landing at Wattisham to refuel and then returning to Matlaske. By the time the last three Whirlwinds had landed, the destroyers – now reduced to five as HMS *Walpole* had been forced to return with engine bearing problems – had located the German flotilla. Their torpedo attacks were pressed home with extraordinary determination from ranges as short as 2,400 yards, but none found their mark. Other air and naval attacks did not cause any material damage and by the end of the day, *Scharnhorst* and *Gneisenau* were out of range, even though both were damaged by mines en route.[222]

Despite its heavy losses on 12 February and frequent snow showers, the squadron continued its routine patrols over the coming days. Also during the month the squadron's B Flight commander, Guy Marsland, was posted out to the Far East. His replacement was John van Schaick, DFM, previously of 609 Squadron.

On 9 March, an accident during a training flight cost the life of Charles De Shane when his aircraft (P7036) spun in and crashed while 'dogfighting' with a Spitfire.

Early on 15 March, a British convoy was attacked by the 2nd Schnellboot Flotilla. *S.104* torpedoed and sank HMS *Vortigern*, one of the escorting destroyers, but *S.111* was caught after the battle by British MGBs and heavily damaged. During the morning, 137 Squadron's Whirlwinds maintained standing patrols over the MGBs while ten Spitfires of 412 Squadron set off from Coltishall to find the schnellboote. The Spitfires' attack did further damage to *S.111* that had to be abandoned and sunk, but by the time 137 Squadron attempted a further attack they found nothing but wreckage and bodies in the water.[223]

Two days later, A Flight moved to Snailwell for Army Co-operation practice and remained there until 28 March when B Flight replaced them. The squadron was reunited on 27 April when B Flight returned to Matlaske. Flying at Matlaske was impeded by poor weather and consisted mainly of fruitless searches for E-boats, uneventful convoy patrols, standing patrols over Yarmouth and Lowestoft, and a few patrols to intercept what inevitably turned out to be misplotted friendly aircraft.

On 4 May, 137 Squadron lost another pilot when PO Robert Wright was killed in P7103 after a structural failure. Wright had taken off for dogfighting practice with another pilot who returned with engine trouble. Wright was next seen recovering from a dive at about 4,000 feet when, with a sharp crack that was heard by witnesses on the ground three miles away, the aircraft broke up in the air and crashed on farmland near Aylsham, Norfolk. The subsequent accident investigation concluded that when Wright pulled out of the dive the substantial tail download caused a failure of the joint between the fuselage and the wing roots. The fuselage had then detached from the wings. They also felt that the joint had limited strength reserves, but since Whirlwind production had finished, it was recommended that the joint should be regularly inspected rather than modified.²²⁴

On the moonless night of 8-9 May, Norwich was bombed by a mixed force of forty Dornier 217s, Ju 88s and He 111s. Coghlan, Bryan, Bartlett and Samant were among the pilots scrambled to intercept them. Samant caught a brief glimpse of an enemy aircraft illuminated by the searchlights beneath him. He dived down to attack, but overshot his target and could not find it again.

A week later, Brennan and Brunet had another encounter with the enemy while covering a convoy off Lowestoft on the morning of 15 May. While patrolling in mist at 300 feet, they saw an unidentified aircraft slightly above them and three or four miles away. They went to investigate and when they had closed to about one mile, the unidentified aircraft began to climb steeply allowing the Whirlwind pilots to identify it as a Ju 88. Concerned that the Junkers would reach cloud cover, Brennan opened fire from 800 yards range while still climbing at fifty degrees, firing all of his ammunition in four bursts and believing he saw shell strikes on the Junker's fuselage. The Junker's gunners returned fire and one bullet found its target, wrecking the reduction gear of his starboard engine and obliging Brennan to break away and make a

On 7 November 1941, seconds after this photograph was taken, No. 137 Squadron's Sgt Art Brunet's aircraft (on the left) suffered an engine failure. He jettisoned his bombs and landed safely. (*Robert Bowater*)

successful single-engine landing at Coltishall. Brunet, following Brennan into the attack and climbing up into the clouds, then regained contact with the Ju 88 though a gap in the clouds 500 feet above. He climbed sharply and fired a long burst, but stalled and was unable to find the Ju 88 again.[225]

On 16 May, the squadron encountered the enemy twice, but on neither occasion did combat follow. While on a routine convoy patrol with Brunet in the late afternoon, Brennan saw a Do 217 appear out of the clouds but lost it in the clouds. On a patrol over another convoy, Ogilvie and McPhail saw a Ju 88 two miles away, but this also escaped.[226]

On the morning of 27 May, the squadron was involved in a combat that was initially believed to have resulted in its first victory, but later judged to have been a tragic accident. Brennan and La Gette were patrolling the shipping lanes off the Norfolk coast twenty miles north east of Cromer when they saw what Brennan identified as a Ju 88. Brennan made a stern attack from 200-300 yards followed by La Gette who attacked with a deflection shot from 600 yards. The port wing of the target aircraft then detached and crashed into the sea. It became clear that the aircraft they had shot down was not a Ju 88 but a Blenheim IV of 1401 Meteorological Flight which was last heard from in the same area. Whether Brennan realised his mistake at the time can probably never be known with certainty, although when La Gette landed he clearly believed that the aircraft they had shot down was a Ju 88. What is known is that although Brennan was instructed to orbit the spot where the aircraft had crashed, he turned east out to sea and when queried by La Gette answered simply 'Everything under control.' La Gette landed safely, but Brennan continued on to Holland in P7122 where he strafed ground targets at Ijmuiden before being shot down by flak into the Noordzeekanaal near Velsen. The nineteen-year-old Canadian did not survive. Subsequent searches of the area where the Blenheim had been lost were made by aircraft including twelve of 137's Whirlwinds, but found only a patch of oil and an overturned dinghy.[227]

The squadron lost another Whirlwind on 29 May when Jowitt's aircraft suffered an internal glycol leak in one its engines while returning to Matlaske from a dawn patrol. Believing that the engine was on fire, Jowitt parachuted successfully while his aircraft (P7118) crashed near Itteringham.

June saw more practice flying and further Army Co-operation exercises, and the next contact with the enemy came on 20 June when four pairs of Whirlwinds were scrambled during the evening. Mercer and Ashton, the last pair, were patrolling at 1,500 feet when they found a Do 217 off the coast forty miles east of Yarmouth, crossing their path about 2,000 yards ahead and 1,000 feet below them. As they dived down towards the Dornier, it dived to sea level. Ashton made two attacks and Mercer used up all his ammunition in three bursts while diving down from 800 feet, believing he saw a handful of shell strikes. He followed the Dornier for twenty miles and then returned to base.[228]

In the evening of 26 June, Bryan and O'Neill carried out a shipping reconnaissance patrol from Ijmuiden to the Hook of Holland, but found no shipping. As they set course for home they saw a Ju 88 that they chased to the Dutch coast. Unable to close any nearer, both pilots fired from 800 yards, but saw no results. That night, the Luftwaffe raided Norwich and in addition to 68 Squadron's Beaufighters and 610's Spitfires, Ashton, Waldron and Jowitt were sent to patrol over the city. Waldron was the only pilot to make contact, firing at a Do 217 from very short range in a dive, but, blinded by the muzzle flashes of his guns, was unable to see results.[229]

At the end of June, three new sergeant pilots joined the squadron: Robert Woodhouse, John Barclay and Alfred Brown. On the evening of 27 June, Brunet and Musgrave briefly engaged a Ju 88 while patrolling a convoy off Yarmouth. After a long chase, Brunet fired two short bursts from extreme range before having to drop back with overheating engines. Musgrave also fired two short bursts before losing sight of the Junkers in cloud.[230] The squadron lost another Whirlwind on the last day of June 1942 when Len Bartlett overshot when landing at Matlaske in very poor weather and collided with a stationary Lysander of 1489 Flight. With its back broken in the impact, P7101 was damaged beyond repair.[231]

Late in the evening of 3 July, three sections of 137 Squadron's Whirlwinds were patrolling off the coast waiting to be vectored onto two enemy aircraft as they crossed out over the coast on their homeward journey. This proved to be an unnecessary precaution as two Ju 88s of 2/Küstenfliegergruppe 106 were shot down over land by Spitfires of 303 Squadron. Early in the morning of 6 July, Bartlett and Roberts were scrambled and vectored after a lone Luftwaffe reconnaissance aircraft. Forty miles off the English coast, Bartlett saw a Ju 88 at sea level about four miles away. Bartlett reported the sighting to Roberts and to his controller and then dived to sea level in pursuit. Bartlett was rapidly closing when the Junkers suddenly climbed towards cloud base at 7,000 feet. Initially, the Ju 88 outclimbed the Whirlwind and closing to 400-300 yards, Bartlett fired all of his ammunition and was certain that he saw strikes on the fuselage. As on so many previous occasions, the enemy escaped into cloud. Roberts did not get close enough to open fire and the Ju 88's gunners managed to score a single bullet strike on Bartlett's aircraft (P7111).[232]

There was no further contact with the Luftwaffe until the evening of 23 July when Waldron and Robert Smith were tasked with escorting a convoy off Yarmouth. Soon after take off, Waldron's aircraft suffered a partial electrical failure putting his lights, gunsight and radio out of action. He gestured to Smith to inform him of his problems and the pair continued their patrol. After twenty-five minutes, the convoy advised Smith that an aircraft was some

A Whirlwind recently delivered from a maintenance unit to No. 137 Squadron and yet to have her codes painted on. Seen at RAF Matlaske in the summer of 1942. (*Robert Bowater*)

distance away to the east at sea level. Smith saw it about ten miles away and just below the cloud base, and set off in pursuit with Waldron following. To avoid being seen by the enemy, the Whirlwind pilots climbed to the cloud base at 400 feet, dipping below the cloud every thirty seconds or so to check the position of the enemy. Ten minutes later, the Whirlwinds emerged from the cloud about 500 yards astern of their target that they identified as a Ju 88. Smith dived down and fired a short burst from 400 yards at which point the Ju 88 pulled up sharply to starboard into the clouds. Smith and Waldron caught further glimpses of the aircraft through gaps in the clouds and fired again, but lost contact with the Ju 88 and made no claim to have damaged it.[233]

First Victory

After these inconclusive combats, 137 Squadron's first victory came on the cloudless evening of 25 July. McClure (P7104) was leading Robert Smith (P7012) patrolling a convoy six miles off Yarmouth. As was frequently the case, a Whirlwind was flying at 2,000 feet for a good long distance view with the other at sea level where a raider could be spotted silhouetted against the sky. On this occasion it was Smith at sea level who first saw an unidentified aircraft a mile away to starboard flying in the opposite direction. Smith radioed the aircraft's position to McClure who immediately identified it as a Ju 88 and saw it turn away to the east. The Whirlwind pilots accelerated towards the Junkers with McClure diving down at 380 mph and experiencing return fire from the Ju 88's dorsal gunner as he closed to 800 yards. Smith, gaining on the Ju 88 slowly, was first to attack, firing a one-second burst from 500 yards astern and seeing his cannon fire hitting the sea beneath the tail of the enemy aircraft. He then saw McClure diving in at high speed to port of the Ju 88 and edged off to starboard to get out of his way. McClure, however, overshot slightly and as he turned away, his aircraft was hit in the starboard engine by the Ju 88's gunner. Smith then renewed the attack, firing his remaining ammunition from 250-200 yards and seeing strikes on the starboard engine. McClure had now turned and, although glycol was streaming out his Whirlwind's starboard engine, approached for a second attack. McClure fired a two-second burst from 100-50 yards and saw strikes on the starboard engine and the centre of the fuselage. The Junkers pulled up slightly to fifty feet and McClure finished his ammunition in a further four-second burst before the Ju 88, with its fuselage and starboard engine now burning, stalled and slammed into the sea. The Whirlwind pilots filmed the wreckage but saw no sign of survivors. Smith then escorted McClure back to Matlaske where he made a successful single-engine landing. There were no survivors from the four-man crew of Ju 88A-5 (WNr. 649), a 3(F)/33 aircraft operated that day by 3.(F)/122.[234]

Two days later, Freeman and Furber, patrolling north of Cromer, inconclusively engaged a Do 217 before it escaped into cloud, but on 29 July, Rebbetoy and O'Neill had better luck. They were engaged on one of five convoy patrols flown by the squadron that day, when fifteen miles north east of Happisburgh at 20:45, O'Neill, flying at low level with Rebbetoy above, saw a Ju 88 crossing in front of them about 200 yards away. Rebbetoy turned in towards the Ju 88 and fired a one-second burst from 250 yards. O'Neill then fired a two-second burst and saw cannon strikes on the nose area of the Junkers that then dived to 2,000 feet before climbing steeply. The Whirlwinds followed and Rebbetoy fired from 100 yards and saw strikes on the fuselage and starboard engine before he broke away underneath the Junkers. O'Neill fired two more bursts, but Rebbetoy saw his tracer passing just underneath the target. The Ju 88 continued to climb and Rebbetoy finished his ammunition in a further burst from 100 yards dead astern and saw more strikes. With white glycol smoke pouring from its starboard engine, the Junkers then dived steeply before levelling off at sea level. O'Neill exhausted his ammunition in a final attack and the Whirlwind pilots followed the Ju 88 for a further fifteen miles before a fire broke out in the starboard wing and the aircraft crashed into the sea. They saw an inverted dinghy in the water, but there was no sign of the crew. Their victim was Ju 88D WNr. 1515 of 3.(F)/122 operating from Creil, twenty miles north of Paris. The body of the pilot, Uffz. Rudolf Pilz, was washed ashore in Denmark two months later, but his three crewmates remain missing.[235]

Between 2-11 August, the Typhoons of 266 Squadron moved to Matlaske to stand in for 137 Squadron that was detached to Drem in Scotland for Exercise Dryshod. Dryshod was a large-scale army exercise in which three army brigades 'invaded' an imaginary German-held coastline along a line between Girvan on the west coast of Scotland and Edinburgh in the east. South of the line three further brigades formed the 'German' defence. 137 Squadron was one of twelve bomber, fighter and Army Co-operation squadrons providing air support for the attacking force. Dryshod proved to be something of a rest for many of the squadrons taking part, including 137, as poor weather prevented much flying. The exercise concluded on 9 August and the Whirlwinds returned to Matlaske on 11 August.

The first action after the squadron's return to Matlaske came on 18 August. In the late afternoon, Bartlett and de Houx set off to search for enemy shipping off the Dutch coast. They found no shipping, but did spot a dinghy in the sea about forty miles off shore and on their return Luing and O'Neill were briefed to locate it. They found no dinghy, but O'Neill spotted a Ju 88. In conditions of near darkness and heavy sea mist, O'Neill fired a short burst and observed cannon strikes on the Junkers. Luing also fired but was blinded by the muzzle flash of his own guns and could not see the results of his fire. The Ju 88 escaped into the murk and was not seen again.[236]

A No. 263 Squadron Whirlwind leaves the dispersal area at RAF Drem in 1940. (*Robert Bowater*)

On 19 August, while much of Fighter Command was engaged with the large-scale amphibious raid at Dieppe, 137 Squadron plied its usual trade of convoy patrols and interceptions. Van Schaick and Brown were between Cross Sands and Smiths Knoll on a routine patrol when Brown, patrolling at sea level with van Schaick 1,000 feet above, saw a Ju 88 coming towards him through the mist. Brown radioed van Schaick about the aircraft and turned to get behind the Ju 88, but van Schaick's starboard engine cut and was unable to follow and lost contact with Brown and the enemy. Brown fired at the Ju 88 from long range and fired four more bursts, closing from 500 to 300 yards. He observed strikes on the enemy aircraft and smoke from one of its engines, but return fire damaged one of the propellers of his Whirlwind (P6976) and put his radio out of action. The two Whirlwinds returned independently with Brown claiming the Ju 88 as damaged.[237]

A more conclusive engagement took place an hour later when, following several vectors from ground control, Bryan and Roberts intercepted a Dornier about fifty miles out to sea off Happisburgh. The aircraft, Do 217E-4, WNr 5370 of 5/KG40, was returning to Soesterberg after a sortie to monitor British shipping movements. The Dornier was 1,000 feet below the Whirlwinds, slightly to one side and flying in the same direction. As Bryan and Roberts dived down, the Dornier turned underneath them into their attack and the dorsal gunner opened fire. Roberts (P7046) fired a short burst from 200 yards while turning with the Dornier, but saw no results. Bryan (P7121) fired all of his ammunition in three bursts from astern and saw cannon strikes on the fuselage and port engine. Roberts renewed the attack from astern, after which the Dornier's crew bailed out and the aircraft stalled and crashed into the sea at about 10:25. Bartlett and O'Neill later escorted a Walrus of 278 Squadron to the scene to look for survivors and after searching for fifteen minutes, saw one man in the water. The Walrus landed and rescued Oblt Adolf Wolf, exhausted but otherwise unhurt, and returned to Coltishall. There was no sign of Wolf's three crewmates and their bodies were washed ashore on the Danish coast two months later.[238]

Early in the morning of 20 August, Bartlett and Barclay were patrolling the shipping lanes off Yarmouth in pouring rain and with dense cloud down to 300 feet. Bartlett was flying at 2,000 feet and Barclay at sea level when Barclay saw a Ju 88 at which he fired three short bursts from long range. The Junkers then climbed where Bartlett also saw it briefly before the bomber vanished into the clouds. This was the last eventful operation for the squadron from Matlaske as 137 Squadron moved to Snailwell airfield near Newmarket on 24 August for a period of intensive training flying.

CHAPTER 11

The Whirlibomber

In September 1941, Tom Pugh had suggested that the Whirlwind should be modified to carry bombs to increase its hitting power in ground-attack operations such as those carried out in August. Fighter Command rejected the idea at the time, but by the summer of 1942, found itself in a very different situation. The Command had learned that fighter-only operations over France rarely provoked a reaction from the Luftwaffe and had also taken responsibility for the 'Channel Stop', the blocking of the central portion of the English Channel to enemy shipping. For both roles it needed fighter-bombers, but the Hurricane Bomber, the only fighter-bomber in its inventory at the time, was in very short supply. Almost all Hurricane production was shipped to other theatres or supplied to the Russians. In mid-1942, Fighter Command had just two Hurricane Bomber squadrons and the availability of replacement aircraft for them was so poor that Freeman warned Sholto Douglas that he might have to disband or re-equip one of them. While it may seem perverse for Fighter Command to ask for the Whirlwinds to be converted to fighter-bombers when so few aircraft were available and production had finished, in effect it doubled its fighter-bomber strength from two squadrons to four at a time when it desperately needed such aircraft.

On 3 July, Fighter Command informed the Air Ministry and MAP that it would like the Whirlwinds to be converted to fighter-bombers as a matter of urgency.[239] By early August, Westland had completed the design and ordered the government-supplied components such as the bomb selection and fusing switches needed to convert fifty aircraft. The modification consisted of a simple welded, tubular reinforcing structure installed in each wing to which the standard Mk III Universal Carrier was bolted. On the Hurricane Bomber, the carrier was provided with an aerodynamic fairing, but none was developed for the Whirlwind because of the small number of aircraft involved.

Later in August, P6997 arrived at A&AEE Boscombe Down for handling and performance trials carrying bombs and Hicks was attached to A&AEE from

263 Squadron to help with the test flying. A&AEE completed its methodical tests by 12 September, but by then 263 Squadron had dropped its first bombs in action. The Boscombe Down pilots found that the Whirlwind's handling was only slightly affected by the bombs, but at high speeds the aircraft's natural tendency to fly with the left wing low became highly noticeable and pronounced aileron flutter was detected. The aircraft's handling was acceptable with just the starboard bomb, but with the port bomb only, lateral control was poor and the aircraft flew with the left wing low at all speeds. The Whirlwind's ailerons were fitted with servo tabs to reduce control loads, but these were not controllable by the pilot so there was no way of trimming out this condition. A&AEE recommended that bombs should be dropped in pairs or, at least, the port bomb should always be dropped first.[240] Inevitably, the bomb racks affected performance: maximum speed was reduced by 20 mph to 318 mph at 15,000 feet and ceiling reduced to 27,500 feet.[241] The bombs made little difference to performance implying that the unfaired racks caused most of the additional drag. To check that they would clear the aircraft's large flaps, A&AEE tested the Whirlwind with a wide variety of weapons including anti-submarine bombs, depth charges, smoke-laying containers and the American M.43 and M.58 500-lb bombs. Operationally, the Whirlwinds usually carried 250-lb general purpose bombs or, occasionally, the 500 lbs equivalent. For practice, adaptors could be fitted allowing four 11.5-lb practice bombs to be carried under each wing.[242]

Long before A&AEE had completed its tests, modification kits became available at 25MU and on 15 August, 263 Squadron was made non-operational and moved to Colerne where the Whirlwinds were modified. Approximately twenty-man hours were required to install the reinforcing structure, wiring and cockpit switches for each aircraft, mainly because the outer wings had to be removed to install the reinforcement.[243] Cliff Rudland was the first squadron pilot to fly the Whirlwind with bombs loaded. He found that maximum speed was reduced by about 25 mph at sea level and also noted aileron flutter at diving speeds, which also sometimes occurred at lower speeds at low altitude.

The conversion of the Whirlwinds into fighter-bombers presaged a new career at low level, but the most significant operational flying during August was against the highest flying adversaries of all – the Junkers Ju 86. On the morning of 28 August, an unidentified aircraft was plotted crossing the French coast at high altitude and tracked until it crossed the English coast, but was then lost until it was seen over Bristol. Before an air raid warning could be sounded, the aircraft, a Ju 86R operating from Beauvais, had dropped its single 250 kg bomb that fell in the city centre, killing forty-eight people and injuring many more. 10 Group scrambled fighters to intercept it, including Brearley and Reed in their Whirlwinds, but none could reach the raider's high altitude. In the afternoon, Gill and Yates were among those who attempted to

Head-on shot of a Whirlibomber, fully loaded with two 250-lb bombs. (*Robert Bowater*)

intercept a similar raid over Cardiff, but again the enemy was too high to be caught.[244]

On 1 September, Rudland, who was posted put to 19 Squadron, was replaced as A Flight Commander by Blackshaw and, a few days later, the flight gained another new pilot when Flt Lt Arthur Johnstone was posted in as a supernumerary. Johnstone had previously served with 430 Flight (operating Gloster Gauntlets and Vickers Vincents) during the campaign in Ethiopia and Eritrea where he had been awarded the DFC for, among other things, destroying an Italian aircraft on the ground using a flare pistol.

By the end of August, most of the aircraft had been converted to carry bombs and the pilots moved to Warmwell to start bombing practice on 7 September. However, during their first day at Warmwell, a tanker was reported at sea near the Channel Islands. Fighter Command's two Hurricane Bomber squadrons were unavailable so four Whirlwinds were prepared to make an attack. The aircraft moved to Bolt Head that afternoon and early the following morning took off for the very first Whirlibomber operation. Sixteen Spitfires of 312 and 313 Squadrons escorted Woodward, Blackshaw, Warnes and Brearley, but there was no sign of the reported tanker.[245]

Into the Limelight

The following afternoon the same four pilots and aircraft took off to find another large ship reported near Cap de la Hague. The Whirlwinds flew at sea level with three anti-flak Spitfires of 118 Squadron on each side, twelve more of 66 Squadron providing close support and a further six aircraft of 118 Squadron as rear support. After twenty minutes, the leading pilots saw four ships heading towards Alderney: a pair of small coasters escorted by two Vorpostenboote, trawlers converted for escort work and usually heavily armed. The anti-flak Spitfires of 118 Squadron attacked immediately. Woodward and Warnes followed closely behind and attacked the furthermost ship of the leading pair. Woodward opened fire at extreme range and fired all of his ammunition before bombing. Warnes saw Woodward's bombs explode on the ship's waterline but could not fire during his run as Woodward was immediately in front of him. Although confident that his bombing had been accurate, Warnes was unable to see its results. Turning away after their attack the pilots saw the ship on fire amidships and apparently sinking.

Blackshaw and Brearley followed the other section of anti-flak Spitfires to attack the nearest ship of the leading pair. Like Woodward, Blackshaw fired his cannon before bombing, but his bombs were near misses. Brearley fired all his ammunition, but could not observe the results of his bombing although both pilots thought the ship was listing after their attack. When the rear support Spitfires arrived six minutes later, the pilots saw just two ships afloat. This led 263 Squadron to believe that it had sunk the other two, but the attack had not been as successful as first believed. The 305-ton MV *Henca* received a direct hit forward, quickly settled by the bows and rolled over. *V207* was raked by cannon fire and casualties aboard were grievous: one man dead and nineteen injured. Nonetheless, she returned to Cherbourg that evening under her own power. *V209* and MV *Tinda* were undamaged. The Germans abandoned attempts to either sink or salvage the MV *Henca* and the wreck, drifting out

20 March 1942: S/L Robert Woodward DFC on Whirlwind P6991 HE-R. (*Niall Corduroy*)

to sea supported by her own cargo of timber, was reported as a hazard to shipping some days later.[246]

After the months of monotonous, low-profile convoy patrols from Fairwood Common and Angle, this operation put the Whirlwinds in the limelight. *The Times* announced that 'Fighter Command's latest fighter-bombers, Whirlwinds, which have been modified to carry two bombs outboard of the engines, were used for the first time yesterday when they sank two of four armed trawlers attacked off Cap de la Hague.'[247] On the evening of 10 September, Woodward, Blackshaw, Coyne and Bill Lovell flew an uneventful shipping reconnaissance along the French coast, but this was the last operation before the entire squadron formally moved to Warmwell on 13 September. The pilots continued bombing practice and quickly achieved average bombing errors of just 20 yards at very low altitudes and around 60 yards when bombing from 500 feet. Reporting on the squadron's experience with the Whirlibomber, Woodward observed that when dropped at low level over rough seas, the 250-lb bombs tended to skip over the water for 30-40 yards before exploding so, provided bombs were dropped short, accuracy for length was not important. However, in calmer water, the bomb could skip for 100 yards or more and explode near the aircraft. Because of this he felt that 500-lb bombs would be dangerous for shipping attacks and that four 250-lb bombs would have been preferable for such bombing.[248]

A fully loaded Whirlwind taxiing to take off. The usual bomb load was two 250-lb bombs, although they could carry two 500-lb bombs if necessary. However, they rarely did so as the heavier bombs stressed the wings. (*Robert Bowater*)

137

While 263 Squadron started operations in its new fighter-bomber role, 137 Squadron left Matlaske on 24 August and moved to Snailwell near Newmarket where it began intensive practice flying, especially night flying. The squadron's next operation was a feint attack at Lille on the morning of 3 September. The intention was that the Luftwaffe would mistake the twin-engine Whirlwinds for bombers and attempt to intercept. They would then be engaged either by twenty-four close-escort Spitfires of 411 and 485 Squadrons or by a following sweep by thirty Typhoons of 56, 266 and 609 Squadrons.

The twelve Whirlwinds took off at 10:00, but Rebbetoy returned early with technical problems. The remaining aircraft set course with their escorts and thirty miles off the Belgian coast began a fast climb to 12,000 feet. Crossing into Belgium, the formation turned south towards Lille and was joined by the Typhoon wing flying a few thousand feet higher. At Diksmuide, the Whirlwinds and their escorts turned for home while the Typhoons continued to sweep southwards into France before they too set course for base. None of the sixty-five pilots taking part reported seeing an enemy aircraft.[249] This was 137 Squadron's last operation before its aircraft were converted to carry bombs. After a period of practice flying, the squadron moved from Snailwell to Manston in Kent on 16-17 September. At the same time, A Flight Commander Len Bartlett was posted out to command Hurricane-equipped 253 Squadron. Acting Flt Lt Joe Holmes arrived from 263 Squadron to replace Bartlett and Sqn Ldr John Wray arrived as a supernumerary squadron leader in late September.

Flight Lieutenant Joe Holmes, Flight Sergeant Graham Smith RAAF, Flight Sergeant Fred Green and Pilot Officer Don Tebbit in front of a bombed-up No. 263 Squadron Whirlwind at dispersal in Knighton Wood, RAF Warmwell, in 1943. (*Robert Bowater*)

CHAPTER 12

Rhubarb and Roadstead

When 263 Squadron moved to Warmwell on 13 September, the airfield was somewhat crowded. 175 Squadron's Hurricane Bombers were still there even though the unit was non-operational and 266 Squadron arrived with its Typhoons three days later. 263 Squadron's B Flight was temporarily based in a tent until it blew down in a gale, but the squadron gradually took over the dispersals and buildings as 175 Squadron moved out. There were many personnel changes during September. Joe Holmes left for 137 Squadron and the squadron's three American pilots, Norman Crabtree, Bill Lovell and Rick Reed, all transferred to the US Army Air Force.

On 21 September, the squadron lost another pilot and aircraft in an accident. King and Jardine took off in the early afternoon to practice flying in cloud, but were recalled shortly due to the deteriorating weather. Turning for home, the pilots lost contact with each other and eyewitnesses saw Jardine's aircraft (P7003) dive out of low cloud and crash a few miles from the airfield. An examination of the wreckage found no obvious technical problems and was assumed that Jardine had simply lost control in the clouds.[250] The squadron's first few weeks at Warmwell were spent mainly on night flying practice and the unit only returned to operational flying on 1 October. Early that day, three minesweepers were reported off Lézardrieux by reconnaissance aircraft and subsequently attacked by Typhoons. Warnes led Gill, Brearley and Adams from Bolt Head, escorted by twelve Spitfires of 312 Squadron, to stage a second attack. Unable to establish their position when they crossed the French coast they returned.[251]

An evening shipping attack on 3 October also did not go entirely as planned. During a routine shipping reconnaissance, 501 Squadron found a 3,000-ton cargo ship in Braye Bay, Alderney. Later, Woodward, Blackshaw, King and Ridley took off from Warmwell and met with five anti-flak Spitfires of 501 Squadron and a further twelve of 118 Squadron to provide rear support. Although the Whirlwinds throttled back to 180 mph, the anti-flak Spitfires struggled to keep up and only a single Spitfire appears to have crossed the target area. In order to attack out of the sun, Woodward led the Whirlwinds to the Casquets before turning east towards Alderney. Running into the target at mast height out of a hazy yellow evening sky, they were still two miles away from Alderney when the first flak bursts appeared around them. In the harbour they found the large merchant vessel and two smaller ships. Woodward bombed the large ship closely followed by Ridley who saw his leader's bombs fall slightly short and to the left of the target. Ridley and Blackshaw also bombed the large ship, but were unable to observe the results of their bombing, while King bombed one of the smaller ships before crossing the harbour and firing all his ammunition at a flak post. The flak was intense. Woodward's aircraft was hit just as he bombed, Ridley's and King's were hit while leaving the target zone and a Spitfire of 501 Squadron was also damaged. A few minutes into the return journey the starboard engine of Woodward's damaged aircraft began to overheat and smoke. Woodward shut the engine down and 118 Squadron's Spitfires closed protectively around to escort him back to the English coast. Ridley and King joined Blackshaw and returned to Warmwell without further incident.[252]

On 8 October, another Whirlwind was written off when Johnstone attempted to take off with the propellers in coarse pitch and ended up in trees at Warmwell. Johnstone suffered only mild concussion, but P7014 was beyond

Whirlwind P70043 was delivered to No. 263 Squadron as HE-A on 21 May 1942, but was lost on 7 November 1942 when she flew into high ground in France. Her pilot, twenty-seven-year-old Canadian Flying Officer Don Gill, was killed and is buried in a Cherbourg cemetery. (*Robert Bowater*)

repair. The squadron was strengthened in October by the arrival of five more pilots: Flt Sgt Don Tebbit returned to the unit after spending sixteen months with an Anti-aircraft Co-operation unit, PO Arthur Lee-White joined from 59 OTU and John Barclay, Don McPhail and Dattrateya Samant were posted in from 137 Squadron.

Don Gill and Stuart Lovell flew another unproductive search for shipping around the Channel Islands at low level on 12 October with four Typhoons of 266 Squadron providing rear cover. They found no ships, but the Whirlwinds again encountered fierce and accurate flak from Alderney.[253] There was little other operational flying during the rest of the month partly because of poor weather and of restrictions on attacks on surface vessels when the Royal Navy was operating in the Channel Islands area in connection with the numerous commando raids staged on the Channel Islands and the Cherbourg peninsula.

On 25 October, the squadron was delighted to receive a gift of £100 from the Fellowship of the Bellows in Argentina, the sponsors of many of its aircraft. In accordance with squadron traditions, some of the gift was promptly spent on a party.[254] Three days later, another of the squadron's Whirlwinds was wrecked when Flt Lt Cooksey of 1487 Flight, which provided target-towing facilities at Warmwell, forgot to lower the undercarriage of P7120 while

No. 263 Squadron Whirlwind P7120 HE-D was presentation aircraft *Bellows Argentina No. 6*. She flew with 263 Squadron between 26 February and 28 October 1942 when she was written off in a crash. The pilot, on his first flight in a Whirlwind, forgot to lower the undercarriage before landing. (*Robert Bowater*)

landing after an experience flight. On the last day of October, the squadron returned to operations over France. Harvey, Ridley, Brearley and Wright took off to attack railway targets in the Cherbourg peninsula, crossed the French coast at Cap de Carteret and followed the railway line towards La Haye-du-Puits. Harvey spotted and orbited a small goods train, but did not attack as it was in a station. Instead, all four pilots bombed the railway line nearby and reported several direct hits before heading for home. For once, no flak was encountered.[255]

Poor weather during the first week of November prevented any operational activity, but the squadron was occupied with a team of photographers from British Movietone News taking pictures for the South American market. 7 November dawned grey, but brightened by mid-morning and at 10:30, Gill, Abrams, Coyne and Cotton took off from Warmwell to attack railway targets on the main line between Valognes and Carentan. Crossing the French coast just south of St-Vaast, they soon ran into dense low cloud and heavy rain. They crossed the single-track railway between Vaudreville and Montebourg, and carried on towards the main line near Valognes which they probably crossed without seeing it in the murk. Coyne radioed to say that he and Cotton intended to return to the single-track railway seen earlier. They quickly found the line and a lone locomotive. Coyne fired a long burst of cannon fire at the locomotive, but his bombs overshot. Cotton bombed the line. The pair then returned uneventfully although, halfway back, their controller warned them that there were enemy aircraft nearby. Gill and Abrams also found a railway line that Abrams bombed as he crossed it. He then saw Gill's Whirlwind (P7043) turning underneath him and the indistinct explosions of Gill's bombs on or near the line. Abrams then lost contact with Gill who did not return, presumably having fallen victim to flak.[256]

Brearley and Yates returned to the same target area on 16 November. Crossing the coast at Quinéville, they found the Valognes-Carentan railway line and followed it south to the stretch between St-Côme-du-Mont and Carentan which was characterised by a high concentration of bridges where the line crossed numerous small rivers and canals. Both pilots bombed bridges from 100 feet. Yates saw Brearley's bombs overshoot the bridge and explode on the tracks, but was sure that his own bombs had hit the track, but less certain that they had hit the bridge. The pair continued south to Carentan before backtracking up the railway line where Brearley fired a short burst at a line of freight wagons. On the return journey and shortly after crossing the coast near Quinéville, Yates saw what he later identified as a ninety-ton schnellboot. He fired a two-second burst at it from 800 yards and closing but observed no results. The pair then returned to base.[257]

On 19-20 November, the squadron flew the first all-Whirlwind anti-shipping operations with four Whirlwinds providing the anti-flak screen for four Whirlwind bombers. The target was a pair of torpedo boats reported to be between le Havre and Cherbourg, but nothing was seen on either day. Three rhubarb operations were mounted on 26 November, but only Coyne and Samant found targets, the other pilots turning back at the French coast because of a complete absence of cloud cover. Lack of cloud cover also prevented Coyne and Samant from proceeding inland to their designated objective of railway targets north of la-Haye-du-Puits, so instead attacked coastal targets. Coyne fired at a pillbox and bombed the harbour at Diélette while Samant bombed camouflaged huts, thought to be a radio station, near Piereville.

On 1 December, the squadron flew a shipping reconnaissance as a part of an unusual formation comprising Brearley, Lovell, Tebbit and Barclay's Whirlwinds with four P-51 Mustangs of 400 Squadron for flak suppression and a close escort of four Spitfires of 118 Squadron led by the Middle Wallop wing leader Wg Cdr Tom Morgan. Morgan led the formation at sea level to Cap Lévi, turned west to follow the coast past Cherbourg as far as the Casquets rocks and then on to a point a few miles north of Jersey before turning for home. They found no shipping, but while returning observed a small group of Bf 109s about ten miles north of the Casquets. Morgan ordered the Mustangs to escort the Whirlwinds home while the Spitfires broke away and became involved in an inconclusive combat with the Messerschmitts.[258]

'Triumph and Tragedy' – Roadstead 45

On 7 December, a day of high winds and low cloud, eight Whirlwinds of 263 Squadron mounted Roadstead 45 to attack shipping in the Channel Islands. Twelve Spitfire VBs of 66 Squadron led by Sqn Ldr Harold Bird-Wilson provided anti-flak support with a further eight Spitfires of 118 Squadron as escort. The formation flew at sea level with the anti-flak aircraft leading in line abreast and dropping their long-range tanks before reaching the Channel Islands. They skirted a few miles to the west of Guernsey before turning towards Jersey where Bird-Wilson saw a large slow-moving convoy of barges and lighters just off St Brelade's Bay. The Whirlwinds followed the anti-flak aircraft closely and the first section of four aircraft split into pairs, left and right as arranged, to attack separate targets. Woodward and Williams bombed a cargo ship estimated at 800-1,000 tons, which had already been attacked by six of the anti-flak Spitfires. Woodward's bombs overshot by about 20 yards, but Williams' ones fell squarely on the stern. During the attack, Woodward's aircraft (P7105) was seen to come under fire and Wright then saw Woodward, with glycol smoke pouring from both engines and the propellers turning slowly, ditch in the water between the convoy and the shore.

Harvey and King attacked the smaller vessel immediately behind that bombed by Woodward and Williams. Harvey's bombs straddled the bows, but King did not release his. King's usual aircraft was one with the bomb release button on the throttle control, but on this occasion he was flying P7057 that had the bomb release button on the control column next to the gun camera switch that King pressed by mistake. The remaining four pilots (Lovell, Yates, McPhail and Wright) lined up to attack the third ship in the convoy, but Wright had to shear away to avoid the blast of Lovell's bombs and attacked a barge instead. One of Lovell's bombs was seen to explode by the stern of the third ship, but Yates' bombs failed to drop since he too was flying an unfamiliar aircraft with a very stiff bomb release button. McPhail (P6987) flew through a heavy flak burst on his run in to the target and was then seen to crash into the water at high speed. After the attack, the remaining Whirlwinds returned to Warmwell with each section of three aircraft escorted by a flight of 118 Squadron. All were short of fuel by the time they had landed.

McPhail was presumed to have been killed, but the squadron hoped that Woodward, who had appeared to have made a controlled ditching close to the shore, was a prisoner of war. Unfortunately, both were lost. On the German side, the MV *Kromwijk* (622 GRT) rolled over and sank, the *Derfflinger* (197 GRT) took a bomb hit forward and ran aground, but was later refloated, and

P6987 HE-L flew over 200 hours with No. 263 Squadron between 4 January 1941 and 7 December 1942 when she was shot down by flak while attacking a convoy off Jersey. Her pilot, twenty-three-year-old Canadian Pilot Officer Don McPhail, was killed. (*Robert Bowater*)

the convoy suffered four dead and nine injured.[259] Two days after Woodward's loss, Geoff Warnes took command of the squadron while Flt Lt Donald Ogilvie arrived to replace Warnes as B Flight commander.

On 14 December, the Whirlwinds stood in for 266 Squadron, which had been released for the day, flying standing patrols that were the RAF's only defence against the Luftwaffe's elusive, low-flying Jabos (Bf 109 and Fw 190 fighter-bombers). On one such patrol in the afternoon, Coyne and Cotton were repeatedly radioed vectors to intercept a pair of enemy aircraft, but despite flying to within sight of the French coast, the only aircraft they found was a Halifax. On their return to England, they met a pair of Fw 190s of 10/JG2 returning to Caen. The first that the Whirlwind pilots knew of this was when Cotton saw a stream of tracer passing behind his aircraft. Coyne and Cotton turned to meet the 190s attack, the 190s also turning and climbing so that the two pairs of aircraft were again approaching each other head-on, but with the 190s a little higher than the Whirlwinds. Cotton pulled up and fired a short burst at one of the Fw 190s, but thought his fire had passed behind it. He then made a second, long-range attack from the beam. Coyne made two attacks from astern after which the Whirlwind pilots saw one of the Fw 190s producing black smoke that appeared thicker and blacker than usual for German aircraft at high boost. Short of fuel, the Whirlwinds broke off combat, escaped into cloud and landed at Hurn. Although Coyne thought he had hit one of the Fw 190s, neither suffered any reported damage.[260]

The last two weeks of 1942 were marked by gale-force winds, pouring rain and dense fog. Almost no operational flying took place at Warmwell, but the enforced break did at least allow the squadron to celebrate Christmas in its usual style. On the second day of the New Year, the squadron detached four pilots and aircraft to Predannack to attack German minesweepers thought to be operating off Île Vierge, but because of poor weather the attack was delayed until the afternoon of 7 January. Brearley, Lee-White and Ridley took off with nine anti-flak Spitfire Vs of 130 Squadron and a further twelve of 234 Squadron as close escort, but found nothing except a floating mine.[261] Brearley, Ridley and Cotton repeated the operation on 10 January with 19 Squadron providing the anti-flak screen and 130 Squadron the close escort, but the only shipping found was a group of six fishing vessels a few miles off the French coast.[262] A few days later, the four pilots at Predannack were replaced by King, Yates, Williams and Stuart Lovell.

Back at Warmwell, which was waterlogged and largely unserviceable for operational flying, Warnes was asked to carry out trial drops with parachute containers. The standard parachute container was one of the few stores that had not been cleared by A&AEE when it tested the Whirlwind bombing installation, but 263 Squadron experienced no difficulty in loading them onto the bomb racks. The containers did not foul the flaps and with the containers loaded with sandbags Warnes found the handling of the aircraft to be much the same as with 250-lb bombs. Warnes reported that 'The containers were dropped from 500 feet, the parachute opening practically instantaneously, and there will be no difficulty in dropping these containers in a very small space.'[263]

On 15 January, two 313 Squadron Spitfires collided off the French coast while on escort duties. One spun into the sea, but the other struggled back to within fifteen miles of Portland where the pilot ditched. Shortly after midday, Blackshaw and Macaulay escorted a Defiant of 276 (ASR) Squadron to the scene. Blackshaw and the Defiant pilot saw the pilot in his dinghy, but as the Defiant turned sharply to orbit the spot its engine cut. The pilot managed to restart the engine, but by then he had lost sight of the dinghy. Blackshaw and Macaulay, weaving above the Defiant, also lost sight of the dinghy while trying to follow the Defiant's turns. No radio fixes could be given because of the poor radio reception for which the area was noted and further searches, including one by six more Whirlwinds, failed to relocate the dinghy or pilot.[264]

Whirlwind by Night

On 15 January 1943, 263 Squadron staged its first night operations. Blackshaw and Warnes carried out an entirely uneventful shipping reconnaissance around the Channel Islands returning to Warmwell shortly before midnight. Brearley flew alone deep into the Cherbourg peninsula on a gloomy night with the full moon largely obscured by cloud. Passing down the east coast of the peninsula, he met accurate flak from two ships off Pointe de Barfleur and circled to attack, but failed to locate them again. Crossing the coast at St-Vaast, he dropped a bomb on a train heading west between Carentan and la-Haye-du-Puits, and another bomb on the railway tracks nearby. Circling, Brearley saw that the train had stopped and was shrouded in smoke.[265]

On 18 January, the detachment at Predannack tried once more to locate the elusive German minesweepers. Stuart Lovell, King and Yates, accompanied by twelve Spitfires of 19 and 130 Squadrons, swept from Île de Batz to just north of Île d'Ouessant where a small group of Fw 190s was seen. 130 Squadron remained with the Whirlwinds while 19 Squadron engaged the German fighters. In the ensuing combat, the pilots of JG2 shot down one 19 Squadron aircraft and seriously damaged another.[266] The pilots at Predannack made a final attempt to find the minesweepers on 21 January, but were recalled shortly after take off. Two days later they returned to Warmwell to be reunited with the rest of the squadron.

February brought a marked increase in the tempo of 263 Squadron operations. The month also saw the first use of the Whirlwind as a dive bomber

Scramble! Two No. 263 Squadron Whirlwinds get airborne from RAF Fairwood Common in 1942. (*Robert Bowater*)

when, towards the end of the month, 263 Squadron attacked Maupertus airfield on three successive days. During the month, Warnes and Blackshaw were both awarded the Distinguished Flying Cross and Joe Holmes returned from 137 Squadron to take command of B Flight, replacing Donald Ogilvie who appears not to have flown operationally during his two months with the squadron.

The month opened with fine weather but Warmwell did not dry out enough to allow operational flying until 5 February. A rhubarb sortie set off to attack railway targets in the Cherbourg peninsula, but returned from the French coast because of a lack of cloud cover. Heavy rain that night then prevented any further flying until 7 February when practice flying recommenced. On 8 February, Warnes, Brearley and King demonstrated the parachute containers tested earlier by Warnes prompting praise for the accuracy of the drops although Brearley's containers failed to release. The following day, P6991 was wrecked when the port engine failed on take off. Macaulay kept the aircraft airborne for nearly two miles before force landing in a field. He was unhurt, but the Whirlwind was damaged beyond repair.

On 10 February, B Flight moved to Fairwood Common while A Flight at Warmwell was again busy working with the cameramen of British Movietone News. A Flight returned to the offensive on 12 February with a rhubarb sortie

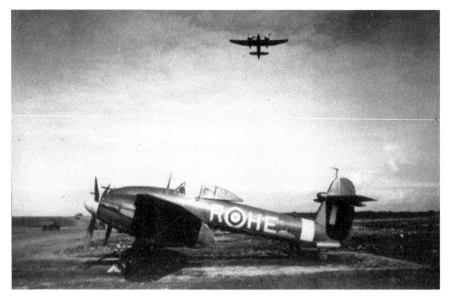

No. 263 Squadron Whirlwind P6991 HE-R seen on 20 March 1942 on the day the Whirlwind was officially taken off the 'Secret List'. The aircraft in the air is P7120 HE-D being flown by F/L Cliff Rudland. (*Robert Bowater*)

P7062 flew with both Whirlwind squadrons, but was lost in a crash on 19 February 1943 during an Army Co-operation exercise. As HE-L with No. 263 Squadron, she clipped a tree during a low-level pass and spun into the ground near Chiseldon, Wiltshire. Her pilot, thirty-year-old Australian Flight Sergeant Frank Hicks, was killed instantly. (*Robert Bowater*)

to the Cherbourg peninsula. Harvey and Williams took off from Warmwell at 08:30 and crossed the French coast at Cap de Carteret in perfect rhubarb weather with dense cloud at 600 feet and good visibility below. Following the railway towards la-Haye-du-Puits, they found two trains. Harvey fired a short burst at one, experiencing light flak as he did so. As he prepared to bomb the second, Williams radioed 'My port engine has been hit.' Harvey saw a sixty-foot-long stream of fuel pouring out of the port wing of Williams' aircraft. Harvey led Williams back up the railway line to cross the coast at Portbail where Harvey dropped his bombs on a railway siding. The pair flew out to sea on a direct course for home with Williams setting the speed, but when they were two miles off the coast at Surtainville, Harvey observed the propellers of Williams' struggling aircraft hit the sea. The Whirlwind (P7052) bounced, hit the water again and sank within a few seconds. Harvey circled and saw Williams in the water, waving and trying to inflate his dinghy. Harvey orbited several more times, but lost sight of Williams in the swell and left for home. An hour and a half later, Harvey took off again as the navigator of a 276 Squadron Walrus, but no trace of Williams was found and the sea conditions were by now too dangerous for the Walrus to land.[267]

Morning rhubarb operations on the 14-15 February were abandoned off the French coast due to the lack of cloud cover, but a night operation on the 15 February met with more success. Warnes and Blackshaw took off at 20:30 to search for shipping around the Channel Islands and, if no targets were found at sea, to attack railway objectives in occupied France. They failed to locate shipping and Blackshaw found no targets inland, but Warnes discovered a train at Carentan. The train was very close to civilian housing so Warnes bombed the line nearby instead.[268] The following night, the same pair of pilots operated over France twice. Warnes bombed a goods train south east of Carentan and Blackshaw attacked a railway bridge in the same area. They both went out again later, but it was then too dark for any targets of opportunity to be found.[269] The pilots had better luck on the morning of 18 February when Ridley and Cotton bombed the railway line south east of Portbail while King and Macaulay attacked the lock gates at Ouistreham, where Macaulay saw King's bombs explode on target.[270]

The following day another Whirlwind and pilot were lost during an Army Co-operation exercise near Wroughton when Hicks, carrying out dummy low-level attacks with Harvey, Macaulay and King, clipped a tree with a wing of P7062 during his third attack and was killed instantly when the aircraft spun in and crashed. On 20 February, while B Flight was still detached at Fairwood Common and the servicing echelon remained at Warmwell, A Flight moved to Harrowbeer.

Dive Bombers

Warnes had previously proposed that the squadron should practice dive bombing so that it could form the bombing element in circus operations. This new technique was put to the test in late February in a series of attacks on Maupertus airfield. The first attack was carried out on 26 February by Warnes, Ridley, King, Blackshaw, Cotton and Coyne with close escort provided by twelve Spitfire Vs of 312 Squadron and escort cover by a further twelve Spitfires of 129 Squadron. Twenty-four Spitfires of 504 and 616 Squadrons, all with long-range tanks and led by Sqn Ldr John 'Killy' Kilmartin, formed a freelance wing that would follow the others back over the French coast and then to patrol around Cherbourg to engage German fighters attempting to intercept the attack. All five squadrons operated from the small airfield at Ibsley. The Whirlwinds and their close escort climbed over the English Channel to 15,000 feet, but because of unexpectedly strong winds they crossed the French coast five miles west of Cherbourg rather than at the planned crossing point at Barfleur. This necessitated a wide orbit around Cherbourg to bring them to the target. Heavy flak from Cherbourg obliged the Whirlwind pilots to make a rapid descent to 11,000 feet and turned underneath the freelance wing, which continued south at 18-19,000 feet. The Whirlwinds bombed the airfield in forty-five-degree dives from south to north releasing their 250-lb bombs at 5-6,000 feet with one bomb fused to explode on impact and the other after a three-second delay. Four bomb bursts were seen on the airfield and another two miles south of the target. The escorting Spitfires stayed with the Whirlwinds during their dive down to sea level and then escorted them back to base. Kilmartin led the freelance wing to Valognes where it circled for a while before re-crossing the coast at St-Vaast, but no enemy aircraft were seen.[271]

The following day, pilots of A Flight attacked Maupertus again, but this time as a diversion to an 8th Air Force raid on the U-boat facilities at Brest. Warnes, Cotton, King, Blackshaw and Coyne, with 129 Squadron providing close escort and 504 and 616 Squadrons as a freelance wing, made landfall at Barfleur as planned. Over the target they peeled off at two-second intervals into eighty-degree dives from 15,000 to 5,000 feet accompanied by 129 Squadron. The freelance wing, again led by Kilmartin, crossed into France 3-4,000 feet above the Whirlwinds and then followed them out after they had bombed. Five miles out to sea they left the Whirlwinds and turned back to patrol off the coast. Kilmartin's controller informed him that enemy aircraft were approaching and the Spitfire pilots jettisoned their long-range tanks, but again no enemy aircraft were seen. The value of this operation as a diversion to the main attack on Brest was in any event diluted because the seventy-eight B-17s and B-24s taking part arrived at their rendezvous point late, had difficulty in forming up and eventually bombed Brest nearly one hour after the Whirlwinds' diversionary attack.[272]

On 28 February, both flights took part in the last of this series of attacks on Maupertus. B Flight returned to Warmwell from its temporary exile at Fairwood Common and, accompanied by Warnes, formed the first wave of the attack. Six aircraft of A Flight, operating from Ibsley, formed the second wave, due to bomb twenty minutes after the first. The first wave (Warnes, Holmes, Brearley, Abrams, Tebbit and Wright) took off, met their escort of thirty-four Spitfire Vs of the Czech Wing over the airfield and set course exactly on time at 15:00. They climbed out over the Channel and crossed the French coast at Barfleur at 15,000 feet with their close escort of 313 Squadron. The freelance wing of 310 and 312 Squadrons flew 3,000 feet above them and dropped their long-range tanks before crossing the coast. South of Maupertus, the Whirlwind pilots turned and began their dives. The technique was much the same as that used on the previous days: the aircraft were trimmed very nose-heavy using the elevator trimmer and put into an eighty-degree dive at 425-430 mph with the engines throttled right back. The aircraft was then lined up on the aiming point using the gunsight and immediately before bomb-release the nose was lifted slightly to correct for bomb trail. Bombs were seen to fall in the centre, south-west corner and north-west corner of the airfield and despite the steepness and speed of the bombing dive, 313 Squadron managed to stay with the Whirlwinds and reformed around them as they crossed out over the French coast west of Cap Lévi. Neither the Whirlwinds nor the close escort experienced any flak during their attack and, although told by their controller that enemy aircraft had been plotted nearby, none of the pilots of the freelance wing saw any sign of the enemy.

Blackshaw, Coyne, King, Cotton, Ridley and Simpson formed the second wave and were escorted by the Ibsley and Portreath Spitfire wings. Twelve Spitfires of 130 Squadron provided close escort and 602 and 616 Squadrons the freelance wing. In addition, 504 Squadron was positioned over Alderney at 25,000 feet to deal with aircraft attempting to interfere with the freelance wing on its way out of the target. The second wave followed the same route as the first and bombed in similar manner. 130 Squadron followed the Whirlwinds down with three Spitfires to starboard, four to port and four more in line abreast further behind. As the Whirlwinds and their escorts left the target area, two Fw 190s were seen closing in on the reforming Whirlwinds. One of the Focke-Wulfs got onto the tail of Cotton's aircraft, but was shot down into the sea by Jaco Andrieux of 130 Squadron.[273]

In contrast to the hectic pace set in February, the squadron did very little operational flying during the first two weeks of March 1943. B Flight at Fairwood Common carried out bombing practice and convoy patrols while A Flight at Harrrowbeer did no operational flying at all. The two flights were reunited at Warmwell on 14 March and that afternoon attacked the Maupertus airfield. The attack was carried in two waves of Whirlwinds twenty minutes apart. Holmes led Abrams, Stuart Lovell, Yates and Wright from Warmwell as the first wave with an escort of twelve Spitfires of 312 Squadron. The second wave (Harvey, Macaulay, Coyne, King, Cotton and Ridley) took off from Ibsley with a heavier escort of twenty-four Spitfires of 504 and 616 Squadrons led by Wing Commander Peter O'Brien while 130 Squadron acted as a freelance squadron with a further twelve Spitfires. Both waves crossed the French coast at Barfleur, bombed Maupertus from south to north in a dive from 15,000 down to 10,000 feet and saw explosions in the airfield area. While 504 Squadron escorted the Whirlwinds back, 130 and 616 stayed to patrol, but no enemy aircraft were seen.[274]

The following day, the squadron sent a detachment to Bolt Head to operate as the second wave of Ramrod 59, a two-stage attack on St-Brieuc airfield by twelve Venturas of 2 Group followed twenty-five minutes later by 263's Whirlwinds, but poor weather at Bolt Head caused the Whirlwind attack to be cancelled. The Whirlwinds stayed at Bolt Head for a few more days, but the weather remained too hazy for the operation to be attempted.[275] Thick sea haze also forced a formation of twelve Whirlwinds and their escort to turn back on the evening of 19 March from an operation to locate and attack a large convoy that had been reported south of Guernsey.[276]

On 20 March, 263 Squadron moved ten Whirlwinds to Predannack to operate from there during the full moon period. That evening, nine Whirlwinds carried out an attack against the 200-foot-high granite viaduct at Morlaix that was a choke point for rail traffic between Lannion and Guingamp to the east and St-Pol-de-Léon and Brest to the west. For this operation, the Whirlwinds carried two 500-lb bombs rather than the usual 250-lb weapons. Warnes was first off at midnight with the others following at five-minute intervals. Warnes crossed into France at 2,000 feet, but was immediately and persistently illuminated by searchlights. Meeting accurate light flak, he jettisoned his bombs and returned home at sea level. Blackshaw and Wright did not find the target and also jettisoned their bombs. Brearley, Simpson, Abrams, Harvey and King all found and bombed the target. Harvey saw a fire on the top of the viaduct immediately after Abrams had bombed, but no other results were seen.[277]

During the night of 21 March, the same nine pilots attacked the Morlaix viaduct, but again only five of them bombed the primary target. Hydraulic failure prevented King from retracting his aircraft's flaps so he jettisoned his bombs over the sea and returned to base. Blackshaw experienced problems with his port engine's constant speed unit that made it difficult to fly an accurate course. He bombed a railway bridge, but did not observe the results. Abrams' aircraft suffered from a faulty compass and crossed the French coast near Île Vierge thirty miles too far west. He flew east towards the target but, running short of fuel and still some way from target area, decided to bomb a bridge over the River Penzé south of St-Pol-de-Léon. Wright found the primary target but was held persistently by searchlights. Unable to complete a bombing run due to accurate flak, he jettisoned his bombs south of Morlaix. The five pilots who bombed the viaduct discovered that flak had been strengthened, or at least fully alerted, compared with the previous night. Despite this, most made dummy runs before bombing. Holmes saw one of his bombs hit the viaduct and Brearley observed one of his hit the top of the viaduct and the other explode at the base. The remaining three pilots were unable to see the results of their bombing.[278]

The following night, the same nine pilots were again operating over France, this time against the viaduct at le-Ponthou seven miles to the east of Morlaix. Wright returned early with technical problems and the others found thick ground haze over the target and only Warnes, Abrams and King found the viaduct. As on the previous nights, the Whirlwinds crossed the channel at five-minute intervals at sea level, climbing to cross the French coast at a variety of heights between 3-7,000 feet. Unable to find the target in the haze, Simpson and Blackshaw jettisoned their bombs in the sea, Brearley and Harvey bombed a cutting in the main railway line east of the viaduct, and Holmes bombed a single-track railway north of it. After twenty minutes of searching, Warnes found the target and after eight dummy runs bombed from 500 feet but could observe no results in the haze. Abrams also found and bombed the viaduct, but unfortunately his bombs did not explode. Last to bomb and guided by the moon glinting on the railway tracks, King made two dummy runs before bombing and two more runs over the target to look for damage, but could see none in the poor visibility. In marked contrast to the attacks on Morlaix, none of the pilots experienced any flak.[279]

First Class Rhubarb

The squadron returned to Warmwell and the next eventful operation was in daylight on 26 March when the squadron sent four pairs of aircraft to attack targets in occupied France. Wright and Tebbit were first to take off, tasked with attacking railway targets near la-Haye-du-Puits, but made landfall at Cap de Flamanville, which they mistook for Cap de Carteret ten miles further south. Searching too far north, they failed to locate railway targets and so bombed the main road to Cherbourg a few miles north of Barneville. Wright's bombs were seen to explode at the edge of the road, but Tebbit's were not observed. Coyne and Yates had more success in attacking their allotted target: the lock gates at Ouistreham. In perfect rhubarb weather with good visibility below dense cloud at 1,000 feet, they crossed the French coast west of Ouistreham at Langrune-sur-Mer where they saw a small goods train. The driver stopped the train and ran along the tracks before both Whirlwind pilots made cannon attacks. They then flew east to bomb the lock gates at Ouistreham. Coyne's bombs were seen to explode on target while Yates' were heard to explode but were not seen. Light and medium flak were experienced during the attack and Coyne's aircraft (P7108) was hit in the fuselage by a 40-mm shell that shattered the radio and oxygen bottle. The pair returned without further incident to Warmwell where Coyne's aircraft was patched up before being flown to Westland on 28 March for full repair.

Abrams and Lee-White were assigned the electrical sub-station at Saint-Lô as their primary target. They both bombed in a shallow dive from 300 down to 100 feet, firing short bursts of cannon fire before bombing. Lee-White saw Abrams' bombs explode on the target and his own among huts nearby. The last pair, Brearley and Simpson, intended to attack targets in the Carentan area, but found no cloud cover and returned to base. After the attack, the A Flight diarist wrote 'First class Rhubarb' and was duly celebrated in a Weymouth pub that evening.[280]

263 Squadron flew no further operations until 4 April, but the interim period was put to good use. A number of new pilots had joined the squadron

The business end of a Whirlwind. Flight Sergeant Bill Watkins of No. 262 Squadron in the cockpit at a Knighton Wood dispersal, RAF Warmwell, in the summer of 1943. The four 20-mm cannons could fire a weight of shells equivalent to 600 lbs per minute. Each gun magazine held just sixty rounds. (*Robert Bowater*)

at the end of February, but opportunities for practice flying had been limited by the squadron's operational commitments and the frequent detachments to other airfields. The pause in operations and the return of the aircraft from Predannack allowed training flying to restart and the new pilots – PO Paul Mercer and Sergeants Rob Beaumont, Norman Blacklock, Len Gray, Harold Proctor, John Purkis, John Thould, William Watkins and George Wood – carried out their first Whirlwind flights in the last days of March.

The return to operations in the early morning of 4 April opened the most operationally intensive month in the squadron's history thus far. It also provided a further illustration of the high price frequently paid by Fighter Command even during militarily unproductive operations. Six Whirlwinds took off from Warmwell at 07:40 to find and attack a group of E-boats reported to be at sea near Alderney. Of these there was no sign, but an escorting 129 Squadron Spitfire suffered an engine failure on the return flight and ditched in the sea. The pilot had died by the time he was recovered by a Walrus and the 504 Squadron Spitfires escorting the Walrus ran into Fw 190s of JG2. In the ensuing combat, 504 Squadron's commanding officer was shot down and killed and another Spitfire damaged.

On 6 April, 11 Group staged a two-part operation against the steelworks and power station at Caen-Mondeville for which 263 and 257 Squadrons and

A No. 263 Squadron Whirlwind sat in her Knighton Wood dispersal at RAF Warmwell in the summer of 1943. Out on the airfield are several Hawker Typhoons of No. 257 Squadron. (*Robert Bowater*)

the Ibsley Wing were borrowed from 10 Group. The first part of the operation was carried out successfully by seven Typhoon bombers of 181 Squadron escorted by 257 Squadron's Typhoons, although the pilots reported that cloud was beginning to form over the target area.

For the second part an hour later, eleven of 263 Squadron's Whirlwinds operating from Tangmere were escorted by 485 and 610 Squadrons of the Tangmere Wing with thirty-six Spitfires of the Ibsley Wing as freelance wing. Holmes led the Whirlwinds at 18:25 to rendezvous with their close escort over Selsey Bill, but on crossing the coast at Ouistreham at 12,000 feet, they found dense cloud 4,000 feet below and abandoned the operation.[281]

On 9 April, Holmes led six Whirlwinds from Harrowbeer, escorted by long-range Spitfires of 312 and 313 Squadrons to search for shipping reported by 313 Squadron off the north coast of Brittany. As on many previous occasions all that was found were rocks.[282] In preparation for an attack on shipping reported near Brest, the squadron detached six A Flight aircraft to Predannack on 11 April. They did not operate from there until 13 April and then against a rather different target. On 13 April, B Flight moved to Exeter and flew an uneventful shipping reconnaissance before joining their colleagues at Predannack to fly the next operation – Circus 22 to attack Brest-Guipavas airfield. Ten Whirlwinds took off at 17:30 on a bright blue evening and met their escort over Predannack. 65 and 602 Squadrons of the Portreath Wing provided close escort while 313 Squadron provided escort cover. All thirty-five Spitfires operated from Perranporth led by Wg Cdr Peter O'Brien. The formation set off at sea level with the close escort in three groups of eight, one group on each side and one behind the Whirlwinds with the escort cover behind and above. Lee-White had problems starting P7059, took off late and flew on to the target alone. Over the Channel, the main formation climbed rapidly to 14,000 feet crossing the French coast near Île Vierge. On reaching the target area, the Whirlwinds echeloned to port, peeled off into their bombing dives and released bombs between 6-7,000 feet from south east to north west. Several bomb bursts were seen in the dispersal areas of the airfield. The close escort dived with the Whirlwinds and the formation crossed the coast at 4,000 feet, dropping to sea level over the Channel. Several enemy aircraft were seen in the distance on the return journey, but none approached and there were no combats.[283]

After the operation, B Flight returned to Warmwell while the six aircraft from A Flight remained at Predannack with a small team of ground crew. That same night, six schnellboote of the 5th S-Boot Flottille attacked Convoy PW323 off Lizard Point, sinking one of the cargo ships and an escorting destroyer. At first light on 14 April, 263 Squadron flew two escorted operations to search for the schnellboote which were now believed to be returning towards Cherbourg. Harvey and Lee-White flew from Predannack while Warnes, Lovell and King took off from Warmwell ten minutes later. Neither formation found the boats, but south of Start Point, Harvey saw a Lancaster in the sea with its crew of seven in a dinghy. The flak-damaged 103 Squadron aircraft had ditched returning from a raid on La Spezia the previous night. The Whirlwinds and four of the escorting Spitfires of 65 Squadron orbited the spot while a further pair of Spitfires climbed to transmit radio fixes. A Walrus rescued three of the crew and the others were collected by boat, but the Lancaster eventually sank during an attempt to tow it ashore the following day.[284]

The final operation of the day was intended to be an attack by five Whirlwinds against shipping reported in the Aber Wrac'H and Aber Benoît. Harvey led Thyagarajan, Macaulay, Abrams and Simpson from Predannack at 15:30 to rendezvous with their escort of twelve long-range Spitfire Vs of 65 Squadron. 312 and 313 Squadrons were briefed to carry out a simultaneous diversionary sweep north of Morlaix. The Whirlwinds and their escort crossed the Channel at sea level and made landfall near what Harvey thought was the lighthouse at Île Vierge to the north east of the target area. Accordingly, he led the formation to starboard flying south west along the coast. However, the lighthouse was the Phare du Four of similar design and also situated on an offshore rock, but south west of the Aber Wrac'H. By turning to starboard, Harvey was leading the formation away from the target. By the time he realised his mistake, the formation was approaching Pointe de St-Mathieu and had spotted what Harvey identified as a dredger moving slowly eastwards. Harvey, Thyagarajan and Simpson bombed the ship in a beam attack from north to south while Abrams attacked with cannon. Harvey's bombs were not observed and Thyagarajan's landed just off the port bow while Simpson's were seen to explode amidships. The 474-ton crane-carrying buoy tender *Emile Allard* sank within minutes.

Macaulay then detached from the formation to attack a small steamship one mile away that he bombed with unobserved results. He was later seen escorted by a number of 65 Squadron's Spitfires and attempted to rejoin the formation. Shortly afterwards, the Spitfire pilots heard Macaulay report that he had engine problems and was going to force land in France. The formation continued on to just off Camaret-sur-Mer where three armed trawlers were spotted. Harvey made a cannon attack on one and Thyagarajan, Abrams and Simpson attacked another, which was also bombed by Abrams, the only Whirlwind still carrying bombs. All saw cannon strikes on their respective targets but Abrams' bombs were not observed. Strangely, one or more Junkers W 34s had stumbled inadvertently into the area. Harvey fired at one without result and another was claimed shot down by 65 Squadron. The Whirlwinds and Spitfires then withdrew at sea level between Île d'Ouessant and the mainland returning to Predannack. No more was heard of Macaulay, but he may have decided to try to get home in his stricken aircraft rather than force land in France as Lt Wilhelm Godt of 8/JG2 claimed a Whirlwind shot down near Île d'Ouessant at the time the Whirlwinds were withdrawing.[285]

The squadron carried out uneventful escorted shipping searches on 15-16 April while the ground crews worked hard to re-establish aircraft serviceability that had declined during the period of detachments and operations. By the evening of 16 April, fifteen of the squadron's eighteen Whirlwinds were serviceable and that night eight aircraft set off to attack the power station and steelworks at Mondeville on the eastern outskirts of Caen. It was a cloudless night with a bright moon, but also with a strong wind that caused many of the pilots to make landfall further west than planned and only three of the eight found the primary target. Simpson and Lee-White saw their bombs explode in the target area while King bombed from 100 feet but was unable to observe results. Of the pilots who found themselves off course, Harvey and Abrams bombed railway tracks, and Blackshaw bombed a trawler off Ouistreham. Warnes was troubled by an unserviceable compass and made landfall well off course at Cap de la Hague before searching unsuccessfully for ships or trains. Brearley took off in P6995 at 22:35, but was not heard from again and was presumably a victim of coastal or ship-borne flak. His body was washed ashore near Swanage a few weeks later.[286]

The following night – again cloudless and with a bright moon – 263 Squadron sent out nine aircraft to operate individually against railway and

Close formation. The closest aircraft, P6995, flew almost 300 hours between 18 March 1941 and 17 April 1943 when she failed to return from a sortie over France. Her No. 263 Squadron pilot, twenty-seven-year-old Canadian Flying Officer Eddie Brearley, was killed. (*Robert Bowater*)

shipping targets over an area encompassing almost all of German-occupied France that was within their range. Three did not return. Cotton took off first to look for E-boats around Guernsey and Sark. If found, he was then to summon the other pilots to join him in attacking them. Two miles north of Guernsey, ominous noises from one of his engines caused him to return to base. When his aircraft was inspected, the cause of the noise was found to be no more serious than a badly fixed cowling panel.

Abrams was briefed to look for shipping along the Normandy coast from Houlgate to Saint-Marcouf, hoping to find the armed trawler that had fired at Blackshaw off Ouistreham the previous night, but nothing was heard from him after he took off from Warmwell in P7099 at 22:45. Lee-White searched unsuccessfully for shipping and then bombed Fort Saint-Marcouf before returning to Exeter with his radio and IFF unserviceable. Coyne found no trains in his patrol area between Bayeux and Airel so bombed the railway tracks at Neuilly-la-Forêt observing a bomb explode on the track and the other beside it. Blackshaw intended to look for shipping as far as Granville and then followed the railway inland to hunt for rail targets, but Exactor control problems forced him to return to base. Harvey's target was the railway between Bayeux and Caen, but like Abrams, no more was heard of him after he took off in P7090 at 23:00. He was awarded the DFC two weeks later.

No. 263 Squadron Whirlwind P7099 at her Knighton Wood dispersal, RAF Warmwell, in 1943. She failed to return from a mission over France on 17 April 1943, presumably crashing into the English Channel. Her pilot, South African Flying Officer Basil Abrams, was never found. (*Robert Bowater*)

Simpson looked for trains around la-Haye-du-Puits but found none and after searching around Alderney for shipping, returned home with his bombs. King (P7117) was briefed to look for trains between Isigny and St-Lô. He was last heard on the radio at 23:45 and failed to return. Warnes was the last pilot to take off, intending to search for trains between Carentan and Valognes, but finding no trains, dropped his bombs on the track and saw their explosions on either side.[287] Early the following morning, ten of 616 Squadron's Spitfires searched along the Normandy coast but found no sign of the missing Whirlwind pilots. All three have no known grave. Despite the heavy losses of the previous night, 263 Squadron staged twelve shipping reconnaissance sorties on 18 April, but no shipping was found.

Coyne and Lee-White were luckier on the night of 19-20 April. Coyne saw a small group of ships eight miles north east of Guernsey heading towards Alderney. Coyne at first thought they were fishing boats and flew towards them at 100 feet to investigate. At closer range he identified a very small merchant vessel, two coasters, a tug and a number of motor barges. He attacked the small merchant vessel in a beam attack from mast height, but even though it was a cloudless and brightly moonlit night, was unable to observe results. He experienced no flak until he had passed over the ship and was up moon. Lee-White took off twenty minutes after Coyne to patrol to the east of the Cherbourg peninsula. After his attack, Cotton radioed Lee-White to inform him of the convoy before returning to Warmwell. Lee-White changed course to search for Coyne's convoy, but was unable to find it so continued with his intended patrol to the east of the peninsula. Off Saint-Marcouf, he found two armed trawlers heading south, one of which he bombed. Like Coyne, he experienced no flak until after bombing, but was also unable to observe specific results. Two-and-a-half hours after Coyne's attack, Warnes, Blackshaw, Simpson and Cotton took off but failed to find the convoy and assumed that it had reached the safety of harbour.[288]

High winds, heavy rain and low cloud prevented operational flying during much of late April; however, 27 April brought better weather and a successful shipping attack near Jersey. Warnes led Tebbit, Lee-White, Blackshaw, Simpson and Cotton off from Exeter at 16:35 to rendezvous at Anvil Point with twenty-two Spitfires of 616 and 504 Squadrons led by Wg Cdr Morgan. Five miles south of Jersey, they found a mixed convoy of ships steaming north in line astern: the motor barges *Nestor* and *Tonkin*, freighters *Maas* and *Mazagan*, and the motor schooner *Helma* escorted by minesweepers *M4611* and *M4613*. Morgan led the anti-flak Spitfires of 504 Squadron out of the sun directly into a beam attack closely followed by the Whirlwinds. All six Whirlwind pilots bombed successfully. Warnes, Blackshaw and Cotton singled out the larger of the two freighters, Tebbit one of the motor barges, Simpson a 'converted yacht' (almost certainly the *Helma*) and Lee-White the leading escort vessel. The escorting Spitfires then reformed around the Whirlwinds and landed safely at Warmwell, the only damage to any of the aircraft being to Lee-White's P7040, the tailplane of which had been damaged by flying debris during his attack. The *Helma* (187 GRT) sank almost immediately and *M4611* (previously the *Étienne Rimbert*) was severely damaged and, with dead and wounded aboard, towed into St Helier harbour where she promptly sank. The boat was later raised and put back into service. *M4613* was damaged by cannon fire and the SS *Maas* (941 GRT), attacked by Warnes, Blackshaw and Cotton, was so severely damaged that she never sailed again under her own power. She was later towed to Le Havre and put into dry dock to be sunk in a Lancaster raid in June 1944 before repairs could be completed.[289]

That night, a large German convoy consisting of the 5,000-ton freighter *Butterfly* with heavy escort was engaged in a confused action with British destroyers HMS *Albrighton* and HMS *Goathland*, and a group of motor torpedo boats off Sept-Îles. The *Butterfly* was heavily damaged and later sank as did the submarine chaser UJ1402, but HMS *Albrighton* was heavily damaged and two of the MTBs lost. As dawn broke on 28 April, the British naval forces disengaged and at 08:15, 263 Squadron moved six Whirlwinds to Exeter to operate against the remains of the convoy. Warnes, Blackshaw, Simpson and Cotton took off at 10:15. Twenty-four Spitfire Vs of the Exeter Wing led by Wg Cdr František Doležal provided the escort, 310 Squadron acting as anti-flak aircraft and 313 Squadron providing escort cover. North of Sept-Îles, Doležal spotted a convoy of eight ships and led the formation behind the convoy and turned to attack the rearmost ships from the starboard beam. The anti-flak Spitfires made their cannon attacks and the Whirlwinds then bombed three of the ships. All bombs were seen to hit their targets, but the only serious damage appears to have been to *Vorpostenboot V722* that made it to Brest with her many dead and wounded. Flak during the attack was intense and one of 310 Squadron's Spitfires was shot down into the sea and two others were damaged. Cotton again returned with another damaged Whirlwind, but landed safely despite an 18-inch shell hole in the starboard wing of P6981.[290] After this operation, the aircraft returned to Warmwell and staged a further shipping strike with six aircraft escorted by twenty-four Spitfires of the Ibsley Wing. They patrolled uneventfully north of Île-de-Bréhat, but found no trace of the shipping reported there.

On 29 April, Sgt Ken Ridley returned to the squadron after a five-week attachment to No. 1 Specialised Low Attack Instructors School. He arrived just in time to take part in another shipping strike the same day. For this hastily arranged operation, escort was provided by twenty-four Spitfire V and VIs of 129 and 616 Squadrons of the Ibsley Wing led by Wg Cdr Morgan. Warnes, Tebbit, Ridley, Blackshaw, Simpson and Cotton rendezvoused with the escorting Spitfires at The Needles and set course across the Channel at sea

No. 263 Squadron Whirlwinds
P6985 HE-J, P6987 HE-
L and P6969 HE-V on a
demonstration flight out of
RAF Exeter in January 1941.
(*Robert Bowater*)

level with the Whirlwinds in two vics of three, the anti-flak Spitfires of 129 Squadron in line abreast ahead and those of 616 in line abreast behind and slightly above. The formation swept from Pointe de Barfleur down the east coast of the Cotentin peninsula to Isigny (where the target shipping had been reported) and then turned along the coast following the shipping lane almost as far as Ouistreham. Near Luc-sur-Mer, a group of ships was seen. Morgan led the anti-flak aircraft in for an immediate attack and Warnes followed to bomb a small patrol vessel that was seen to explode. The pilots then recognised the other ships as fishing boats and called off further attacks.[291]

On 30 April, seven Whirlwinds flew to Predannack from where four performed an uneventful shipping reconnaissance to Île d'Ouessant escorted by the Spitfires of the Portreath Wing. Four Fw 190s were observed fifteen to twenty miles off Ouessant but did not engage.[292] By the end of April, the squadron was beginning to suffer from shortages of serviceable aircraft and operational pilots. Macaulay, Brearley, Harvey, King and Abrams had been lost on operations during the month, Stuart Lovell had been posted to 257 Squadron on 23 April and the operational workload of the squadron was now borne by just eight pilots: Warnes, Blackshaw, Lee-White, Cotton, Coyne, Simpson, Tebbit and the newly-returned Ridley. The shortage of aircraft, pace of operations, frequent detachments to forward airfields and the need to conserve airframe hours all conspired to limit training flying by the other, less experienced pilots. During intensive operations it was inevitable that aircraft would be lost or damaged, but there were now very few Whirlwinds available at MUs to replace them. Accordingly, 10 Group relaxed the squadron's readiness commitment, requiring only that it keep available for operations as many pilots and aircraft as it could.

On 2 May, Blackshaw led five Whirlwinds escorted by the Ibsley Wing to search for a tanker reported near the Channel Islands, but found nothing and concluded that the Casquets rocks had again been reported as a ship. The following day dawned bright, cold and windy, and in the early afternoon, Blackshaw led six Whirlwinds from Exeter to look for minesweepers reported in the Channel Islands area. 310 and 313 Squadrons led by Wg Cdr Doležal provided the escort. They swept from Guernsey to Sept-Îles and on to Île de Batz, but found no trace of the minesweepers. On the return journey, ten miles north of Île de Batz, the escorts were warned of enemy aircraft in the vicinity and dropped their long-range tanks. 310 Squadron became involved in a dogfight with six Fw 190s, losing one Spitfire and pilot with another fighter returning damaged with its pilot wounded. The Whirlwinds were not attacked and all returned undamaged.[293]

The squadron carried out unproductive shipping searches on 5, 6 and 11 May. On 7 May, John Thould wrecked P7057 when he stalled while landing at Warmwell in a strong crosswind. He was promptly sent on a refresher course. On 14 May, 263 was briefed to bomb a cargo ship, believed to be the *Sonderburg*, in the Bassin Napoléon III in Cherbourg Harbour. Warnes selected a dive bombing attack from 12,000 down to 5,000 feet. Warnes, Mercer, Holmes, Simpson, Blackshaw, Ridley, Coyne and Lee-White took off at 21:00 and met up over Warmwell with their escorts of the Ibsley Wing. With 504 Squadron as close escort, 129 Squadron as escort cover and 610 Squadron as top cover, they flew at sea level before making a fast climb to 12,000 feet and crossed the French coast at Querqueville. Warnes formed the Whirlwinds into echelon starboard and then led them in a turn to port to bomb out of a conveniently placed cloudbank and a glaring, yellow sunset. The Whirlwinds peeled off successively into seventy/eighty-degree dives at 400 mph, released their bombs at 5,000 feet and dived down to sea level where the Ibsley Wing reformed to escort them to Warmwell.[294]

The following day, the squadron prepared for another shipping attack that evening, which was cancelled. Instead, many of the pilots met Lord Trenchard, founding father of the RAF, who was visiting the station. That night, Lee-White and Coyne took off to search for shipping around the Cherbourg peninsula and the Channel Islands respectively. Lee-White patrolled as far as Isigny and when passing Pointe de Barfleur at 1,000 feet on the return journey, saw a convoy of eight or nine ships steaming east. Lee-White identified the ships as a minesweeper, three or four E-boats, a 2,500-ton cargo vessel and three other freighters. He dived to sea level and kept his distance from the convoy, working around to the north of the ships in order to attack from up moon. He bombed the cargo ship at the rear of the convoy from mast height. As he pulled up, he heard a large explosion and saw a burst of flame in the centre of the ship that then subsided. Patrolling west of Jersey, Coyne spotted two vessels five miles offshore. At first he thought they were fishing vessels and by the time he recognised them as E-boats, it was too late to turn in to bomb them. He circled the area and saw the ships briefly on two further occasions, but was unable to get into position to attack before lack of fuel obliged him to return home. As soon as Lee-White had landed and reported the convoy's position, Warnes, Blackshaw, Holmes and Simpson were briefed to attack it. They took off at intervals, but neither Warnes nor Simpson found any trace. Holmes reached the end of his patrol line at Île St-Marcouf, turned for home and, as he approached Pointe de Barfleur, saw flak firing ahead of him. He flew on to investigate and just off Pointe de Barfleur saw a cargo ship estimated at 1,000 tons. He aimed his bombs at the ship in a quarter attack off the starboard bow, but was unable to observe results. Blackshaw took off immediately after Warnes and was heard on the radio at 02:00. He was next seen circling Exeter, Harrowbeer and then Exeter again with his navigation lights off. P7094 finally crashed a few miles away from Exeter presumably out of fuel after a flight of two hours and twelve minutes. Blackshaw's body and partly opened parachute were found 500 yards away from the wreckage of his

A No. 263 Squadron Whirlwind parked in a fighter pen at RAF Harrowbeer in 1943. (*Robert Bowater*)

aircraft.[295] Four days later, Jim Coyne was promoted to flight lieutenant and replaced Blackshaw as A Flight commander.

In the morning of 16 April, the squadron performed two operations in search of a merchant ship. The first was recalled due to communication problems at Middle Wallop. Warnes, Simpson, Coyne and Lee-White carried out the second operation with an escort of twelve Spitfires of 504 Squadron. The shipping target was not located but seven miles west of Casquets, Coyne saw two Fw 190s approaching the formation from ahead and slightly to port. The Whirlwinds flew in loose line abreast with the Spitfires in line astern on either side. The two Focke-Wulfs turned in to fire at the Spitfires on the left of the Whirlwinds and then broke away over and in front of the Whirlwinds allowing Coyne and Lee-White to fire at them. Lee-White fired a two-second burst from 600 yards with considerable deflection and saw cannon strikes in the sea on either side of the Fw 190 and a bright flash in the fuselage. Coyne fired a short burst at the second Fw 190 from 400 yards and observed shell splashes in the sea around it. 504 Squadron detached a section of aircraft to pursue the Fw 190s but made no further contact. The Whirlwinds that were still armed with bombs returned to base with 504 Squadron. Coyne and Lee-White believed they had damaged the Fw 190s, but neither of the aircraft from NAGr 13 were hit.[296]

The next eventful operation was against shipping reported between Cap de la Hague to Cherbourg on the night of 21-22 May. Having briefed Holmes, Cotton, Coyne and Lee-White to follow when their aircraft were ready, Warnes took off at 00:25. He found the ships off Nacqueville and reported that they consisted of a single cargo ship of around 3-4,000 tons escorted by four armed trawlers in a compact formation. Warnes then orbited the convoy and radioed its position before bombing the cargo ship from the port beam up moon. Warnes then patrolled a few miles north of the convoy, broadcasting directions and encouragement to the following pilots, together with a running commentary relayed to the squadron intelligence office by the Middle Wallop Operations Room. Holmes then arrived on the scene and bombed the cargo ship from 300 feet. During his attack, his Whirlwind (P7040) suffered minor damage from the intense light flak. During Holmes' attack, Warnes saw explosions on or near the ship followed by a column of smoke. Cotton also bombed the cargo ship after firing a short burst with his cannons. The German defences were now fully alert and Warnes was unable to witness Cotton's attack because of the spectacular flak and glare of the searchlights at Cherbourg and Querqueville. He did, however, see a brief burst of flame from the cargo ship. Cotton weaved away from the target towards the French coast, but a single 20-mm shell in the rear fuselage of his aircraft wrecked the hydraulic system and air speed indicator, and partially jammed the rudder controls. Despite this, Cotton landed P7108 safely at Warmwell on his fourth attempt. By the time Coyne arrived, the cargo ship appeared to be sinking so he bombed one of the leading escort ships. Warnes saw a brief, flickering flame after Coyne's attack and short of fuel turned for home. Lee-White was the last to arrive. The starboard engine and cooling system of his aircraft were damaged by a 20-mm shell when he was 400 yards from the convoy, but he went on to bomb one of the escorting trawlers from mast height in a port beam, up moon attack. He turned over the French coast, coaxed his damaged aircraft up to 1,500 feet and radioed his intention to parachute. He then found that the slipstream had subdued the flames and decided to try to get home. Lee-White struggled slowly over the Channel with the starboard engine ticking over until he reached Warmwell where he appeared 'like Jehovah to the Israelites as a beacon of flickering fire'. As he landed, the flames erupted again and Lee-White jumped out of the burning aircraft while it was moving. The fire crew extinguished the flames before they reached the fuel tanks, but P7059 was beyond repair.[297]

On 23 May, 129 Squadron reported a shipping convoy near Guernsey and, despite the shortage of aircraft, 263 Squadron staged another successful attack. At 07:45, Holmes led Ridley, Coyne and Cotton on Roadstead 70 to attack the convoy. Over Warmwell, they met up with eight Spitfire VIs of 616 Squadron as anti-flak aircraft and ten Spitfire Vs of 129 Squadron as close escort. With the anti-flak aircraft flying ahead and escorts on either side, the Whirlwinds headed out toward the Channel Islands at low level. Running through the Little Russel Strait between Guernsey and Herm where, as Coyne put it, 'The sea seemed to boil with flak', they found a convoy of seven ships just outside St Peter Port. These were the coasters *Oost Vlaanderen*, *Meteoor* and *Corona*, the steamship *Irene* and three escorting minesweepers of the 46th MS Flottille which had sailed from Jersey under cover of darkness and were now waiting to enter the harbour. With the ships perfectly arranged for an attack from the starboard beam, the anti-flak Spitfires attacked the four leading ships with the Whirlwinds following close behind. Holmes' bombs exploded amidships in a coaster, but Cotton found himself too close to Holmes, so veered away and attacked the next ship, but his bombs fell astern of it. Coyne and Ridley then attacked the same ship. The formation then reformed and returned to base. For the second time in three days, a 20-mm shell found Cotton's aircraft (P7089) and one of his starboard tanks lost a lot of fuel before it sealed itself. Holmes' bombing had been effective and the MV *Oost Vlaanderen* (421 GRT), carrying guns and cement for fortifications on the Channel Islands, sank almost immediately. The ship remains a popular diving site to this day, a gaping hole on the waterline forward of her No. 1 hold a mute testament to the accuracy of Holmes' aim. The *Corona* was also severely damaged and the *Meteoor* less so.[298]

By late May, the squadron had just five or six serviceable Whirlwinds available, but was surprised to learn on 28 May that it would be re-equipped with Vultee Vengeance IV aircraft rather than the Typhoons it had been expecting. The following day, the instruction was rescinded: 137 Squadron would instead re-equip and pass its Whirlwinds to 263. Warmwell was unusually crowded on 29 May with thirty-six Spitfires of the Hornchurch Wing preparing to operate as withdrawal cover for an 8th Air Force raid on Rennes. Despite the congestion at the airfield, 263 Squadron sent six aircraft to attack fifteen ships reported off Barfleur, but found only fishing vessels. Later in the day, pairs of Whirlwinds patrolled over Warmwell while the Hornchurch Spitfires refuelled after their operation. Poor weather restricted operational flying during early June, but on 6 June, Holmes led five Whirlwinds with Spitfire escort to dive bomb shipping in Cherbourg docks, but dense cloud over France forced them to return.

'Another like Bader'

Early June brought further high honours for the squadron. No fewer than four pilots – Cotton, Coyne, Holmes and Lee-White – were awarded the DFC and Warnes the Distinguished Service Order, the only such award won solely for Whirlwind operations. Gp Capt. Stephen Hardy, the Middle Wallop Sector Commander, enthusiastically endorsed Warnes' DSO recommendation: 'Warnes is another like Bader. He has made his squadron into as fine a unit as any in the Command.' Lee-White, who had flown for Faucett Airlines in Peru before joining the RAF, also travelled to London to audition for a BBC radio broadcast in Spanish intended for a South American audience.

With improved weather, a shipping reconnaissance was ordered for first light on 15 June. Lee-White, Wood, Cotton and Ridley took off from Warmwell at 05:43 towards the Channel Islands with eight anti-flak Spitfires of 616 Squadron ahead and four escorting Spitfires of 504 Squadron on each side. Thirty minutes later, they observed five ships heading north east a few miles off Sark: boats of the 24th Minensuchflottille carrying out a routine minesweeping sortie. The Whirlwinds and anti-flak Spitfires climbed to 400 feet before diving down to attack from the port beam. At the same time, the ships' gunners opened fire, putting up an intense barrage that claimed one of 616 Squadron's aircraft. The Whirlwinds followed close behind, Cotton and Ridley attacking the first ship on the port beam of the convoy (M483) and Lee-White and Wood attacking the second, about 150 yards astern (M452). Lee-White and Wood thought their bombing had been accurate, but saw no explosions as their bombs were fused for an eleven-second delay on this occasion. Ridley saw the splashes of Cotton's bombs amidships of the first ship and thought that his own bombing had also been accurate. As Cotton passed over the target, his aircraft (P7000) was hit hard by M452's 20-mm gunners, crashed into the sea and disintegrated, offering little hope that Cotton survived. The Whirlwinds and escort then reformed and returned to base, claiming to have damaged two M-Class minesweepers. In fact, *M483* had received a direct bomb hit in her engine room and sank twenty minutes later. The German flotilla recorded its casualties as two dead, two missing and twenty-four injured.[299] Warnes, Holmes, Lee-White and Ridley were now due to be rested from operational flying. Warnes was posted out to a non-flying role with 10 Group, Holmes became an instructor and Lee-White and Ridley were posted to the Air Fighting Development Unit at Wittering.

John McClure, DFC, arrived from 137 Squadron to replace Holmes as B Flight commander and Flt Lt Ernest 'Reg' Baker, DFC, arrived to replace Warnes as the squadron's commanding officer. For a fighter pilot, Baker's RAF career had been an unusual one. He had flown Sunderland and Catalina flying boats with 210 Squadron and was awarded the DFC in November 1940 after a series of determined attacks on U-boats. After a period on ground duties in Malta, he returned to the UK, transferred to fighters and, at the time of his posting to 263 Squadron, was a flight commander with 182 Squadron flying Typhoon fighter-bombers.

On 16 June, the squadron was released from operations and moved to Zeals with its ten remaining airworthy Whirlwinds for a period of training. A large number of new pilots were posted during late June/early July to replace those lost in the previous few months. Among the new arrivals were Sgts Peter Cooper, Iain Dunlop, Fred Green, William Handley, William Heaton, Richard Hughes, Len Knott, Graham Smith, Denis Todd and George Williams, POs Ken Funnell, Robert Hunter and Douglas Sturgeon, and FOs Eric Holman, Douglas Mogg and Robert Tuff. Two further accidents in late June aggravated the shortage of Whirlwinds. On 20 June, Hughes retracted the undercarriage instead of flaps when landing after his first Whirlwind flight and Watkins hit a tree the following day during an Army Co-operation exercise, but managed to land safely.

CHAPTER 13

137 Squadron – Manston Months

In contrast to the hectic early pace set by 263 Squadron with its Whirlibombers, 137 Squadron spent its first weeks as a fighter-bomber squadron quietly at Manston. Flying was restricted to training flights until mid-October when the squadron resumed shipping reconnaissance sorties. Often abandoned due to poor weather, none of the sorties that were completed found any shipping. Samant, McPhail and Barclay were posted to 263 Squadron, although Barclay would later return, and two new pilots, Sergeants Edmund Bolster and George Walker, arrived from OTU. The first hint of excitement came on a morning shipping search on 25 October. Holmes and O'Neill found no ships, but a few miles off the coast at Dungeness saw four Fw 190s about a mile ahead. The Whirlwind pilots pursued, but could not catch or prevent them from bombing the village of Littlestone-on-Sea. Three days later, Bryan and Brunet had a similarly inconclusive encounter scrambling at 15:45 to intercept enemy aircraft approaching Ramsgate. They saw a Ju 88 off the coast and closed to 800 yards, but the enemy disappeared into dense cloud and was not seen again. That evening, Trafford Leigh-Mallory visited the squadron. He told the pilots they would be used on offensive operations over occupied territory rather than the routine shipping and defensive patrols that had occupied them previously. The first of these operations took place on 31 October. It did not go well and only one of the four Whirlwinds involved returned.

Van Schaick and Waldron were briefed to attack a military camp at Étaples while Furber and Jowitt were briefed to attack a similar target a few miles to the north at Camiers. The four aircraft took off at 11:00, crossed the Channel at sea level and separated into pairs at the French coast. Jowitt and Furber could not locate their target, but met with intense flak. Furber's aircraft (P7102) was hit twice and he saw Jowitt's Whirlwind (P7115) also hit with glycol smoke pouring from the starboard engine. As they crossed out over the French coast, Jowitt asked Furber to transmit a mayday call as he intended to bail out over the sea. Jowitt was last seen climbing to 900 feet before Furber lost sight of him in cloud. He was not found.

Van Schaick and Waldron found their target, a camp of around seventy huts believed to have been originally built by the British Expeditionary Force in 1940 and now used by the personnel of nearby coastal batteries. They also met intense flak. Van Schaick bombed the target camp and saw Waldron following to bomb behind him. Waldron fell victim to the flak and force landed north of Le Touquet where he was captured, uninjured, by the Germans. The port engine of van Schaick's aircraft (P7064) was damaged by flak before he had bombed. As he left the target area he exhausted his ammunition at a stationary goods train, but was then hit again, this time disabling his elevators. Van Schaick flew through overhead telephone wires before crossing out to sea at which point his aircraft was hit for a third time, causing the starboard engine to fail. The Whirlwind lost height and hit the water. Fortunately, a Spitfire pilot of 91 Squadron spotted him in his dinghy and a 277 Squadron Walrus left Hawkinge with an escort of four 91 Squadron Spitfires to rescue him. The Walrus pilot found van Schaick in a minefield and made a crosswind landing between the rows of mines. After overshooting slightly, the pilot then had to turn back and carefully navigate between the mines to reach van Schaick. The Walrus' gunner threw a rope to van Schaick and pulled him into the aircraft. The Walrus successfully took off from the minefield and returned to Hawkinge.

Posed shot for the press at RAF Manston on 5 March 1943. Left to right: Sgt Albert Witham; P/O James Rebbetoy RCAF; F/O Eddie Musgrave DFC RAAF; F/S John Barclay; W/O Art Brunet RCAF; P/O Des Roberts RNZAF; F/L John Bryan; Sgt Aubrey Smith; F/O John McClure RCAF; F/O John Hadow; Sgt Tom Sutherland; F/O Robert Smith DFM; P/O Norbury Dugdale; Sgt Edmund Bolster; P/O Hilt Ashton RCAF; and Sgt Robert Woodhouse. The Bullmastiff was named Lynn and belonged to F/L John Bryan. (*Niall Corduroy*)

After five hours in the water, van Schaick was found to be suffering slightly from exposure, but was otherwise unhurt.[300]

Later that day and in poor weather, 137 Squadron scrambled six Whirlwinds in response to the largest Jabo raid yet staged: an attack on Canterbury by around thirty Fw 190 fighter-bombers with escort. Only McClure and Brunet, one of whose aircraft was already bombed up, requiring the pilot to jettison his bombs in the sea off Margate before he could join the fray, made contact. The two Whirlwind pilots chased a Fw 190 at low level across the airfield and out to sea, firing at it from 600 yards range, but the Focke-Wulf easily outpaced them.

Poor weather during the next week prevented operational flying and the squadron flew its next offensive sorties on the afternoon of 7 November when McClure and Freeman operated from Ford airfield to attack a military camp at Bolbec. They crossed the French coast at Cap d'Antifer, located the main railway line to Le Havre and followed it east towards Yvetot, but became separated in the dense low cloud. McClure bombed a railway bridge at Mirville from twenty feet before flying on to Bolbec where he fired a four-second burst of cannon fire at two large huts in the camp, one of which burst into flames. Unable to contact Freeman via radio, he then returned directly to Manston. Freeman could not find the camp at Bolbec, but did pick up the railway line to the east of Mirville, followed it toward Yvetot and bombed a road bridge over the line before returning to Ford.[301]

With one exception, the remainder of November was characterised by shipping searches that found no shipping and rhubarbs abandoned because of inadequate cloud cover. The exception was on the night of 21 November when Mercer and de Houx set off just before midnight. Mercer patrolled the railway from Lille to Lens and on to St-Omer, but found no targets. He caught a glimpse of the navigation lights of an aircraft slightly above him and apparently approaching St-Omer-Longuenesse airfield, but the aircraft switched its lights off and he lost sight of it. He continued out towards Calais and bombed an electrical installation near Holque. De Houx also failed to find trains and bombed a railway yard near Bourbourg.[302]

In early December, Alec Torrance was promoted to flight lieutenant and became B Flight commander to replace van Schaick who was posted to an OTU. On 10 December, four Whirlwinds took off from Manston at 11:00 to attack a petrol train that intelligence sources expected to arrive at Doullens from Amiens an hour later. The aircraft became separated in low cloud off the English coast and carried on independently, but found cloud down to the hilltops in the target area. They abandoned the operation and searched for alternative targets near the coast. Coghlan bombed an unidentified, camouflaged aircraft at Crécy-en-Ponthieu airfield and strafed flak posts. De Houx followed Coghlan and shortly before crossing out over the French

coast at Baie de l'Authie, was subjected to intense light flak from a group
of buildings which he then bombed. The pair then climbed into cloud and
returned, neither having observed the results of their bombing. The other
pair, Ashton and Robert Smith, bombed railway targets at Auxi-le-Château
before returning home. A later attempt by Bryan and Roberts to attack the
Brugge-Gent canal was aborted when they found insufficient cloud cover at
the Belgian coast.[303]

In the early morning of 15 November, Brunet and Sutherland patrolled
uneventfully from Cap Gris Nez to Cayeux, but in the afternoon, Robert
Smith had a rather more exciting time. Smith took off at 15:50 to flight-test
P7976 to ensure it was serviceable should it be needed for operations that
night. Also airborne were two of 609 Squadron's Typhoons flown by Flt Sgt
Alan Haddon and FO Henry Amor on a routine offshore standing patrol.
Shortly after taking off, Smith saw twinkling lights over Pegwell Bay to the
south of Ramsgate Harbour. He initially thought these were snowflakes, but
it was a flare dropped by an 841 Squadron Albacore on a test flight. Smith
flew towards Pegwell Bay just below the cloud base at 1,000 feet, but saw
nothing unusual and descended to sea level where he felt it would be easier
to see an aircraft at low level. As he descended, he saw four aircraft in a wide
echelon about five miles away and approaching Ramsgate from the south east.
Smith wisely climbed into the clouds. When he emerged, the four aircraft, now
identifiable as Fw 190s, were only about one mile away. Smith made a steep
diving turn onto the tail of one of the 190s, but as he did so the Ramsgate
anti-aircraft guns opened fire. Smith heard strikes in his port wing and a few
seconds later smelled petrol and saw a streak of vapour streaming back from
his port engine nacelle. Nonetheless, he continued on to fire a one-second burst
from 500 yards range at the rearmost Fw 190. He finished his ammunition in
five further short bursts and was certain he had damaged the Fw 190, but
the remaining enemy fighters had now turned and in an attack from the port
beam wrecked the elevator controls of Smith's Whirlwind (P6976).

By this point, the air raid warning had been sounded. Haddon and Amor
were directed towards the enemy aircraft and another 609 Squadron pilot,
PO Peter Raw, also took off to intercept. Smith was now short of fuel in his
damaged port fuel tanks and decided to head inland, but was chased by two
Fw 190s. 609 Squadron's commanding officer, Sqn Ldr Roland Beamont,
saw the Whirlwind and its pursuers and took off in his Typhoon without a
parachute or strapping in. However, by the time he reached the area, the anti-
aircraft defences had opened fire again and the Fw 190s had turned away
out to sea. Using a combination of flaps and elevator trim, Smith landed at
Manston with his aircraft's fuel tanks almost empty. 609 Squadron engaged
the Fw 190s and lost PO Amor who bailed out of his burning Typhoon too
low and was killed.[304]

No. 137 Squadron Whirlwind P6976 SF-X, the mount of Pilot Officer Robert Smith. He received the DFC on 12 February 1943 for his heroic work on Whirlwinds. P6976 was eventually struck off charge and scrapped in November 1943. (*Robert Bowater*)

The Fw 190s of 10/JG26 were again active over England on 19 November, and while on a practice flight, Bryan and Rebbetoy ran into a pair of them. The Whirlwind pilots were flying over Pegwell Bay at 1,500 feet when they saw two Fw 190s to port at sea level over Goodwin Sands. They turned in and made head-on attacks, but saw no results. Bryan fired once and Rebbetoy twice in the subsequent dogfight and both thought that they saw cannon strikes on their opponents. The combat closed with the Fw 190s flying for home, one with copious black smoke pouring from it. Suspecting a trap, the Whirlwind pilots returned to base claiming a Fw 190 as 'probably destroyed'. The only Luftwaffe loss from this operation was a Fw 190 that almost certainly fell to anti-aircraft guns.[305]

Intruders

On the night of 20 December, 11 Group sent seventeen intruder sorties out over occupied Europe: nine Bostons, a 3 Squadron Hurricane, three 609 Squadron Typhoons and four Whirlwinds of 137, the last eight of these all operating from Manston. Sqn Ldr Beamont had long tried to persuade 11 Group to allow 609 Squadron to fly night intruder operations over France and carried out trial sorties that had shown that the Typhoon could be flown and navigated at night, and was perfectly suitable for making low-level ground attacks in the dark. 11 Group had agreed that the squadron could use a small number of aircraft on these operations. If it stopped a train with a cannon attack, it would then report its position to 137 Squadron that would despatch a Whirlwind to complete the train's destruction with bombs.[306] Accordingly on the night of 20 December when Beamont returned from Lumbres (just to the west of St-Omer) having stopped a train in the course of three attacks, Wray took off at 20:30 to finish the job, but turned back with engine problems off the French coast. 137 Squadron flew three other intruders that night. Rebbetoy was briefed to attack an ammunition dump near Torhout while de Houx and Mercer were tasked with attacking a similar target at Houthulst. Rebbetoy failed to find his target and so dropped his first bomb on a freight train north of Roeselare. The bomb exploded alongside the train and blew it onto its side, but his second bomb failed to release during a subsequent attack as Rebbetoy failed to find the right switch. De Houx found the dump at Houthulst easily and dropped a bomb on one of thirty large huts. After a long search, Mercer located the target and dropped his bombs from 200 feet on railway lines in the south-east corner. Both pilots saw their bombs explode but observed no other specific results. They then crossed into France and searched unsuccessfully for trains. De Houx flew on and found an airfield just south west of Douai, believed to be the landing ground at La Brayelle, where he saw four parked He 111s. For some reason he did not bomb the Heinkels and continued on to attack two canal barges, but, like Rebbetoy, 'finger trouble' prevented his second bomb from releasing. Mercer set course for home, but near Oostende observed three armed trawlers travelling south three or four miles offshore. Mercer climbed to transmit a request for a 'fix' on the position and at 01:10 on 21 December, Brunet took off to attack the ships. Brunet searched from Oostende to Mardyck and back, but found no trace of them. Instead, he bombed a small trawler at Zeebrugge. Musgrave also took off to attack the ships seen by Mercer, but was recalled when Brunet reported that there was no sign of them.

The squadron only flew two more operational sorties during 21 December. Shortly before midday, McClure and Woodhouse set off on yet another attempt to attack the supply dump at Auchy-lès-Hesdin. Descending through cloud at 2,000 feet, they found themselves south of the target over the Forêt de Crécy and diving towards the target area. Here they saw a freight train heading towards Crécy-en-Ponthieu. They flew on to look for their target, but, unable to locate it, turned back to attack the train seen earlier. They made almost simultaneous attacks from fifty feet, McClure making a three-quarter attack from the rear of the train while Woodhouse attacked from the other side, his Whirlwind being thrown upwards by the blast from McClure's bombs. Both pilots saw the train toppled over, but became separated while evading intense light flak from the airfield. Woodhouse set course for home while McClure searched for the original target. On finding the supply dump, McClure fired nearly all his ammunition before returning home.[307]

On the morning of 22 December, Musgrave and Sutherland took off in search of trains on the line between Abbeville and Eu. They broke through the cloud east of Eu and followed the line towards Abbeville until they found and bombed a stationary freight train at a small station. They saw three of their bombs explode on the wagons and the fourth on the track, but Sutherland's aircraft (P6998) was hit in the fuselage, tailplane and starboard engine by flak. While Musgrave made two cannon attacks on the train, Sutherland climbed for cloud cover and set course for home. The starboard engine of Sutherland's aircraft seized over the Channel and he overshot when landing at Lympne, doing further damage to the aircraft although he was unhurt. P6998 was dismantled and returned to Westland, but found to be unrepairable.[308]

That night, 137 Squadron sent five aircraft out on sorties over France and Belgium. Coghlan found thick ground mist and returned to base. Wray attacked a train in the St-Pol area, but was unable to observe the results of his bombing. Meanwhile, Beamont of 609 Squadron found a passenger train travelling fast near Rue which, after multiple cannon attacks, stopped on a bridge. Bryan was sent to bomb the stationary train, but was recalled ten minutes later due to deteriorating weather. This did not stop Beamont from attacking the train again. Bryan, followed two hours later by Musgrave, set out to attack a railway yard south east of Gent. After five dummy runs, Bryan dropped his bombs on a large shed with a number of locomotives next to it. He saw his bombs explode but was subjected to intense light flak and saw no specific results. He then made a strafing attack on locomotives nearby and a further attack on another train on his way home. Musgrave was caught and held by searchlights shortly after crossing the Belgian coast near Veurne and was forced to take violent evasive action. Abandoning his attempt to reach Gent, he patrolled west along the coast into France and bombed a railway bridge a few miles inland from Calais, but saw no results.[309]

In the evening of 23 December, Furber searched for shipping and found four armed trawlers a few miles off Boulogne heading south. He bombed the leading ship from thirty feet through intense light flak but saw no results. On returning to base, P7119 had a large hole in the starboard outer wing. Ashton took off just before midnight on an anti-shipping sortie. Off Cap Gris-Nez, he briefly saw two small ships, but lost sight of them before he could attack. After midnight, McClure and Torrance set off on intruder sorties. Torrance returned early with a faulty compass, but McClure found and bombed a train near Ieper (Ypres) before dropping his remaining bomb on a railway track between Roeselare and Kortrijk. These were the squadron's last operational flights in 1942 as poor weather closed in over the Christmas period and practice flying was restricted. Operations recommenced on 3 January 1943 with an uneventful shipping reconnaissance by Bolster and Furber, the latter on his

No. 137 Squadron's Pilot Officer Frederick Furber's aircraft at readiness at RAF Matlaske on 14 August 1942. Note his flying helmet on the mirror above the cockpit. Furber was from Rhodesia. (*Robert Bowater*)

last sortie with the squadron before he was posted to Typhoon-equipped 266 Squadron a few days later.

Early in the morning of 8 January, Robert and Aubrey Smith abandoned a rhubarb operation due to a lack of cloud cover and an evening search by four Whirlwinds and three Albacores found no trace of a large group of E-boats reported to be near Boulogne.[310] Poor weather prevented any further operational flying until 11 January when Robert and Aubrey again attempted a rhubarb operation to attack the supply dumps at Auchy-lès-Hesdin. They crossed into France at Quend Plage in cloud at 5,000 feet, but as they flew west towards their target, found no low cloud and so turned back with the intention of finding alternative targets. Robert bombed a railway bridge over the River Authie and saw one of his bombs explode near the bridge, but the other overshot by 100 yards. Smith found a stationary goods train near Conchil-le-Temple at which he fired a short burst of cannon fire in a dive from 1,000 feet before dropping his bombs where they exploded nearby. Neither pilot experienced flak during the operation.[311]

137 Squadron's next operational sorties were on the night of 15-16 January when four Whirlwinds operated as intruders. Earlier that night, Beamont of 609 Squadron made five separate cannon attacks on a freight train at Morbecque and reported its position on his return. At 23:15, Coghlan took off to finish the train off with bombs. He failed to find it and when Coghlan attempted to

bomb canal barges discovered his bombs would not release. Bryan bombed trains at Ieper and saw one locomotive and wagons derailed. McClure found no trains in the St-Pol area so bombed a signal box while Holmes bombed a drifter three-quarters of a mile offshore north of Oostende.[312]

Two nights later, the squadron flew a further four intruder sorties. Musgrave bombed a train from low level and subsequently saw it lying on its side in a cloud of steam. Brunet returned early and Roberts bombed barges on a canal near Nieuwpoort. The fourth pilot due to operate that night was Jack Luing, but his aircraft crashed on take off and caught fire. Luing sprinted clear and was unhurt, but P7051 was destroyed when a bomb exploded.

The Whirlwinds were out again on the night of 19 January. Mercer was briefed to attack railway targets in the Roeselare area, but returned with engine trouble. Rebbetoy took off next, briefed to locate railway targets in the Hazebrouck area and in particular a passenger train carrying German personnel returning from leave and expected by intelligence sources to arrive at Calais at 20:10. He duly found a passenger train with fifteen coaches approaching Calais from Gravelines. He bombed the train from 250 feet derailing coaches and made two cannon attacks. Coghlan patrolled the Diksmuide, Ieper and Hazebrouck areas, and bombed six railway wagons on an embankment south of Ieper. Bryan found a passenger train on the Brugge-Gent line near Sint-Maria-Aalter that he bombed from 150 feet. His bomb derailed the locomotive and the first two carriages which he then attacked with cannon. He then saw a freight train approaching from the opposite direction which he also attacked. His second bomb fell near the locomotive, but was not close enough to derail it, after which he exhausted his ammunition in a cannon attack.[313]

After this period of nocturnal sorties, 137 Squadron returned to daylight rhubarb operations on 23 January during which it lost a further two aircraft and pilots. First to take off were Bryan and Walker who bombed a freight train near Neufchâtel-en-Bray before strafing with cannon. They then attacked another freight train at Serqueux and another locomotive near Neufchâtel. McClure and Doig crossed the coast at Bray-Dunes, but met intense flak over Poperinge and separated. McClure went on to bomb two adjacent trains on the eastern outskirts of Ieper, but Doig (P7054) fell victim to flak and force landed. Doig initially evaded capture, but was picked up near Cambrai four days later and became a prisoner of war. Freeman and Brown did not find their briefed target, a supply dump at Hesdin, but made a cannon attack on a freight train leaving the station at Aubigny-en-Artois before bombing another north of Doullens. In this second attack, they derailed and toppled the locomotive and the first five wagons. Light flak was experienced from the second train and the pair climbed into cloud where they separated. Brown radioed Freeman and told him he was okay, but thought he had been hit in the port engine. Brown successfully force landed P7095 near Arras, but no more was heard of him until after the war when his body was found buried nearby. The cause of his death remains unclear. Musgrave carried out his rhubarb alone. First he bombed a goods train at Kortemark, but was unable to observe the results of his bombing due to intense flak. He dropped his second bomb on a small locomotive pulling tanker wagons over a bridge at Vlamertinge before making a cannon attack on a third train in the same area. Coghlan and Smith flew the last sorties of the day. They separated after crossing the French coast just south of le Tréport. Coghlan fired at and then bombed a group of wagons and two freight trains near Neufchâtel-en-Bray. Smith bombed camouflaged trucks and huts in a camp in woods east of Fallencourt. He then made a cannon attack on military trucks north west of Londinières.[314]

On the night of 26 January, a Manston-based Albacore of 841 Squadron searched unsuccessfully for shipping from Dunkerque to Vlissingen, but the crew observed that navigational beacons were lit and early the following morning British radar detected a substantial ship heading east from Calais. McClure and Torrance were briefed to attack it and its escorts off Dunkerque. Diving down to attack through flak from the ships and shore, McClure dropped his bombs, but one of Torrance's failed to drop. Because of the intense flak, neither pilot saw the results of their bombing.[315]

Two Whirlwinds were sent out to look for trains on the morning of 28 January. De Houx's target was the line between Dunkerque and Lille, and Musgrave was briefed to operate further north over the border in Belgium on the lines between Brussel and the ports of Oostende and Dunkerque. De Houx found a freight train with around six wagons pulling out of a station south of Bergues, fired a four-second burst of cannon at the locomotive and saw his shells striking the target. He then bombed from fifty feet and, looking back after bombing, saw a large cloud of steam from the locomotive but no more conclusive results. Musgrave bombed a freight train south west of Tielt before making two cannon attacks on the now stationary locomotive on which he saw cannon strikes and 'much steam blowing out from places not intended by the makers'. As he pulled away from his cannon attack, he saw two Fw 190s about 800 yards away approaching from three-quarters astern. Musgrave turned in to the leading aircraft, but the Fw 190 succeeded in getting onto his tail. Musgrave saw tracer from two bursts of fire passing his Whirlwind before he put the flaps down and throttled back forcing his pursuer to overshoot and pull up into cloud. Musgrave turned south west for the coast and home, but a few minutes later south of Roeselare, one of the Fw 190s reappeared. Musgrave immediately fired a short burst from 300 yards range and using considerable deflection, but saw no strikes and the enemy vanished in the clouds. Musgrave then sought refuge in the clouds and landed safely at Manston at 11:40. Musgrave made no claim to have damaged the Fw

190, but his hasty burst of cannon fire had mortally damaged it. Uffz. Heinz Wälter's Fw 190A-4, WNr. 5622, of 8/JG26 crashed nearby with the loss of its pilot.[316] Freeman and Smith took off that morning to attack supply dumps at Hesdin, but found no cloud cover ten miles off the French coast at Le Touquet and returned home. An afternoon shipping reconnaissance by O'Neill and Walker was similarly uneventful.

There was no further operational flying until 6 February although, while on a practice flight on 3 February, de Houx saw a group of single-engine aircraft off the coast near Felixstowe. He pursued them towards France, but could get no closer than a mile and a half and abandoned the chase. The period did, however, bring the good news that Robert Smith had been awarded the DFC, the first decoration awarded to a pilot with 137 Squadron, although his award was partly for his prior service on Blenheims. On 6 February, the squadron sent three pairs of Whirlwinds out on rhubarb operations, but only Bryan and Brunet found targets. Crossing into France over the Baie de Somme, they separated to search individually for railway targets around Abbeville. Bryan followed the railway line south east and at Hangest-sur-Somme found two freight trains approaching each other. He dropped one of his bombs from 150 feet and saw one wagon blow up and two others derailed. He followed this by dropping his other bomb and making four cannon attacks on the two trains. Brunet made two separate bombing attacks on a collection of railway wagons to the west of Abbeville and attacked an army lorry with cannon, but due to intense light flak from Abbeville did not stay to observe results.

Thus far in 1943, shipping targets had been scarce and the coaster attacked by McClure and Torrance on 27 January 1927 was the only major movement detected in the Channel by British radar during the entire month. However, increased German minesweeping activity in early February hinted at the imminent passage of a significant ship and on the night of 10 February, a large vessel with substantial escort was detected by the Chain Home Low radar network. This was the commerce-raiding auxiliary cruiser *Coronel* (codenamed 'Schiff 14' by the Germans and 'Raider K' by the British) sailing from Dunkerque, escorted by twelve minesweepers en route to begin her first war cruise. Hugging the coast, *Coronel* was engaged by British coastal artillery as she passed westbound between Calais and Cap Gris-Nez, but sustained no damage and continued south past Boulogne. Although the moon was obscured by dense cloud at 3,000 feet with patches of rain and sea fog at lower levels, Brunet, Musgrave and McClure took off at intervals from Manston to look for the *Coronel*, followed by three Fairey Albacores of 841 Squadron. Only Musgrave found the target. After being given several vectors by his controller, he glimpsed a dark shadow and the wake of a large ship about a mile offshore near Hardelot. Flying closer, he also observed five of her escorts. Musgrave flew towards the French coast and found a distinctive feature in the shape of dunes from which a run at ninety degrees to the shoreline would bring him back over the target. During his first two attempts he was immediately caught and held by searchlights and was forced to take such violent evasive action that he could not complete his bombing run. For his third attempt, Musgrave climbed to just beneath the cloud base and passed through the searchlights in a fast dive down to 100 feet. Like the others of her kind, *Coronel* was well equipped with anti-aircraft weapons in addition to powerful surface armament. Forced by intense flak from the ships to take violent evasive action during his approach, Musgrave steadied his aircraft at the last minute and bombed the ship from the port beam. Ten or more streams of tracer passed his Whirlwind as he flew over the masts, a cannon shell tore a large hole in the starboard elevator of P7114 and pieces of shrapnel from a near miss penetrated the cockpit canopy, but fortunately missed Musgrave. However, Musgrave's bombing had been effective. The *Coronel* stopped for ninety minutes for urgent repairs before returning to Boulogne Harbour with one crewmember dead and three injured. The ship was subsequently bombed by the RAF and US 8th Air Force, but was not damaged further. The Germans estimated that it would take three to four months to repair the damage caused by Musgrave's bombs and abandoned their attempt to get *Coronel* out into the convoy routes. The ship left Boulogne on 14 February, returned to Germany and ended the war as a night fighter direction ship.[317]

On 12 February, 137 Squadron returned to daytime rhubarb operations over occupied Belgium. Musgrave and Rebbetoy were briefed to patrol the railways in the Roeselare-Ieper area while Bryan and Brunet set off for similar targets around Gent and Brugge. They found no shortage of targets. Musgrave and Rebbetoy separated after crossing the Belgian coast at Nieuwpoort. Musgrave attacked three freight trains on the line between Gent and Kortrijk while Rebbetoy bombed two adjacent stationary freight trains south east of Roeselare. Immediately after his attack, Rebbetoy saw two Fw 190s closing in behind him, one of which was firing from long range. Fortunately, there was dense cloud at 1,500 feet into which he climbed to evade his pursuers. After orbiting in cloud for a few minutes, he returned home, but not before making a cannon attack on a shunting engine on a line between Oostende and Roeselare. Bryan and Brunet made cannon attacks on a stationary locomotive before bombing and firing at a fifteen-wagon train on a line between Brugge and Torhout. Brunet then returned to base due to malfunctioning Exactor controls, but Bryan continued south down the line past Torhout and attacked another freight train north east of Roeselare.[318] That night and the following one, Whirlwinds and Albacores patrolled uneventfully off Boulogne in the expectation that the *Coronel,* bombed by Musgrave on the night of 10 February, left her harbour.

Rhubarb operations on 15 February were abandoned due to unsuitable weather, but that night, Luing and McClure took off at 22:30 to carry out intruder operations. Luing bombed a stationary freight train north east of Hazebrouck and saw the last four wagons derailed. McClure bombed a pair of trains passing each other between Lillers and Aire-sur-la-Lys despite being caught by a searchlight while attacking. He then flew further south to Bruay-la-Buissière where he found and attacked a freight train with cannon. The following day, Joe Holmes returned to 263 Squadron after five months as a flight commander with 137 Squadron. To replace him, John 'Mike' Bryan was promoted to flight lieutenant and took over 137 Squadron's A Flight. At the same time, John Barclay returned to the unit after four months with 263 Squadron. That evening, de Houx and Mercer flew night intruder sorties over Belgium and France, but neither found trains in their allotted patrol areas. Flying through fierce rainstorms, de Houx found navigation difficult, but eventually found and bombed two canal barges and saw wreckage in the water after his attack. Mercer dropped a bomb on railway tracks south of Ardres and the other on a bridge over the Calais-St-Omer canal, which it missed by ten to fifteen yards.

During the night of 18-19 February, 137 Squadron attempted a record eighteen sorties, but with the tragic loss of two pilots in an accident. At 21:00, Coghlan searched the Belgian railway network from Veurne to Gent via Ieper and Roeselare, but found no trains and so bombed a bridge over the Brugge-Gent canal, but was unable to see the results of his bombing. O'Neill and Sutherland carried out shipping searches, but neither pilot found any ships. Bryan dropped his first bomb on a freight train a few miles east of Roeselare, derailing two of the wagons, and then followed up by firing two bursts of cannon fire at the locomotive. He then flew on to Roeselare and dropped his second bomb on two adjacent stationary trains. Looking back, he observed a large cloud of steam, but flak from the surrounding countryside dissuaded him from investigating further. He then found a passenger train approaching Veurne from Diksmuide that he attacked twice with cannon. During his first attack, he saw cannon strikes on the first coach and strikes on the now stationary locomotive during his second attack. Musgrave flew an anticlockwise orbit over Northern France and southern Belgium searching unsuccessfully for trains. On the way home, he found and bombed a train near the coast heading from Veurne to Dunkerque. De Houx, who took off twenty-five minutes later, found a train heading south on the line from Calais to St-Omer and, when it stopped at Watten, made a head-on cannon attack. Continuing on to St-Omer, he experienced intense flak from airfields at Longuenesse and Fort Rouge and, having found no more trains, bombed the railway line between Veurne and Dunkerque before returning home.

Ashton took off shortly after midnight, but when he reached the French coast at Berck, found the ground obscured by fog with only the hilltops visible. Since it was pointless to continue inland, he flew offshore north towards Calais in search of ships but found no targets. An hour later, Exactor control problems forced Robert Smith to return to base from the same area. Torrance also found poor visibility when he crossed into occupied Belgium near Nieuwpoort. He bombed a barge on a canal before crossing out over the coast where he saw five ships near Nieuwpoort heading towards Dunkerque and climbed to report their position to his controller. Shortly after 01:10, tragedy struck. While taking off, Mercer (P7114) collided with Freeman who was taxiing in P7119. The aircraft caught fire and two of the bombs exploded killing both pilots.

Operations continued and Walker took off just after 02:30 to attack the ships reported earlier by Torrance, but was vectored by his controller onto shipping further west near Calais. He located a convoy of three cargo ships with eight or nine escorts, which revealed their position by firing at him. He dived down from 1,500 to 500 feet to bomb the rearmost vessel, but did not see the results of his bombing. These ships became the focus of the squadron's operations for the rest of the night. Coghlan and McClure returned due to poor radio reception and Coghlan was recalled from a second attempt because the ships were reported, wrongly, to be in harbour. Luing and de Houx found the convoy and bombed some of the escorts, observing no results and experiencing intense light flak. McClure took off for a second time and attacked one of the merchant vessels, but his bombs undershot by fifteen to twenty yards.

Fog and haze prevented any further operational flying until 2 March and practice flying was only possible on a few days. In the interim, Sgt Pilot Albert Witham and FO John Hadow joined the squadron from 55 OTU and PO Norbury Dugdale arrived in early March. There was also news of the award to Eddie Musgrave of a well-deserved DFC.

On 2 March, Bryan flew an uneventful morning shipping reconnaissance and Rebbetoy and Roberts took off at 11:10 to hunt for trains. They flew to Bambecque where they separated. Rebbetoy saw a train at Bergues and orbited for ten minutes waiting for it to leave the town. When it eventually emerged, he saw it was a passenger train on which daylight attacks were

Australian Eddie Musgrave was awarded the DFC on 26 February 1943, but was lost on 17 May 1943. (*Niall Corduroy*)

prohibited and so flew on to search for other targets. He dropped a bomb on a barge on the Canal de la Colme and his second on a group of railway wagons west of Dunkerque. Roberts also failed to find trains and bombed a railway bridge near Bambecque without seeing the results. He then made cannon attacks on a lock gate and another bridge near Bergues. Bryan searched for trains near Diksmuide and bombed one four miles north of Roeselare before making three cannon attacks and strafed another freight train nearby. Bryan had now damaged twenty locomotives. At 13:10, Coghlan (who was to fly alone), Brunet and Walker took off to find railway targets, but found dense low cloud at the French coast. Coghlan returned safely, but Brunet and Walker became separated in the cloud. Brunet gave Walker a course for home, but later heard him make a mayday call. Walker's call was not heard by ground radio stations and no further contact was made with him. Brunet, Luing and Ashton flew searches to look for him to no avail. Walker (P7005), presumably having been hit by flak, force landed north of Boulogne and was captured.[319]

The following day, the squadron carried out formation flying practice in preparation for an official visit to Manston by a large number of journalists and photographers on 4-5 March. The journalists interviewed a number of pilots and 'stories of noble deeds were told, to appear in various stages of distortion in the papers during the next few days'. The photographers were treated to formation flying displays and solo aerobatics by 609's Typhoons and by McClure and Bryan. Poor weather over the next few weeks prevented operational flying, but some practice flying was carried out, including the squadron's first dive-bombing practice in anticipation of a proposed attack on Abbeville-Drucat airfield. Operations restarted early on 11 March when McClure, Aubrey Smith, Barclay and Bolster took off to meet their escort of Spitfire IXs of 64 Squadron in order to look for seven armed trawlers reported between Oostende and Dunkerque. The formation patrolled from Mardyck to Nieuwpoort, but found only fishing boats.[320]

The following day brought news of a DFC for Bryan and the arrival of two new pilots, FO John Davidson and PO Gordon Chalmers. Training flying and dive-bombing practice continued on 13 March, but 137 Squadron was briefed that night to attack a small group of ships that had been detected off Cap Blanc Nez. Ashton was successfully vectored onto the ships, bombed in a dive from 1,500 to 400 feet and saw his bombs explode close to the ship. Barclay returned early because of poor radio reception. Aubrey Smith caught a glimpse of a number of ships, bombed from seventy-five feet and saw his bombs explode, but no other specific results.

On the afternoon of 14 March, the squadron staged Ramrod 44, the long-expected attack on Abbeville-Drucat airfield and the squadron's first dive-bombing operation. The Whirlwinds and their Hornchurch Wing escorts met no opposition and suffered no casualties, but a diversionary sweep by the Biggin Hill Wing was hit hard by JG26 and lost four pilots. Coghlan led Bryan, Brunet, Musgrave, Rebbetoy and de Houx to Hastings where they met their close escort, the Spitfire VBs of 350 and 453 Squadrons, and the escort cover provided by the Spitfire IXs of 64 and 122 Squadrons. The formation set course at sea level before commencing a fast climb to cross the French coast at Cayeux at 13,000 feet. Over the target, the Whirlwinds peeled off into seventy-degree dives to release their bombs between 7,000 and 6,000 feet where they met accurate flak. The escort squadrons saw bomb explosions on the north east side of the airfield and elsewhere in the target area, but observation was difficult in such high-speed dives. Meanwhile, the escort cover squadrons continued their climb to 25,000 feet, but lost sight of the Whirlwinds and their close escort in the haze. They therefore orbited up sun of Abbeville until told that the Whirlwinds and escort were safely out of the target area. They were then instructed to investigate enemy aircraft reported to the west of Le Touquet, but saw nothing except smoke trails of a small number of aircraft which dived away. However, the Luftwaffe was active and the subsequent Rodeo 188 by the Biggin Hill Wing experienced a series of sharp combats with the Fw 190s of JG26 and lost four aircraft and pilots, including the wing leader and two squadron commanders.[321]

Poor weather forced another pause in operational flying until 20 March when ten Whirlwinds were obliged to turn back before reaching the enemy-held coast because of insufficient cloud cover. On 22 March, thick cloud down to sea level forced three pilots to return, but de Houx and Rebbetoy continued and crossed the French coast at Gravelines where they separated. De Houx found no trains, but bombed three adjacent barges on a canal near Merville. Rebbetoy dropped his first bomb on a freight train between Armentières and Bailleul, but the bomb overshot and burst on the track in front of the train that then stopped. He then returned and released his second bomb from treetop height and saw it explode alongside and derail the locomotive. Rebbetoy then made cannon attacks on a second train between Armentières and Lille, and two barges on a canal nearby.

On the afternoon of 24 March, six Whirlwinds took off on Ramrod 46 to bomb the marshalling yards at Abbeville, but turned back over the Channel when they found dense cloud at 7,000 feet. They tried again the following day with more success. Bryan led Torrance, McClure, Luing, Robert Smith and Aubrey Smith at 14:45 to rendezvous over Hastings with their close escort of 453 Squadron's Spitfire Vs and the Spitfire IXs of 64 and 122 Squadrons as escort cover, all led by Sqn Ldr Don Kingaby, the Hornchurch Wing leader. The Whirlwinds bombed in a steep dive from 13,000 to 7,000 feet and the escorts saw at least four bomb bursts in the yards and four more on the edge of the adjacent canal. Robert Smith's aircraft was superficially damaged by flak splinters before bombing and the escort cover Spitfires, orbiting to the north of the target area, skirmished with Fw 190s of JG26, but all aircraft and pilots returned safely.[322]

The remainder of March was taken up with training flying including dive-bombing practice with 500 lbs-bombs. During one of these flights on 30 March, the starboard engine of Davidson's aircraft failed and the undercarriage collapsed in the subsequent heavy landing on Manston's notoriously bumpy runway. Davidson was unhurt but P7104 was beyond repair. On 1 April, a number of the squadron's personnel attended a parade to mark the 25th anniversary of the formation of the RAF and two new pilots, PO Bernard Soulsby and Sgt William Evans, joined the unit. On the same day, Bryan, Hadow and de Houx together with Sqn Ldr Patrick Lee, a pilot temporarily attached to 609 Squadron and flying as a guest on this occasion, took off at 08:00 to look for shipping from the Hook of Holland to Oostende. They found no shipping, but the weather seemed suitable for rhubarb operations. Accordingly, Musgrave and Sutherland took off at 10:30 for the Kortrijk area but returned from the Belgian coast having found the cloud base at 4,000 feet. Two hours later and further south west, Bryan and de Houx found better conditions. They crossed the French coast together at Gravelines and then separated. Bryan flew south east into Belgium and dropped a bomb from 100 feet on a train with four wagons near Roesbrugge and saw the explosion wreck the last wagon. He then attacked a train entering Veurne with cannon and his remaining bomb. Bryan then attacked a third train near Zarren after which pieces were seen to fall off the locomotive. During this attack, Bryan was joined by de Houx who had been searching without success for trains near Ieper, but had only found a passenger train which he did not attack. De Houx dropped one of his bombs and saw it explode just behind the rear locomotive. Bryan then returned to base while de Houx continued searching, again without success, for trains. He eventually dropped his second bomb, which failed to explode, on railway tracks near Torhout. Musgrave tried again at 14:50, but was forced to return due to unsuitable weather.

On 3 April, eight Whirlwinds with Spitfire escort searched from Koksijde to Calais for shipping, but found nothing. They did, however, stray too close to Dunkerque and four Whirlwinds were superficially damaged by flak. The following morning Coghlan led eight Whirlwinds with nine Typhoons of 609 Squadron to look for twenty-four small ships reported near Dunkerque. While flying at sea level five miles off the coast at Deal, Dugdale misjudged his height and his aircraft's propellers hit the water. He was obliged to ditch P7002, but got clear before it sank and was recovered by a rescue launch patrolling in the area. The remaining Whirlwinds swept from le Touquet to Oostende, but failed to locate targets.[323] Later that day, the squadron repeated Ramrod 46 to Abbeville marshalling yards, but this time with 500-lb bombs. Coghlan led Torrance, McClure, Musgrave, Rebbetoy, Ashton, Brunet and Roberts with a close escort of nine Typhoons of 609 Squadron. 122 and 453 Squadrons of the Hornchuch Wing provided escort cover. Over the target, the Whirlwinds bombed in a dive from 12,500 to 7,000 feet and the pilots saw bursts in the centre of the target and one on a large building. Heavy flak was experienced and the tail of Coghlan's aircraft was hit by shrapnel. Halfway across the Channel on the return journey, the escorting Typhoons were instructed to investigate shipping detected by radar off Boulogne. Two of the Typhoons remained with the Whirlwinds while the others made a successful attack on what were identified as a group of Räumboote accompanied by a flak ship. All the Whirlwinds returned safely to Manston by 19:40.[324]

On 8 April, the squadron prepared eight Whirlwinds for a dive-bombing attack on Abbeville-Drucat airfield which was postponed and eventually cancelled due to excessive cloud. A similar dive bombing attack on the railway yards at Brugge the following day was postponed three times before being finally cancelled at 18:00. It was attempted again on 13 April when, just before midday, eight Whirlwinds led by Coghlan took off on Ramrod 50. Twelve Spitfire Vs of 19 Squadron provided close escort and twenty-one Spitfire IXs of 453 and 122 Squadrons made up the escort cover force. Following were the Norwegians of 331 and 332 Squadrons as first fighter echelon and thirty-six P-47s of the US 8th Air Force as second fighter echelon. Ten miles off Oostende, the Whirlwinds and their close escort abandoned the operation when they found a carpet of cloud at 4,000 feet and extending all the way to the target. The other fighters carried on to perform largely uneventful sweeps. The following afternoon, 137 Squadron tried again, this time with more success. The Spitfires of 19 Squadron again provided close escort while Squadron Leader John Ratten led 453 and 122 Squadrons as escort cover. 331 and 332 Squadrons provided the first diversionary fighter echelon while the Biggin Hill Wing (611 and 341 Squadrons) led by Wing Commander Al Deere provided the second echelon. Coghlan, Bryan, Rebbetoy, Roberts, Sutherland, Luing, Robert Smith and Barclay crossed the Belgian coast at Blankenberge with their escort at 9,000 feet, still climbing, before dive bombing the target in a run from south east to north west from 12,000 down to 7,000 feet. The pilots saw their bombs explode on the tracks and a group of engine sheds on the eastern side of the yards. The Whirlwinds and the close escort returned to base safely, despite experiencing flak while crossing the coast in both directions. 453 and 122 Squadrons orbited the target area until the Whirlwinds and their close escort had safely crossed the coast at which point they returned to base. Although enemy aircraft were plotted by British radar, none were encountered. The North Weald and Biggin Hill wings carried out their diversionary sweeps north and south of the main area of operations, but they too were ignored by the Luftwaffe.[325]

That evening, four Whirlwinds carried out anti-shipping operations. Ashton and Aubrey Smith were vectored onto a group of twelve or more

Räumboote near le Tréport and claimed near misses with their bombs. An hour later, McClure and Robert Smith were vectored onto a different group of escorted Räumboote, further north, off Berck. McClure was recalled because of poor radio reception, but Smith bombed one of the ships without observing concrete results.

On 15 April, 137 Squadron sent four aircraft to operate individually in search of German naval units between le Touquet and Berck. Bryan found fifteen ships, identified as 'E and R-boats' heading south in two columns. He bombed in a dive from 1,000 down to 100 feet, but saw only one bomb explosion. Rebbetoy and Musgrave also bombed, but saw no conclusive results, although one of Rebbetoy's bombs produced a large explosion that was seen by Brunet some miles away. Brunet returned to base after radio problems prevented him from being vectored onto the target.

There was no operational flying on 16 April, but practice flights continued, during one of which FO John Hadow, who had been with the squadron for only six weeks, was killed in P7121. Hadow was practicing dive-bombing over the airfield at 10:00 and was seen to pull out of a dive at 5,000 feet when his aircraft flicked over and crashed into the ground.[326] The following night, 137 Squadron flew six sorties to attack railway targets in Belgium and shipping off the coast. Brunet dropped his first bomb on a train on the Oostende-Torhout railway line, blowing the locomotive and first two coaches off the track before attacking with cannon. He dropped his second bomb between two canal barges near Nieuwpoort and then turned for home. On his return journey a few miles off the coast, he saw what he identified as a Dornier Do 217 in the opposite direction. Brunet put his flaps down to reduce speed and turned sharply to port, but was apparently seen by the crew of the enemy aircraft that turned away and disappeared down moon. A few minutes later, Brunet saw tracer passing him from behind and climbed to 3,000 feet and accelerated away. Rebbetoy took off shortly after Brunet and was also briefed to attack railway targets. He dropped a bomb on a locomotive in Hazebrouck and saw it explode, but was then forced to retire by aggressive flak and searchlights. After orbiting for five minutes, he returned to drop his remaining bomb on railway wagons, but saw no concrete results because of the violent evasive action he was forced to take. Searching for further targets, he was illuminated by searchlights and fired at by flak from Merville airfield before finding and attacking another locomotive between Hazebrouck and Bailleul.

At this point, the controller at Swingate reported that shipping had been detected off the coast near Berck and Sutherland took off just before 02:00 to attack it. Sutherland fleetingly saw what he identified as an R-boat followed by an E-boat and bombed the latter in a dive from 2,000 down to 150 feet, but was unable to observe results. Roberts returned early due to an instrument failure, but an hour after Sutherland's attack, Musgrave found

four ships and bombed the rearmost one from starboard astern. As he turned
away, he observed his bombs explode on the ship and then a burning red glow
on the water. Ninety seconds later, there was another explosion and the fires
died out. It seems likely that Musgrave's target was the 300-ton minesweeper
M3817 that was reported sunk on the night in this area. Bryan also saw the
explosions of Musgrave's bombs while he was orbiting the area awaiting his
turn to attack. He dropped his two bombs from 150 feet on one of the ships
and saw swirls in the water immediately behind it but no explosions. All three
pilots experienced intense light flak during their attacks, but Bryan's aircraft
(P7111) was the only one damaged.

Because of poor weather on 18 April, there was little flying during the day
and the squadron sent out a single Whirlwind that night. McClure found and
bombed a passenger train on the line between Roeselare and Kortrijk, derailing
the locomotive and first coach. He dropped his remaining bomb on a long,
slow-moving freight train near Gent before making a cannon attack on the,
now stationary, target. A slight and temporary improvement in the weather
allowed operations to restart on 20 April and the squadron flew ten night
sorties. McClure and Ashton flew to Abbeville-Drucat airfield, but the airfield
lights were turned off and there were no other signs of activity, so the two
pilots searched for trains instead. Ashton failed to find a target and returned
to base with his bombs, but on the southern outskirts of Abbeville, McClure
found a stationary locomotive that he bombed from 100 feet. He then dropped
his remaining bomb on a group of railway wagons further south. Musgrave
and de Houx were briefed to attack railway targets and de Houx patrolled
the Armentières area and as far south as Lille and Lens, but failed to find a
target. On the way home, he was illuminated by searchlights near Gravelines,
met intense and accurate flak and, to facilitate evasive action, jettisoned his
bombs in fields. Musgrave crossed the coast at Bray-Dunes and patrolled in
a large counter-clockwise orbit from Ieper to Kortrijk, Gent and Brugge, but
found nothing. He dropped his bombs singly on a barge near Kortrijk and
another near Gent before making a cannon attack on a small passenger train
south east of Eeklo. Crossing the coast at sea level at Nieuwpoort and passing
through intense light and heavy flak, Musgrave saw six ships heading north
east towards Oostende. He attacked one of the ships with a long burst of
cannon fire, only breaking away when 100 yards from the target. He then
climbed to 3,000 feet to ask his controller for an emergency homing, the
standard method of securely reporting the sighting of a worthwhile shipping
target so that its position could be pinpointed.

These ships had also been seen and attacked at about the same time by one
of 609 Squadron's Typhoons and at 01:55, 137 Squadron sent six Whirlwinds
to find and attack them. Woodhouse returned early with engine problems and
Torrance, Robert Smith, Ashton and Barclay failed to locate the ships despite

searching from Calais to Blankenberge. Aubrey Smith was the only pilot to find a target: an E-boat a few miles off shore at Blankenberge that he bombed in two separate attacks. The boat stopped after his first attack and believed he had achieved a direct hit with his second bomb, but there is no record of a Kriegsmarine vessel being significantly damaged in this attack.

After a period of poor weather, the squadron returned to the offensive on the morning of 25 April with three pairs of aircraft staging daylight rhubarb operations, unfortunately with the loss of one of the squadron's most experienced and effective pilots. Bryan and Rebbetoy were first off and found perfect weather conditions with dense cloud at 1-2,000 feet and good visibility below. Near Roeselare, they saw a small freight train moving very slowly. By this point it was normal for trains to carry a small number of anti-aircraft guns for protection, but as Bryan commenced his bombing run, he saw two guns in the wagon immediately behind the locomotive and machine gun and cannon fire from the other wagons. Suspecting a trap, Bryan broke away and ordered Rebbetoy to do likewise, but seconds later saw Rebbetoy attacking the train. He observed Rebbetoy's cannon fire hitting the locomotive and first truck, but then saw his aircraft (P7058) hit the ground, disintegrate and burst into flames. The twenty-six-year-old Canadian did not survive. Bryan continued his patrol across the French border to Cassel, but the only trains he saw were in stations and could not be attacked. On his return journey, he successfully bombed lock gates on the Calais-St-Omer canal and made a cannon attack on a stationary locomotive nearby. De Houx and Witham searched unsuccessfully along the railway from Torhout to Roeselare, Kortrijk, Gent and Brugge and then bombed a group of canal barges south of Brugge which they then strafed with cannon.

McClure and Woodhouse took off a few minutes later to patrol the railways in the Gent area. McClure dropped his first bomb from fifty feet on the locomotive of a small freight train and saw it and a number of wagons derailed. He dropped his second bomb on a barge near Gent. Woodhouse dropped his first bomb on a railway bridge near Deinze and his second on a barge. The pair then found a long freight train heading towards Gent that they attacked with cannon. McClure exhausted his ammunition in a second attack and then, as he pulled away, observed two Fw 190s coming in to attack from astern. Fortunately, the cloud base was only at 1,000 feet and Woodhouse climbed into the safety of the clouds as six streams of white tracer passed to his left. McClure was uncertain if he could reach the cloud cover in time, so stall-turned to approach the enemy aircraft head on. Even though McClure had no ammunition left, this desperate tactic caused a Fw 190 pilot to dive underneath McClure who was then able to escape into the clouds.

On 29 April, Torrance led eight of 137 Squadron's Whirlwinds on Ramrod 66, a dive-bombing attack on the railway yards at Eu. This operation provided a fine illustration of the importance of timing in these heavily choreographed operations. The Spitfires of 411 Squadron provided close escort, 122 and 453 Squadrons of the Hornchurch Wing acted as escort cover, and the Typhoons of 609 Squadron acted as withdrawal cover. The Whirlwinds flew to the rendezvous point at Hastings and orbited while waiting for their escort to arrive. 411 Squadron duly arrived, but of the escort cover squadrons there was no sign. After a further twenty minutes of orbiting, Torrance – unwilling to expose the 137 pilots to the unnecessary hazard of continuing the operation largely unescorted and aware that nearly half an hour's fuel had been consumed – ordered the Whirlwinds to return to Manston and land. The Hornchurch Wing, delayed by haze and poor visibility, decided to dispense with the rendezvous altogether and headed directly for the target expecting to find the Whirlwinds there. The nine Typhoons of 609 Squadron formed up over Hastings and had commenced their climb out towards France when they saw the Whirlwinds and 411's Spitfires behind and below them orbiting Hastings. Believing that the Whirlwinds were about to set course, they also made for France where they carried out an uneventful sweep. When the Hornchurch Wing returned to base, the wing leader, John 'Killy' Kilmartin, called Manston and had a less than cordial conversation with Torrance whom he believed should have continued with the operation and taken a chance on finding the escort cover in the target area.[327]

For the first eleven days of May, continuous strong winds precluded any operational sorties, but training continued, during which P6976 was damaged beyond repair when both main wheel tyres burst and a wing hit the ground while landing on 1 May. Four sorties on 12 May were abandoned because of the weather, but 13 May had improved allowing 137 Squadron to send six Whirlwinds on night anti-shipping patrols. Sutherland and Musgrave took off just before midnight and were vectored onto a group of twelve to fifteen minesweepers heading south between Cap Gris-Nez and Boulogne. Sutherland bombed from 200 feet and Musgrave ten minutes later in a dive from 1,500 to 150 feet before making a cannon attack. Intense flak from both ships and shore prevented both pilots from observing the results of their bombing runs. O'Neill and de Houx set off for the same target an hour later. O'Neill located the minesweepers off Hardelot but lost sight of them while turning into attack. Shortly afterwards, he observed light flak from the south and investigated. While diving down to avoid the flak, he caught sight of two ships which he bombed, although one bomb failed to release. De Houx was fired at near Boulogne, but was then vectored by his controller on to a target further south off le Touquet where he failed to find a target. Later, Bryan and Witham took off to attack the same target but were ordered by their controller to orbit Manston and instructed to land as enemy aircraft had been plotted in the target area.

As dawn broke on 14 May, Bryan and Musgrave took off to patrol the French and Belgian coast hoping to find shipping. Bryan's patrol was uneventful, but Musgrave found and bombed a minesweeper a mile offshore between Calais and Blankenberge. He saw one of his bombs burst near the stern of the ship before making a cannon attack. That evening, the squadron sent three aircraft to look for shipping. Woodhouse patrolled from Boulogne to Gris-Nez, but failed to find the enemy. Ashton, patrolling further south, discovered a merchant vessel with heavy escort off le Touquet that he bombed from fifty feet and saw a brilliant flash as one of his bombs exploded. Barclay who was twelve miles away saw the flak firing at Ashton's aircraft and a reddish-blue flash, but when he flew towards the position found no sign of the ships.

15 May was another hectic night, opening with an uneventful shipping reconnaissance flown between Boulogne and Zeebrugge at dusk by Bryan and three other pilots. O'Neill and Musgrave failed to find trains in their respective patrol areas and bombed barges near Veurne and Kortrijk respectively. On his way home, Musgrave located a freight train four miles north of Torhout and made two cannon attacks. Barclay and Ashton, taking off thirty minutes later, also failed to find trains. Barclay bombed railway tracks and Ashton bombed canal barges near Aire before attacking them with cannon.

On the following night, 137 Squadron flew eight night sorties. Bryan was first to patrol railways in the Hazebrouck area. He found the airfield lights lit at St-Omer, but saw no aircraft or trains. He eventually bombed a group of around thirty barges on the Canal d'Aire just north of Béthune, but his bombs overshot. Bryan followed with two cannon attacks on the barges before strafing the locomotive of a freight train near Hazebrouck. Crossing back out over the coast at Bray-Dunes, Bryan saw flak to his right, believed to be aimed at Brunet who had taken off just after midnight to attack railway targets, but instead attacked fifteen E-boats off Nieuwpoort. Brunet bombed one of the ships from fifty feet and saw bomb splashes alongside. He then climbed to 1,500 feet and turned up moon to make a cannon attack on another ship. Turning away, Brunet saw no sign of the ship and believed he had sunk it, but no German vessel appears to have been lost that night. Sutherland and de Houx were diverted from their planned attacks on railway targets to look for the E-boats attacked by Brunet, but found no sign of them.

The last four operational sorties of the night were on airfields. Barclay failed to locate the airfield at Poix, so dropped his bombs on the airfield at Moyencourt-lès-Poix nearby. Half an hour later, McClure found the airfield lights at Poix illuminated and dropped his bombs from 1,500 feet through intense light flak. Ashton and Aubrey Smith found and bombed their targets at Amiens-Glisy and Calais-Marck respectively. While these eight operational sorties were taking place, the new pilots on the squadron carried out night flying practice. Among them was Bernard Soulsby who was held for nearly fifteen minutes by 'friendly' searchlights and fired at by heavy and light flak despite having IFF switched on, lowering his undercarriage and flashing the code letter of the day. McClure and several of 609 Squadron's Typhoons were also illuminated and shot at on their return from their sorties. Fortunately, no aircraft were damaged.

On 17 May, 137 Squadron flew fourteen operational sorties. Ten aircraft operated against shipping and a further four flew intruder sorties, but during the night lost one of its most effective and popular pilots. The Swingate controller directed de Houx on to what appeared to be a group of eight loaded barges accompanied by two minesweepers off Dunkerque. He dropped his two bombs from low level, up moon on one of the minesweepers and saw a large red explosion amidships before returning to make a cannon attack. Sutherland, Witham and Bryan also bombed the same ships and Musgrave took off at 01:10 in P7063 to attack shipping off Gravelines. Having made his bombing attack, he told his controller at 01:32 that he was making a second attack with cannon, but no more was heard of him. It was assumed that Musgrave had fallen victim to the shipboard flak. His body was later washed ashore in France. Brunet found what he identified as a mixed group of seven E- and R-boats leaving Gravelines. Diving down from 1,500 to 100 feet, he bombed the rearmost boat and saw it listing after his attack before returning to attack with cannon. De Houx took off for a second time just before 02:00 and was again vectored onto a group of four minesweepers heading south west off Gravelines. He bombed the leading vessel in an up moon attack from fifty feet though intense light flak from all four ships. Sutherland was recalled while en route to attack the same ships, but near Goodwin Sands saw a disturbance in the sea and a large patch of oil that he presumed to be from a crashed aircraft. Soulsby found five minesweepers off Nieuwpoort, bombed the leading vessel and then attacked with cannon. Further south off Dunkerque, he made a cannon attack on one of three E-boats. Ashton also found shipping off Nieuwpoort in the form of a minesweeper or merchant vessel of around 600 tons with four large loaded barges. He attacked the minesweeper with bombs and cannon and saw his shells strike although he was unable to see the results of his bombing. Ashton then exhausted his ammunition in a further attack on the barges.

While these anti-shipping operations were taking place, B Flight sent four Whirlwinds to patrol the railways in the Gent area, but two of the pilots found targets at sea on their outward journey and attacked these instead. McClure was first off, shortly before midnight. He crossed the French coast just north of Dunkerque in a dive from 5,000 feet and found two trains between Kortrijk and Oudenaarde. He attacked one with his first bomb and cannon fire before turning his attention to the second. After making two runs, McClure failed to release the second bomb and strafed the locomotive with cannon. On his return journey, he saw an estimated twenty-five E- or R-boats off Dunkerque and climbed to report their position to his controller. Torrance took off a few minutes after McClure and on his way to the target saw a small group of E-boats north east of Oostende, one of which he bombed in a quarter stern attack from 200 feet. Torrance failed to see the results of his bombing as he flew through intense light flak from the ships and a few bursts of heavier flak from the shore. Barclay located a group of minesweepers off Dunkerque on his outward journey and bombed the leading ship from 100 feet in a dive from shoreward, but observed no results due to the intense and accurate light flak. Aubrey Smith found no trains on his sortie, but west of Gent saw a column of army trucks, some of which he thought were towing guns. He bombed in two separate attacks from fifty feet before making a further two passes with cannon and saw one of the trucks completely destroyed, another burning, a third blown on its side and others damaged.

After this night of intensive operations, Bryan and Brunet carried out a first-light shipping reconnaissance and flew at sea level from Gris Nez to Oostende and back, but saw nothing of importance and returned to Manston at 05:45. Poor weather prevented any further flying during the rest of the day and during daylight on 19 May. The squadron returned to operations on the evening of 19 May, the last night of the full moon period, and sent nine aircraft to attack airfields and two others to attack railway targets. Flying at 300 feet on his way to Amiens-Glisy airfield, Bryan encountered a Ju 88 head on and pulled up violently to starboard to avoid a collision. He turned sharply to attack, but the Ju 88 was lost down moon. He continued on to the target, bombed from 600 feet and saw his bombs explode close to two large buildings. The flak was intense but returned without being hit. Torrance and McClure were briefed to bomb Poix airfield, but were unable to find it and bombed railway tracks instead. Ashton arrived over Poix to find the flare path lit and an unidentified aircraft taking off. He dived and fired a three to four-second burst of cannon at the aircraft before dropping both bombs. Aubrey Smith also attacked Poix and saw his bombs explode near buildings and observed around fifteen dispersed aircraft on the airfield. De Houx orbited the area around Amiens-Glisy at 4,000 feet, but was unable to locate the airfield and therefore bombed Crécy-en-Ponthieu airfield, his bombs exploding among a group of buildings. Brunet found Amiens-Glisy and bombed from 200 feet, even though he was held by searchlights and subjected to intense flak. In thickening cloud and ground haze, neither Soulsby nor O'Neill located Poix airfield and bombed railway tracks near Gamaches on their return home. Sutherland and Roberts were briefed to look for trains in the Diksmuide and Kortrijk areas respectively. Sutherland failed to find trains and bombed two groups of barges south of Brugge. Roberts flew into a thick bank of fog from the east and returned to base before crossing the coast.

Due to poor weather, 137 Squadron carried out no operational flying and very little training during the following week. There were also substantial personnel changes. Coghlan had commanded the squadron for an extraordinary nineteen months and was posted to a staff position with 11 Group. His place as squadron commander was taken by John Wray. Dugdale, O'Neill and Robert Smith were posted out and three new Australian pilots, Sgt Pilot Alfred Emslie and Flight Sergeants John Gates and Clarence Neal, arrived. The squadron was called to readiness in the afternoon of 30 May for an attack on no less than thirty E-boats reported near Vlissingen, but a subsequent Typhoon sortie returned with the information that these were fishing boats.

On the evening of the 1 June, Wray led eight Whirlwinds on Ramrod 82 to dive bomb the railway yards at Eu with close escort provided by Spitfires of 167 and 485 Squadron (to which New Zealander Des Roberts was posted the following day after eight months with 137 Squadron) and escort cover by 401 Squadron. Two Spitfire squadrons were to provide top cover and a further six squadrons were briefed to perform three separate sweeps on support of the operation. The Whirlwinds rendezvoused with their escorts near Eastbourne, but the operation was abandoned when thick cloud down to 4,000 feet was discovered off the French coast.[328]

The next eventful operation took place early in the morning of 6 June when Wray and de Houx, escorted by two of 609 Squadron's Typhoons flown by Flt Lt Erik Haabjørn and FO 'Manu' Geerts, searched for shipping reported near Cap Gris-Nez. Off the French coast at Ambleteuse, they found a group of four minesweepers. Haabjørn attacked the leading vessel with a long burst of cannon fire from 800 yards closing to fifty yards after which it was bombed by Wray, his bombs observed by Geerts as direct hits. Geerts' attempt to attack the second ship was hampered when he found de Houx's Whirlwind in his sights. De Houx fired a five-second burst of cannon before releasing his bombs. He could not see the results of his bombing due to the intense light flak that slightly damaged his aircraft (P7055). All aircraft returned to base just over thirty-five minutes after taking off.[329]

There was no operational flying on 7-8 June, but the squadron learned that it was to move from Manston to Southend and to re-equip, not with the Typhoons it had been expecting, but with Hurricane IVs. The squadron duly moved to Southend on 12 June, but retained its Whirlwinds for the remainder of the full moon period and continued to operate with them over France. On the evening of 13 June, Bryan, McClure, Brunet and Ashton flew their Whirlwinds to Manston and took off shortly after 01:00 to attack Poix airfield. Bryan could not locate Poix and so dropped his bombs on railway wagons near Abbeville while the other three turned back before reaching the French coast due to unfavourable weather.[330]

Whirlwind P7055 served with both Whirlwind squadrons. P7055 flew in excess of 260 hours and was involved in several accidents between 24 March 1941 and 2 March 1943 when she failed to return from a sortie over France. Her No. 137 Squadron pilot, Sergeant Gerry Walker, was taken prisoner. (*Robert Bowater*)

On 14 June, the squadron moved six aircraft to Manston to operate against airfields and railway targets. Ashton, Brunet and Barclay took off just before 01:00 on 15 June to attack airfields at Poix, Amiens-Glisy and Abbeville respectively. Ashton eventually found Poix when the runway lights were suddenly switched on. He bombed in a dive from 8,000 to 700 feet and saw his bombs explode on the southern side of the runway. Ashton also fired a long burst of cannon fire at a taxiing aircraft and saw strikes nearby. Brunet could not locate Amiens-Glisy, but attacked a stationary freight train at Flixecourt with cannon fire and a bomb. On his return, he inadvertently strayed over Abbeville airfield and was greeted by accurate flak with minor damage to his aircraft (P7092). Brunet dropped his second bomb and saw it explode close to the runway. Barclay found thick cloud over the French coast and returned to base. The remaining three pilots set out to operate against trains at 02:25. McClure and de Houx bombed barges near Diksmuide and Roeselare while Bryan a train near Roeselare with cannon and bombs.[331]

The following day, the first Hurricanes were delivered, but the squadron sent six Whirlwinds to Manston from where five operated against airfields in the early hours of 16 June. Wray took off at midnight to attack Poix, but immediately after crossing the French coast at Cayeux saw a Fw 190 passing across in front of him. He pulled round to port and fired a one-second burst of cannon, but having pulled a tight turn at low speed (with bombs still on) and dazzled by the muzzle flashes of his own guns, could not claim a result and lost sight of the Focke-Wulf. He continued to the village of Poix, found no flak or airfield lighting and dropped his two bombs where he knew the airfield to be. McClure found and bombed Amiens-Glisy while Bryan and de Houx bombed Veurne airfield before separating. De Houx then attacked a tug and two barges on the Gent-Brugge canal while Bryan attacked two barges on the same canal before making three cannon attacks on a freight train. Brunet could not find the airfield at Veurne so bombed two barges on the Ieper canal, scoring a direct hit on one. All pilots experienced intense flak near the coast while crossing in both directions.[332]

11 Group sent out seventeen intruder sorties on the 17 June including eight Whirlwinds which took off at ten to fifteen minute intervals from midnight to 02:00 to attack the airfield at Poix. Six found and bombed the target but Brunet, en route to Poix, observed two E-boats off Quend-Plage, north of the Somme Estuary. He bombed the second boat and saw his bombs hit the water fifteen to twenty feet short. The boat turned through ninety degrees and stopped after which Brunet returned for a cannon attack. Barclay, who had returned from an earlier attempt due to an electrical failure, took off again at 02:00. He could not locate Poix, but attacked a stationary freight train in a siding near Rue during which the port fuel tank of his aircraft (P7111) was hit by flak.[333]

Lack of cloud cover prevented operations on 18 June, but six Whirlwinds moved to Manston the following evening to operate against airfields. De Houx and Luing went to Amiens-Glisy, Ashton and Barclay to Poix and Bryan and Brunet to Abbeville. All found and bombed their targets and returned safely. While Ashton and Barclay were bombing SKG10's forward base at Poix-Nord, a young German pilot was waiting on the airfield in his Fw 190 to take off with his colleagues for a fighter-bomber attack on Ramsgate. The Whirlwind pilots would meet him again later. A little after 03:00, while waiting with the other pilots in the Manston briefing room for Bryan and Brunet to return from Abbeville, John Wray heard the sound of an unfamiliar aircraft overhead and was told that a Fw 190 had landed on the airfield. Wray rushed out, detained the unsuspecting German pilot and cautiously moved the Focke-Wulf to a hangar. Uffz. Werner Öhne of 1./SKG 10 had taken off at 02:00, but facing weather that was far worse than forecast and with his radio unserviceable, became disoriented. Believing he was over France, Öhne jettisoned his bomb and made a perfect landing at Manston. He was the second SKG10 pilot to land in error there in a month: Uffz. Heinz Erhardt had arrived on 20 May to become the guest of 609 Squadron. Öhne's undamaged aircraft, Fw 190A-5

(WNr 2596), was flown to Farnborough the following day, given the RAF serial PN999 and extensively tested.[334]

137's Whirlwinds went to Manston for the last time on 21 June. Five aircraft, all armed with two 500-lb bombs, took off between 01:15 and 02:08 on 22 June to attack Poix airfield. Wray, Bryan, Luing and Ashton all found and bombed the target. Unable to find Poix despite a lengthy search, Barclay bombed a stationary freight train near Rue. On his return to Manston, the starboard throttle control failed in the fully open position and the engine soon lost power. Shortly afterwards, the port engine ran short of fuel – he had been airborne for nearly two hours – and Barclay landed, wheels up, in a field near the airfield. Barclay was unhurt, but P6993 was wrecked.[335]

With the end of the full moon period, 137 Squadron Whirlwind operations came to a close and 263 Squadron pilots collected the nine remaining, serviceable Whirlwinds from Southend. Those 137 Squadron pilots who had not yet done so went to the Specialised Low Attack Instructors School (SLAIS) at Milfield, Northumberland, to train on the Hurricane IV, rockets and 40-mm cannon that it could carry. 137 Squadron returned to operations on 23 July when Bryan, Brunet, Chalmers and Davidson staged successful train-busting sorties to Kortemark with their Hurricanes. July and August also brought news of the award of DFCs for McClure (by then posted to 263 Squadron as a flight commander), de Houx and Brunet and a second DFC for Bryan.[336]

No. 137 Squadron Whirlwind P6993 HE-A flown by F/L Mike Bryan demonstrates the aircraft to the press at RAF Snailwell on 5 March 1943. (*Robert Bowater*)

CHAPTER 14

Then There Was One

At the end of the full moon period, 137 Squadron ceased operations and transferred its nine serviceable Whirlwinds to 263 Squadron. This welcome increase in the number of aircraft available to 263 Squadron was offset by the loss of several of the unit's most experienced pilots: Holmes, Ridley and Lee-White left at the end of their operational tours. McClure arrived from 137 Squadron to replace Holmes as B Flight commander and new pilots, Flt Lt David Ross and FOs Robert Tuff and Eric Holman, joined the unit. With the training of the new pilots completed at Zeals, 263 Squadron returned to Warmwell on 12 July and returned to operational duties. July brought unseasonable weather and, other than six shipping searches, which all met shore-based flak but found no shipping, there was no operational flying. Poor weather and high winds made accidents inevitable and the new pilots wrecked two more Whirlwinds. Len Knott stalled while landing after an engine failure during the evening of 13 July. P7110 was wrecked and Knott severely burned in the ensuing fire, but made a full recovery. On 1 August, Peter Cooper bounced P6981 while landing in a strong crosswind. The aircraft dropped a wing into the ground and cartwheeled twice, losing both engines in the process. The aircraft then caught fire, but Cooper walked away unhurt.

After a typically uneventful shipping reconnaissance in the morning of 3 August, the squadron sent ten Whirlwinds to Predannack to stage an evening attack on Brest-Guipavas airfield. Eight of the Whirlwinds with a close escort of twelve Spitfire Vs of 453 Squadron and twelve Spitfire VIs of 616 Squadron were briefed to be over the target at 20:30. Twelve Spitfires of 610 Squadron were to be over the target at 4,000 feet eight minutes before the Whirlwinds to ensure local air superiority in advance of the attack followed by eleven Typhoons of 266 Squadron at 7,000 feet two minutes later. These were followed by twenty-four Spitfires of 165 and 131 Squadrons of the Exeter Wing at 10,000 feet. In addition, 302 and 317 Squadrons were to act as a freelance wing over the target at 16,000 feet two minutes after the Whirlwinds' attack.

Baker, Gray, Mercer, Beaumont, McClure, Graham Smith, Simpson and Coyne met their escorts over Predannack and flew at sea level before making a rapid climb to cross the French coast at 12,000 feet. The Whirlwinds then turned with their escorts to dive bomb the airfield from the south east from 13,000 to 7,000 feet. The explosions of six of the sixteen bombs dropped were seen within the airfield perimeter and four of these were among the buildings. Six Fw 190s were seen during and after the attack, one of which fired at one of the Whirlwinds during its dive, but there were no other combats and none of the Whirlwinds or escorts were damaged. The escort cover squadrons were less fortunate: 266, 610 and 131 Squadrons each lost an aircraft to the Fw 190s of JG2.[337] The Whirlwinds stayed at Predannack overnight and the following morning searched from Île d'Ouessant to Cap de la Chèvre, south of Brest. They failed to find shipping and returned to Warmwell.

On 8 August, the unit lost another experienced pilot when Jim Coyne, at the end of his operational tour and due for a rest, was replaced as A Flight commander by Ross.

Westland's Chief Test Pilot Harald Penrose poses Whirlwind P7110 for the camera of photographer Charles E. Brown. P7110 was delivered to 263 Squadron on 15 October 1941 and after 349 flying hours, she crashed at RAF Warmwell on 13 July 1943. (*Niall Corduroy*)

The E-boat Kings!

Under cover of darkness at 04:00 on 11 August, Korvettenkapitän Werner Lützow of the 4th Schnellbootflottille led four boats from his flotilla and three from the 5th Flotilla from Brest to the Aber Wrac'h in preparation for a mine-laying sortie off Plymouth that night. An earlier signal announcing his intentions was intercepted, decrypted, translated and distributed to the Operational Intelligence Centre in London by 03:08. Later that morning, 263 Squadron moved ten Whirlwinds to Predannack to mount an attack. By 09:30, Lützow's seven boats were anchored in the Aber Wrac'h, but his announcement of their safe arrival together with that of a Sperrbrecher was also quickly decrypted and distributed. Just before 03:00 and less than one hour after the distribution of the second signal, Baker, Ross, Proctor, Blacklock, McClure, Wood, Tebbit and Purkis took off to rendezvous over the airfield with their escorts of the Polish Portreath Wing led by Sqn Ldr Wienczyslaw Baranski. After crossing the Channel at sea level, Baranski recognised the target area and led the Whirlwinds and eight anti-flak Spitfires of 302 Squadron directly into the estuary while 317 Squadron climbed to 2,000 feet to cover the withdrawal of the attacking force.

In the estuary were seven schnellboote: five anchored mid-stream and another two, together with the Sperrbrecher, at the pier on the southern shore. The anti-flak Spitfires climbed, split into two sections and dived down to make their cannon attacks with the Whirlwinds following closely behind. Baker led Proctor, Ross and Blacklock to attack the ships close to the pier while McClure, Wood, Tebbit and Purkis targeted those midstream. The pilots claimed direct hits on the armed trawler and four of the schnellboote. A fifth schnellboot was seen burning. Flak from the shore was intense but there was little from the ships. A bullet hole in an engine nacelle of one of the Whirlwinds was the only damage. The Whirlwinds and their escorts reformed at Île Vierge and returned at sea level to Predannack. The attack was not quite as spectacularly successful as the squadron believed at the time, but the German boats had been hit hard. *S121* of the 5th Flotilla received a direct hit and quickly sank after its ammunition exploded with the loss of its captain and ten crew. *S84* and *S136*, also of the 5th Flotilla, were slightly damaged. Of the four boats from the 4th Flotilla, *S117* was severely damaged, two others lightly so and Lützow and a crewman on *S110* were slightly injured by splinters, although the boat was undamaged.[338]

The following day, 263 Squadron set off from Predannack to dive bomb Brest-Guipavas airfield escorted by the Ibsley Wing, but found dense cloud from 7,000 to 10,000 feet, fifteen miles off the French coast. The Whirlwinds and their close escort returned, but the three Spitfire and two Typhoon squadrons providing target cover continued on to the target and were engaged by Fw 190s returning without loss. As 263 Squadron's Intelligence Officer wryly noted, 'Whirlie-bait caused successful combats for the wing.' Later that night, the first of the full moon period, Simpson and Smith searched individually for shipping, but only found fishing boats.

An early morning reconnaissance by four Whirlwinds to the Channel Islands on 13 August was similarly uneventful and the only excitement was the arrival at Warmwell of the cameramen of British Movietone News to interview and film *The E-boat Kings*.[339]

Poor weather prevented daylight flying on 14 August, but an extensive programme of night-flying practice took place and Baker and McClure carried out individual shipping searches in the late evening. McClure failed to locate the enemy, but Baker, flying P7113, found an E-boat travelling fast from Jersey towards Guernsey. He attacked up moon from twenty degrees of the port beam and saw his bombs explode. While turning after his attack, McClure thought he saw two men swimming amid floating debris. Baker continued his patrol towards Île de Bréhat in deteriorating weather with low cloud and occasional rainstorms, but without encountering the enemy. Flying a few miles north of Guernsey on the return journey, he saw what he identified as a He 111 passing him on a parallel course 1,000 yards away and silhouetted against the moon. Baker turned and climbed beneath and slightly to port of the bomber to avoid being seen, closing slowly to 100-150 yards at which point he opened fire with a two-second burst. The port engine of the Heinkel burst into flames and the bomber made a shallow diving turn to port. Baker followed and fired again after which the aircraft crashed into the sea. Baker returned home to claim the Heinkel as destroyed, but the identity of the aircraft he attacked is uncertain.[340]

On 15 August, the squadron was asked to keep aircraft ready as fighters and removed the bomb racks from six Whirlwinds, but only two were scrambled. Simpson and Graham Smith were given numerous vectors on to an unidentified aircraft, but saw no sign of the enemy. In the mid-afternoon, eight Whirlwinds were bombed up for another attack on Brest-Guipavas airfield. Baker returned early with engine control problems, so Ross took the lead, but again the presence of solid cloud near the target forced the Whirlwinds and the thirty-five close-escort Spitfires to return. The Spitfires and Typhoons of the target cover and freelance wings continued on to the target where 266 Squadron lost three Typhoons and pilots to JG2.[341] That night, the squadron flew two shipping patrols. Other than some unusual flares, Tuff failed to find the enemy, but Beaumont mistook forts on the Cherbourg outer mole for ships and flew up moon to investigate. Unwittingly straying into the harbour, he found a number of barges and a coaster which he bombed. Inevitably, he attracted considerable attention from the harbour defences and did not stay to see the results of his attack.[342]

On 16 August, the squadron was asked to prepare fourteen Whirlwinds to move to Predannack at first light the following day, so the only operational flying were two uneventful night shipping searches. Before dawn the following morning, the aircraft moved to Predannack to mount another attack on Brest-Guipavas airfield. Following the period of intensive training flying, the squadron had twenty operational pilots and could now stage this type of operation on a larger scale. Twelve Whirlwinds took off just before 09:00 and met with twenty-two Spitfires of the Ibsley Wing as close escort and a further twenty of the Portreath Wing as escort cover, but were again forced to return from the French coast by dense cloud. Four shipping searches that night were also uneventful with the exception of that flown by Beaumont. He did not locate the enemy but experienced undercarriage problems on his return to Warmwell. He used the emergency blow down system to extend the undercarriage and flaps, but then the port engine failed. He jettisoned his bombs in a field near the airfield and made a successful single-engine landing.[343]

On 18 August, the pilots spent the morning searching local fields for Beaumont's bombs, but a number of them appear to have only found pubs. They also attended a farewell party for Coyne on 20 August, but there was no further operational flying until 21 August when Baker bombed a trawler off Cherbourg and observed a large explosion near its stern. With the full moon period over and the weather too poor for daylight rhubarb raids into France, the squadron performed convoy patrols until the end of August. During this period of enforced inactivity, the pilots became enthusiastic model makers with six Whirlwinds and a Hurricane built.[344]

Canadian F/L Jimmy Coyne climbs onboard a Whirlwind at RAF Warmwell in the summer of 1943. (*Niall Corduroy*)

Starkey – 'A Piece of Harmless Play Acting'

In early 1943, the Allies began planning an interlinked series of deception operations designed to persuade the Germans to retain forces in France, Norway and the Balkans, and thereby reduce the forces available to oppose both the Russians and the forthcoming invasion of Sicily. Among these was Operation Starkey, an amphibious operation against the French coast near Boulogne designed essentially as a deception operation, but intended to be followed through if the situation seemed promising. The Starkey plan was repeatedly diluted. The Admiralty was uneasy about deploying battleships in the confined waters of the Channel and much of the specialised shipping needed for a real amphibious operation was in the Mediterranean. The Admiralty was already committed for the invasion of Sicily and Italy, and neither the US 8th Air Force nor Bomber Command wanted to divert their forces from targets in Germany to support what Bomber Command leader Arthur Harris described as 'at best a piece of harmless play acting'.[345]

The air plan for Starkey was intended to be consistent with that for a real invasion and called for repeated attacks on coastal gun positions, airfields and transport infrastructure in the area of the 'bridgehead'. In total, 25,227 Starkey sorties were flown between 16 August and the abandonment of the operation on 9 September. 263 Squadron's Whirlwinds flew only twenty-four sorties out of this total so their contribution was but a minor one. The squadron flew fourteen Whirlwinds to Manston on the morning of 7 September in order to carry out Starkey Ramrod 42 on 8 September. In this three-part attack, nineteen Mitchells were to attack gun emplacements near Wimereux. The Whirlwinds were to bomb gun emplacements at Hardelot, just south of Boulogne, which would also be attacked by Typhoon bombers of 181 Squadron. The Whirlwind pilots were originally briefed for a low-level attack, but this was changed at the last minute to a dive-bombing attack. Baker, Beaumont, Proctor, Purkis, Ross, Todd, McClure, Heaton, Watkins, Williams, Wood and Cooper (the latter flying on his first operation) took off just after 17:00 on 8 September and flew to Hastings to meet their escort. Unfortunately, the orders for the escorts appear to have arrived late and there was confusion about the correct 'zero hour' for the operation. The eight Typhoons of 1 Squadron and a further eight of 609 Squadron (now led by ex-Whirlwind pilot Sqn Ldr Patrick Thornton-Brown) found no sign of the Whirlwinds at the rendezvous point and after waiting for twenty minutes, returned to base. The Whirlwinds had arrived earlier and went out alone. Unfortunately, Baker's aircraft suffered a propeller control failure and he turned back. Ross also turned for home as his radio was unserviceable and, unable to make radio contact with their section leader, Beaumont, Purkis and Todd followed him. Only Proctor of the first section joined up with the other six and carried on to the target. The seven

For Operation Starkey on 8 September 1943, the Whirlwinds of No. 263 Squadron had their noses painted white and sported black/white stripes beneath the wings for the three-day exercise. (*Robert Bowater*)

Whirlwinds dived from 14,000 to 5-7,000 feet and saw at least six bomb explosions in the target area. Flak was light and none of the Whirlwinds were hit. The eight Typhoons of 181 Squadron also bombed successfully seventeen minutes later.

The amphibious force was due to sail for Boulogne the following day. Overnight distinctive black and white identification markings were applied with temporary distemper to the Whirlwinds and other aircraft operating at low level close to naval forces. The pilots were up early for a briefing at 05:00. The morning's operations were repeated attacks on five groups of coastal gun batteries along an eight-mile stretch of the French coast straddling Boulogne. Most of the attacks were to be carried out by small forces of medium bombers and each target was to be attacked four times at roughly thirty minute intervals from 08:30. 263 Squadron's target were the gun positions at Hardelot that were to be attacked thirty minutes later by twelve Typhoons of 3 Squadron. Nos 1 and 609 Squadrons were briefed to provide escort. Baker, Blacklock, Ross, Tuff, Mercer, Holman, McClure, Handley, Purkis, Todd, Wood and Beaumont took off at 08:00, met their Typhoon escort over Hastings, and climbed to 14,000 feet over the Channel. Holman returned early due to faulty propeller controls, but the others reached their target and bombed in a dive down to 4,000 feet. The aircraft returned to Manston and were quickly refuelled and rearmed for a repeat attack, but the amphibious force had turned back as arranged and the second mission was not called for. During the day, the weather deteriorated and a planned attack on St Omer Longuenesse airfield later in the afternoon was cancelled while the Whirlwinds were taxiing out and 609 Squadron's Typhoons were warming their engines.[346]

Their work at Manston completed, a flight of Whirlwinds returned to Warmwell that evening. The others returned the following morning, but

Baker's aircraft (P7096) hit a ridge while landing and the port undercarriage collapsed. The following pilots diverted to Middle Wallop and waited there until the stricken Whirlwind had been removed from the runway at Warmwell. After their return, the remainder of the day was spent scrubbing off the temporary black and white markings, but heavy rain and storms prevented night operations.³⁴⁷ The weather remained poor for the next few days and only convoy patrols were flown. The squadron detached eight aircraft to Predannack for three days, but the bad weather prevented any operational flying. The squadron returned to night operations on 16 September with six shipping searches, but only two found targets. Baker was briefed to patrol from Cap de la Hague and down the eastern coast of the Cherbourg peninsula to Isigny. Between St-Vaast and Île Marcouf, he saw what he identified as a pair of E- or R-boats in front going south in line astern. He turned and bombed the leading boat up moon from the starboard beam from about fifty feet. Orbiting behind the boats, he made a cannon attack on the second boat. Baker saw the splashes of his shells hit the water and lifted the nose of his aircraft to bring his fire onto the target, but saw no strikes or damage.

Later that night, McClure flew a reconnaissance patrol of the Channel Islands area. Offshore of Guernsey passing Pleinmont Point, he also saw what he identified as two E- or R-boats ahead of him. In a shallow dive from 800 feet, he bombed the rearmost boat from astern and saw his bombs explode slightly astern and to the starboard of it. He was then illuminated by searchlights from the shore which, together with light flak from the boats, discouraged him from repeating an attack.³⁴⁸

Night Ranger

On the night of 17-18 September, the squadron played a leading role in a carefully planned operation intended to cut the Rennes-Brest railway line in ten separate places. Eight targets between Morlaix and Lamballe were assigned to 263 Squadron and the other two, further inland between Lamballe and Rennes, to 264 Squadron's Mosquitoes. Both squadrons would then return later that night and the following one to attack any trains stranded on the disrupted railway network. The Whirlwind pilots were briefed to cross the French coast at the nearest flak-free point to their objectives and not to be distracted by other targets on the way.

On 17 September, the squadron moved fourteen Whirlwinds to Bolt Head and eleven took off in rapid succession between 01:22 and 01:31 that night. Ross, Beaumont, Mercer, Heaton, McClure, Simpson and Smith operated individually while Baker, Purkis, Proctor and Blacklock were briefed to collectively attack the single most important target: the viaduct at le Ponthou.

Beaumont and Ross' targets were two small railway bridges to the west of Lamballe, but with the moon partly obscured by cloud, neither pilot found the bridges and so bombed nearby railway tracks. Heaton and Mercer were tasked with bombing two points on the line between Guingamp and St Brieuc. Heaton found the track where the line passed through the Forêt de Malaunay and bombed in two runs. During the second attack, Heaton saw a locomotive and strafed it with cannon fire. Mercer also found his target just to the north east of Plouvara and was confident that his bombs had fallen on or very close to the tracks. McClure and Simpson's targets were on the line between Guingamp and le Ponthou, but the starboard propeller of McClure's aircraft stuck in coarse pitch on take off and, rather than risk a night landing at the short airfield at Bolt Head, returned to Exeter. Simpson found his target to the east of Plouaret and bombed down the line although he was unable to see any specific results. Baker, Proctor and Blacklock found the viaduct at le Ponthou and bombed the tracks at both ends of it between 02:08 and 02:15, but Purkis crossed the coast too far west to reach the target and so bombed the line south west of Morlaix. Smith found and bombed the track between Morlaix and le Ponthou, the most westerly of the briefed targets. All pilots landed safely by 03:30, and although those attacking the targets at le Ponthou and near Morlaix had seen searchlights, none had experienced any flak. Before the others had returned, Holman and Watkins set off to look for trains on the same line. Holman found and bombed a train east of Plouaret and then made a second attack with cannon, but Watkins failed to locate trains and bombed the track west of Plouaret. 264 Squadron's three Mosquitoes also found and bombed their targets between Lamballe and Rennes. However, on the following day, south-west England was shrouded by fog and mist and all offensive operations by 10 Group were cancelled, including the planned follow up attacks on trains.[349]

On 21 September, the squadron sent nine Whirlwinds to Predannack for an attack on Brest-Guipavas, but both this and an anti-shipping operation from Bolt Head the following day were cancelled due to unsuitable weather. Meanwhile, FO Len Unwin and PO Alex Barr, two Canadian pilots who had joined the unit a few days earlier, flew the Whirlwind for the first time. The squadron resumed offensive operations on 23 September with Ramrod 85, a dive-bombing attack on Morlaix airfield. Late in the morning, eight Whirlwinds led by McClure and twelve Spitfires of 610 Squadron took off from Bolt Head. They flew at sea level before climbing to cross the French coast at 10,000 feet to the west of Île-de-Batz where the escorting Spitfires dropped their long-range tanks. The formation turned left towards its target and the Whirlwinds peeled off into their bombing dives. The bombing appeared to be good with explosions seen across the airfield and among buildings. Halfway down the dive at 8-9,000 feet and just after releasing his bombs, George

A Whirlwind makes a high-speed, low-level pass over the photographer. (*Robert Bowater*)

Wood's aircraft (P7113) was hit hard by flak and spiralled out of control. Wood was not observed to have bailed out of his stricken Whirlwind and was posted 'missing, presumed killed'.[350]

The squadron abandoned an attack on Brest-Guipavas airfield on 25 September due to dense cloud over the target area. Returning at 100 feet, many of the pilots jettisoned their bombs in the sea. Among them was Sgt Green (P7040). A few seconds later, his aircraft was rocked by an explosion in the sea, believed to have been caused by an acoustic mine detonated by either the bombs or the noise of his aircraft. The explosion damaged his starboard engine, but he made a successful single-engine landing at Warmwell.[351]

Poor weather prevented any further operational flying until the first week of October when the squadron flew abortive daytime shipping searches on 2, 4 and 7 October. The awards of a second DFC for Baker and a DFM for Simpson were also announced that week. With the beginning of a new full moon period, the squadron resumed night operations on 8 October with eleven sorties to hunt for shipping off the French coast. Baker and Holman took off first to search the Cap de la Hague-Isigny and Channel Islands areas respectively. Holman's patrol was uneventful, but Baker was repeatedly held by searchlights while patrolling the north coast of the Cherbourg peninsula. Near Île Marcouf, he found a ship up moon and ahead of him that he identified as either an E- or R-boat. Baker bombed it at mast height from thirty degrees astern, but did not see his bombs explode. He was again held by searchlights from the shore which he evaded by flying inland before returning to search for the ship. Unable to find it, he returned to Warmwell.

Blacklock and Heaton were next to take off on a shipping patrol. Blacklock failed to locate the enemy around the Channel Islands, but, while patrolling at 1,300 feet between Alderney and Cap de la Hague, Heaton saw tracer fire rising towards him from a ship down moon ahead of him. As he descended, he was the subject of shore-based flak batteries which hit his aircraft (P7097) and damaged the rudder controls. Heaton flew out towards Alderney and radioed to report the presence of a possible target before returning to Warmwell. Shortly after 22:00, Baker, Proctor, Tuff, Beaumont, Simpson, Mercer and Ross set off to attack the ship reported by Heaton. Off Cap de la Hague, Baker found a ship of around 2,500 tons heading towards Alderney. In dim moonlight and dense sea haze, Baker bombed the ship from ten degrees astern and saw the indistinct explosions of his bombs. Throughout his attack, Baker experienced concentrated and accurate fire from the ship and shore-based batteries. Because of the opposition and the deteriorating weather, Baker instructed the following pilots to abandon the operation and return to base. Dense fog had now descended at Warmwell and the Whirlwinds were diverted to Tangmere. Simpson reported that his starboard engine had failed and was jettisoning his bombs. He then reported that his other engine was overheating and losing power. His aircraft then crashed short of the runway killing Simpson instantly.[352]

The Blockade Runner

Night fog rolled in at Warmwell on the following four nights, but the squadron returned to operations on 13 October when Proctor and Mercer flew a night shipping reconnaissance in search of a very specific target: the blockade runner SS *Münsterland*. The blockade runners sailed unescorted between ports in occupied France and Japan bringing tin, manganese, tungsten, natural rubber and edible oils from Japanese-conquered territories in the east and taking machine tools, optics, chemicals and technical samples in the opposite direction. The SS *Münsterland* (6,408 GRT) had made just one blockade running voyage, arriving in Bordeaux from Kobe in May 1942 after three months at sea. She had remained in Bordeaux during the blockade running season of 1942-1943 and by October 1943, was one of nine ships in the Biscay ports available for a renewed blockade running programme during the coming winter. British intelligence kept a close watch on this fleet, but when the SS *Münsterland* left Bordeaux in the first week of October, she headed not for the Azores and the South Atlantic, but northwards for Brest. Her days as a blockade runner apparently over, she was to return to Germany either to refit or to join the Baltic trade.

The squadron searched again on the following three nights, usually without bombs in order to cover a larger search area, but found no sign of SS *Münsterland*, which, unknown to the British, had been docked at Brest since 9 October. On the night of 17-18 October, 263 Squadron took a temporary break from searching for the blockade runner to stage another pre-planned attack on railway targets. A first wave of aircraft were to cut the main line in five places between Caen and Cherbourg and the second wave would then search for trains on the disrupted network. Because the aim of the first group was to cause structural damage to railway bridges, its Whirlwinds were armed with 500 lbs rather than 250-lb bombs. Shortly after 02:20 on 18 October, Ross, Mercer, Todd, Baker, Cooper and Dunlop took off. Dunlop could not locate his target, a railway junction near Valognes, or a railway line, so he crossed the coast and jettisoned his bombs in the sea. Ross, Cooper and Todd found and bombed the railway bridge over the River Vire south west of Isigny-sur-Mer. Ross saw one of his bombs explode on the railway track at one end of the bridge. Cooper's were near misses on the riverbank, but Todd's were not observed.

Mercer's target was a railway bridge near Condé-sur-Seulles to the south east of Bayeux. He saw a train approaching and waited until it had reached the bridge. Mercer then bombed in a dive to 600 feet and saw one of his bombs fall short, probably in the river, but thought his other bomb may have hit the train. The train then stopped and Mercer made two cannon attacks, experiencing intense flak as he did so. Several of the pilots, including Mercer who was over twenty miles away at the time, saw a spectacular explosion away to the north west. This was Baker's work. At his briefed target, the tracks south east of Valognes, Baker had found a stationary train that he bombed in a dive down to 700 feet. The result was far beyond that normally expected from such an attack. A sheet of yellow flame followed by numerous green and white explosions led Baker to believe that he had hit a train carrying either ammunition or fuel. He then followed the line past Valognes and found another freight train on which he made two cannon attacks. Crossing back out over the French coast, he saw lighthouses on the Channel Islands illuminated so made a brief search for shipping on his return to Warmwell.

Beaumont, Proctor, Purkis and Blacklock formed the second wave and took off forty-five minutes after their colleagues. Beaumont, Proctor and Purkis failed to locate trains and bombed the railway tracks near Sottevast, Flottemanville and Brouay respectively. Also unable to bomb the enemy, Blacklock dropped his first bomb on the tracks near Le Molay-Littry. Continuing his patrol, he found a pair of adjacent stationary trains which he strafed with cannon fire and dropped his remaining bomb from seventy feet between the two trains. He then crossed the coast and off Îles Saint- Marcouf saw a small ship to his left and made an up-moon cannon attack in a shallow dive from 400 to

Rob Beaumont on the wing of a Whirlwind in the summer of 1943. (*Niall Corduroy*)

100 feet. He orbited and repeated the attack, then orbited again, but despite a bright moon and good visibility, could not locate the ship.[353] Twelve hours after the Whirlwind's attacks, a pair of 257 Squadron Typhoons found no shortage of trains in the Cherbourg peninsula and claimed to have damaged no less than seven locomotives as well as a steam excavator at a mysterious new construction site at Sottevast.

Later on 18 October, the squadron again moved four Whirlwinds to Predannack to resume the search for SS *Münsterland* that night, but strong winds prevented operational flying. In violent gales and pouring rain, the squadron returned to small scale operations on 19 October. Proctor and Dunlop went looking for trains in the Cherbourg peninsula and found two near Flottemanville. Both pilots made cannon attacks and Proctor dropped a bomb on one of the trains. While Dunlop was turning to make a further attack, a flak shell hit the starboard wing of his aircraft and severely damaged the aileron controls. The two Whirlwinds crossed back out over the coast at Quinéville and Proctor advised his controller that Dunlop was in trouble. Two Typhoons of 257 Squadron were sent out to escort the Whirlwinds back to Warmwell where Dunlop landed successfully, despite the damage to his aircraft's controls. Blacklock and Beaumont flew across the Channel in pouring rain to find perfect weather conditions in their patrol area along the railway between Bayeux and Saint-Lô. Flying west along the line, they spotted a long freight train a few miles north of Airel. Blacklock attacked the train with cannon from the rear before bombing it from abeam and then circled to make a further cannon attack. Beaumont bombed from astern before making two long cannon attacks from the beam. The pilots saw bomb explosions in one of the wagons, on the tracks in front of the train that then stopped, and in a field alongside the line. They returned to Warmwell in pouring rain and a 45 mph crosswind blowing directly across the runway. Beaumont landed safely, but Blacklock overshot slightly and, with no fuel for a second attempt, retracted the undercarriage to bring his Whirlwind to a halt before it ran into barbed wire at the edge of the airfield. Blacklock was unhurt and Westland repaired his aircraft on site.[354]

The poor weather persisted over the next few days and the next operational flying took place on 21 October when Ross, Holman, Tebbit and Gray took off in pairs to attack railway targets in the Cherbourg peninsula, but were recalled when a standing patrol of Luftwaffe fighters was detected off Cherbourg. They tried again in the late afternoon, but Tebbit and Gray returned off Pointe-de-Barfleur due to a lack of cloud cover. Ross and Holman, flying further west, found a freight train near Portbail and attacked the locomotive with cannon fire. They experienced accurate light flak, but neither aircraft was damaged.[355]

The following day, the same four pilots operated again. This time it was Ross and Holman who turned back because of insufficient cloud cover, but Tebbit and Gray continued on to the railway bridge over the River Vire, south of Isigny, that had been one of the primary targets for the operations of the night of 17-18 October. They bombed the bridge and saw three bomb

Pilot Officer Don Tebbit in the cockpit of No. 263 Squadron Whirlwind HE-C at Knighton Wood, RAF Warmwell. (*Robert Bowater*)

explosions: one a direct hit, one on the railway embankment and the third in the water under the bridge.[356]

On the afternoon of 22 October, SS *Münsterland* left Brest with a heavy escort and the British sent out an improvised and disparate force of the cruiser HMS *Charybdis* and six destroyers to intercept her. German radar detected the approaching British fleet and detached SS *Münsterland* out of harm's way. In poor visibility, the German escorts surprised the British and in a brisk torpedo action at around 01:30 on 23 October, sank HMS *Charybdis* and the destroyer HMS *Limbourne* before disengaging.

Warmwell was only semi-operational on 23 October due to waterlogging caused by previous heavy rain, but the squadron's Whirlwinds were prepared for a night attack on the SS *Münsterland* that had been discovered and photographed by the PRU at Lézardrieux that afternoon. The night passed without the attack being ordered and by the following morning the ship had set sail. At 08:00, twelve Whirlwinds set off to find her. The Ibsley-based Spitfires could not operate as their airfield was waterlogged, so 263 Squadron provided its own anti-flak force. Ross, Barr, Unwin, Holman, Mogg and Funnell flew as anti-flak aircraft with Baker, Proctor, Purkis, Watkins, Handley and Gray carrying bombs. Eight Typhoons of 257 Squadron provided rear cover. They searched from the Casquets to Barfleur but found no trace of the elusive ship. Nor did four reconnaissance sorties flown by other squadrons, but the PRU eventually found SS *Münsterland* in the heavily-defended inner harbour at Cherbourg.

10 Group quickly organised a high-level raid by B-25 Mitchells followed by low-level attacks by 263 Squadron's Whirlwinds and 183 Squadron's Typhoons. The twenty-four Mitchells were escorted by ninety Spitfires from the Ibsley, Perranporth and Churchstanton wings, and the first bombed from 12,500 feet at 15:20. Two or three of the thirty-seven bombs dropped were observed as near misses near the stern of SS *Münsterland* and another was a direct hit on a smaller ship to the west of the primary target. The second group of Mitchells found SS *Münsterland* obscured by cloud and therefore bombed another ship in the outer harbour instead. Several Mitchells were damaged by the intense flak, but no enemy fighters were seen.

Five minutes after the B-25s attack, the eight Whirlwinds, escorted by eight Typhoons of 257 Squadron, approached the target. The Whirlwinds flew just above sea level in two groups of four in line abreast. Baker led the leading section (Proctor, Mercer and Williams) with Ross, Gray, Beaumont and Cooper about 650 yards behind. Approaching Cherbourg, the Typhoons climbed to 12,000 feet over Querqueville while the Whirlwind pilots turned and headed directly into the harbour. Ahead of them they could see SS *Münsterland* moored at the Digue du Homet with two smaller ships astern of her. There were six other vessels identified as minesweepers in one of the other docks.

Baker, Proctor and Mercer of the first section and Gray of the second bombed SS *Münsterland* and Baker also fired a short burst of cannon fire at it. Due to the swirling mass of aircraft ahead of them, Ross and Beaumont fired at and bombed the ship immediately behind SS *Münsterland* while Williams and Cooper bombed the third ship in the row. The Whirlwinds climbed to clear the ships' masts and then hugged the sea. While doing so, Beaumont fired a short burst of cannon at two of the six smaller ships. As the Whirlwinds attacked, the Typhoons of 257 dived down to sea level, passed the target area from west to east and reported seeing two bomb explosions forward of SS *Münsterland*'s funnel and a fire further aft. Crossing the harbour, the Whirlwind pilots were subjected to intense flak, described by Beaumont as 'like a horizontal hailstorm with the hailstones painted red' and all eight aircraft were hit.

As they left the target area, the other pilots saw the starboard engine of Len Gray's aircraft (P6979) smoking heavily. Gray dropped out of formation, force landed in open country near Digosville and became a prisoner of war. Mercer radioed to say that he had been hit over the target but was okay. Mercer stayed with the others, but, as they crossed out over the coast, Baker saw Mercer flying at 150 feet, well above the others and radioed to ask if he was in trouble. Seconds later, Mercer's aircraft (P6986) was hit by a burst of flak from a position at St Vaast. The Whirlwind's starboard wing dropped and the aircraft hit the sea 200 yards offshore and disintegrated, leaving little hope that Mercer could have survived. A number of 257 Squadron's Typhoons returned to search the area but saw no sign of him. Mercer was the last pilot to lose his life in a Whirlwind.

Ross' Whirlwind was also hit over the target. The starboard wing was so badly damaged that he could only keep the aircraft level by bracing his right elbow against the cockpit sidewall in order to force the control column fully left. He broke away and crossed the coast at Réthoville escorted by two 257 Sqn Typhoons. Reaching Warmwell, he found that the starboard wing juddered and stalled at 180 mph and decided that a wheels-down landing was 'unwise'. Instead, he made a perfect high-speed belly landing. He was unhurt but P6974 was beyond repair. The starboard undercarriage of Cooper's aircraft (P7040) was also damaged by flak and collapsed on landing at Warmwell. The other four aircraft suffered only superficial damage although Baker was slightly cut and bruised by fragments of the shattered canopy of his aircraft. Eleven minutes after the Whirlwind's attack, four Typhoons of 266 Squadron flew a low-level reconnaissance over Cherbourg and reported fires on SS *Münsterland* with smoke visible from ten miles away. However, the eight Typhoons of 183 Squadron, which attacked about forty-five minutes after the Whirlwinds, saw no damage or fires. The Typhoons were carrying 500-lb bombs and, to reduce the risk of damage to the aircraft by the shock wave of their own bombs, fused for an eleven-second delay. This made it difficult for the pilots to observe the results of their bombing, but were confident that they had achieved some direct hits. However, the cost was high: three Typhoons and pilots, including the unit's commanding officer, were lost to flak over the target.[357]

With only a handful of serviceable aircraft available, 263 Squadron carried out very little flying over the next few days. On 28 October, the squadron struck SS *Münsterland* that was moored in dry dock inside the heavily-defended port. Ramrod 96 was a multi-part operation involving heavily-escorted Mitchells, Whirlwinds and Typhoons. The first element of the operation consisted of eighteen Mitchells escorted by five squadrons of Spitfires and the Typhoons of 257 Squadron. A few minutes before the Mitchells were due to bomb, sixteen Typhoons of 193 and 266 Squadrons, providing target cover, began the first of four sweeps across the Cotentin peninsula, but saw no enemy aircraft. The Mitchell attack ran into problems from the beginning. Just three arrived on time at the rendezvous and set course for the target with the escort cover squadrons, and another twelve arrived late of which six flew on to the target unescorted. Thus only nine of the bombers bombed the target and one was shot down by flak with the loss of its Dutch crew.

The eight Whirlwinds were next to attack. Baker, Mogg, Watkins, Handley, Ross, Beaumont, Purkis and Proctor were briefed to dive bomb the target rather than the low-level bombing approach used four days earlier. The rapid changes in altitude and high-speed exit from the target area provided a degree of protection from flak at the expense of bombing accuracy. The Whirlwinds reached their rendezvous at Portland Bill a few minutes late, but met with their escorting Spitfires of 610 Squadron over the Channel to be over the target at 12,000-13,000 feet exactly on time at 14:52. They dropped their 500-lb bombs in seventy-degree dives from the south west to the north east, pulling out at 7,000 feet. Flak was pummelling the delayed Mitchells and no Whirlwinds were hit. All of the bomb explosions seen were within a 500-yard radius of Bassin Napoleon III including some on warehouses, but neither the Whirlwind pilots nor those of the Typhoons of 183 Squadron, which attacked four minutes later, claimed to have hit SS *Münsterland*. 610 Squadron's Spitfires orbited just off the coast during the bombing and dived after the Whirlwinds as they left the target area.[358]

A repeat attack the next day was cancelled because of unsuitable weather over the target, but on 30 October, 10 Group staged Ramrod 99 in which 263 and 183 Squadrons were again to attack SS *Münsterland* while Douglas A-20 Havocs of the US 9th Air Force attacked Maupertus airfield. 263 Squadron had just seven serviceable Whirlwinds. Baker, Heaton, Snalam, Green, Proctor, Holman and Dunlop set off at 15:00 escorted by 610 Squadron's Spitfires. Snalam's aircraft lost a bomb ten miles off the English coast and Baker ordered him to return to Warmwell. The six remaining Whirlwinds experienced intense flak while crossing the French coast at Querqueville, some exploding between the aircraft, before turning to bomb from the south west. Baker dived too early and the others levelled out at 12,000 feet and then recommenced their attacks. Even at 7,000 feet when they released their bombs, all pilots were subjected to intense and accurate flak, so Baker continued to dive to 5,000 feet. The 263 Squadron pilots saw two of their bombs explode in the dry dock area and pilots of 183 Squadron observed a further cluster of Whirlwind bombs explode on warehouses west of the dry dock. Despite the intense flak, Dunlop's aircraft (P7108) was the only one damaged, albeit only slightly.[359]

A Fitting End

The squadron performed no operations during the first few days of November and further attempts to attack SS *Münsterland* were cancelled on 4-5 November due to unsuitable weather. On 1 November, however, the squadron learned that George Wood, assumed to have been killed in the attack on Morlaix airfield on 23 September, was not only alive, but back in England. Unseen by his colleagues, Wood parachuted from his disintegrating Whirlwind and landed in trees on the northern edge of the airfield. With no time to hide or bury his parachute, he ran north west and far away as possible to avoid German patrols and the local population. When darkness fell, he tried to cross the Dossen River to reach a convent where he thought he could get help, but sank up to his waist in mud and turned back. He walked back towards Morlaix to a farm that had previously seen Germans searching earlier. Wood was making himself comfortable in a barn when he was discovered at dawn by the farm owner who offered him food, civilian clothing and hid him in a haystack. Over the next month, Wood was moved from one hiding place to another until 30 September where he and six Frenchmen slipped away from Carentec by boat for Plymouth. By daybreak on 31 September, they were sufficiently far away from the coast to start the engine and in the late afternoon, Wood recognised the familiar shape of the Eddystone Lighthouse. Shortly afterwards, they were found by the British minesweeping trawler HMS *Loch Park* and taken to Plymouth.[360] Wood rejoined his squadron in January 1944 and was rested a year later.

On 6 November, the first night of the full moon period, 263 Squadron sent out two pairs of aircraft on shipping patrols. No shipping was found, but Heaton, while passing Cherbourg at fifty feet, was surprised to find flak firing not at him, but at an aircraft flying straight and level with its navigation lights on to the east of the city. He speculated that it was an aircraft of a Bomber Command OTU that was lost. The squadron spent much of the following day searching unsuccessfully for a 257 Squadron Typhoon pilot who had parachuted into the sea early that morning following an engine failure, but that evening four pilots went looking for shipping. Dunlop returned early due to Exactor control problems, Baker and Ross abandoned their sorties due to dense cloud and Proctor found nothing of interest during his patrol of the Channel Islands. On 8 November, heavy mist ruled out any operational flying and on the following night, only one of six shipping searches flown from Warmwell and Predannack found anything. Douglas Mogg thought he saw six ships a few miles offshore south west of Jersey. Intense flak between him and the ships prevented him from investigating further and as he was unsure of what he had seen, returned home without transmitting a sighting report.[361]

On the morning of 10 November, Ross led Proctor, Snalam and Cooper to attack shipping reported between Guernsey and Herm. The Ibsley Wing provided eight anti-flak Spitfires and another eight as escort. Approaching Guernsey at sea level, the formation climbed to obtain a better view down the Little Russel Straight. They saw no ships, but found two tugs and a small cargo ship north west of the island steaming towards St Peter Port. Following close behind the anti-flak aircraft, Proctor fired at the leading tug and achieved two near misses off the port bows with his bombs. Snalam and Cooper bombed the second tug: Snalam's bombs fell just off the stern, but Cooper's were not seen. As one of the anti-flak Spitfires attacked the small cargo ship, Ross also bombed it. He did not see his bomb explosions but thought that he 'couldn't have missed'. The flak was, as usual, intense but only a single Whirlwind was slightly damaged.[362]

That night, the squadron sent out the usual pair of shipping searches. Watkins' patrol around the Cotentin peninsula was uneventful, but Sturgeon found a group of four or five armed trawlers four miles south east of Sark. He climbed and tried to report the ships' position, but could not contact his controller. With the moon largely obscured by patchy cloud, Sturgeon searched for the ships and eventually bombed one of them from 300 feet, but was unable to see the results of his attack. Although Sturgeon had been unable to contact his controller, Watkins, who was searching near Îles Saint-Marcouf, heard his transmission and passed the report on. Four more Whirlwinds were prepared to attack the convoy and Baker took off with Purkis, Green and Cooper following behind. After reaching the target area, Baker told his fellow pilots that the navigational beacons at Alderney, Sark and St Peter Port on Guernsey were all lit and briefed each pilot on his individual search area. There was no sign of the convoy reported by Sturgeon and Baker was the only pilot to locate shipping. He observed a small trawler south west of Sark that he bombed from the port beam at mast height. Baker saw his bombs explode alongside the trawler and continued over Sark before returning to search for the ship again, but it had eluded him. Having not found targets of opportunity, the other three pilots jettisoned their bombs into the sea and set course for home with Baker.[363]

The following night, Proctor and Todd patrolled from Île de Batz to Île d'Ouessant and on to Brest without encountering the enemy. However, Tuff, patrolling from Cap de la Hague around the Cotentin peninsula to Îles Saint-Marcouf, found two tugs entering Cherbourg Harbour. He climbed to 1,000 feet to radio Holman who was patrolling west of Guernsey. Tuff then dived and bombed the rearmost tug from the starboard stern quarter, but his bombs overshot, although one was a near miss. When Holman reached Cherbourg, there was no sign of the tugs which, it was assumed, had by now reached the safety of the harbour.[364]

No operational flying took place on 12 November, but Holman, Medical Officer Peter Green and one of the ground crew were injured at Biggin Hill in a landing accident in the squadron's Airspeed Oxford (T1058). The aircraft swung violently in a strong crosswind, clipped the propeller of a parked Typhoon, tearing off the Oxford's port flap and collided with a building and burst into flames. Holman and his passengers all recovered, but the Oxford was written off.[365]

In October, 263 Squadron's establishment was increased from twelve to sixteen aircraft (plus two reserves), but as there were only twenty-six surviving Whirlwinds and these were being regularly damaged in intensive operations, it was becoming impossible to maintain this level of availability. Therefore, on 15 November, the squadron received the inevitable news that it was soon to be re-equipped with Typhoon bombers.[366]

Early in the morning of 15 November, poor weather forced Green to return home off Île d'Ouessant while on a shipping reconnaissance to Brest, and that night Watkins and Green flew uneventful shipping searches around the Brest area. Bad weather prevented any operations that night by the seven Whirlwinds that the squadron had moved to Ibsley. The seven aircraft returned to Warmwell on 16 November, but persistent bad weather prevented any operational flying for the following week. Operations restarted early on 25 November when four Whirlwinds took off at 08:30 to perform an uneventful escorted shipping reconnaissance of the Channel Islands and on towards St-Malo before turning for home. The squadron also received the good news that Len 'Friar' Gray reported missing on 24 October during the attack on SS *Münsterland* was alive, albeit as a prisoner of war.

At midday, the squadron made a further attempt to attack SS *Münsterland*, but turned back when they found thick cloud over Cherbourg. They went out again just before 16:00 escorted by the Ibsley Wing and although Todd returned early, Baker, Graham Smith, Snalam, Mogg, Ross, Barr and Tebbit found sufficient gaps in the clouds over Cherbourg through which to bomb. They bombed in very steep dives from south west to north east from 12,500 feet and released their 500-lb bombs at 7,000 feet. Flak was intense, accurate and superficially damaged some of the Whirlwinds. Four explosions were seen close to the target and two more in the dry dock at the north end of the Bassin Napoleon.[367]

On the morning of 26 November, the Whirlwinds mounted another attack on SS *Münsterland*. Baker, Barr, Snalam, Williams, Ross, Unwin, Tebbit and Todd, together with eleven Spitfire Vs of 610 Squadron, took off from Warmwell shortly before midday and flew at sea level before climbing rapidly to cross the French coast at 12,000 feet. While the escorting Spitfires orbited near Querqueville, the Whirlwinds turned and bombed although two pilots had a bomb hang up. Some pilots continued their dives down to 4,000 feet and headed out to sea where escorting Spitfires rejoined them. At least eight bomb explosions were seen within 300 yards of the target and others around No. 5 Dry Dock. Again, flak caused superficial damage to the aircraft.[368] Although damaged in these attacks, SS *Münsterland* was repaired by the end of December, sailed to Boulogne and then left for Dunkerque on the night of 19 January. Early the following morning, her luck finally ran out when she was detected by British radar and engaged by coastal artillery batteries. Repeatedly hit and with both engines out of action, she ran aground in fog off Sangatte and later sank. 198 and 609 Squadrons had been briefed to attack her at daybreak, but by the time they arrived the ship had sunk and used the still-visible superstructure for cannon and rocket-target practice.

Martinvast

After its final attack on SS *Münsterland*, 263 Squadron mounted another bombing operation, but against a very different target. Located near Couville and two miles south west of Martinvast (by which name the target was usually known), this was one of a handful of large construction sites that had been detected on the French coast in addition to the large number of standardised 'ski' sites. Thought to be associated with a German secret weapons programme, even if its exact purpose was at the time unclear, Couville was intended as a storage and assembly site for the V2 rocket. In late July, photoreconnaissance revealed the start of work at Couville and by early September, showed a railway spur joining the site to the main Cherbourg-Valognes line. Marauders and Typhoons attacked the site on 11 November and on 25 November, while 263 Squadron was preoccupied with SS *Münsterland*, it was hit again by ninety-one Typhoons. On 26 November, Couville was attacked five times by Bostons, Mitchells, Typhoons (twice) and 263 Squadron's Whirlwinds.

Escorted by 610 Squadron's Spitfires, Baker, Snalam, Ross, Mogg, Smith, Tebbit, Dunlop and Tuff crossed into France (the last time a Whirlwind would do so) at Flamanville at 12,500 feet. They met intense flak all the way from the coast to the target where they turned to bomb from east to west. Bomb explosions were seen in the target area, but flak inflicted minor damage on all eight aircraft and Mogg, flying P7046, was obliged to return on one engine. The formation crossed out to sea near Surtainville and all aircraft returned safely to land at Warmwell at 16:50.[369]

High winds and heavy rain prevented most operational flying for the remainder of the month although Baker, Mogg, Snalam and Blacklock flew a patrol on 29 November to search for mine-destroying Junkers Ju 52s of 1/ Minensuchgruppe 1 believed to be operating off the Normandy and Brittany coasts. 10 Group had ordered these patrols under the codename 'Haunch' on two previous occasions without success and 263 Squadron's patrol ran into violent rainstorms and dense cloud down to sea level. Unsurprisingly, neither the Whirlwind pilots nor those of the escorting Ibsley Wing saw anything of interest. The four Whirlwinds returned to Warmwell just before 11:00 at the end of what turned out to be the last operational Whirlwind sortie.[370]

Despite the number of aircraft damaged during the intensive operations during November, 263 Squadron had twelve serviceable Whirlwinds, but on 2 December, the first Typhoons were delivered. A Flight's diarist noted that '...with their shiny new paint and fittings they rather make the old faithful Whirlwinds look a trifle shabby. Still, the latter have given stout service. The squadron have been very pleased to fly them.'[371] To mark the end of the aircraft's three-and-a-half year career with the unit, Westland treated 263 Squadron to a party on 3 January 1944 and the following morning, twelve hung-over pilots performed a flypast over the factory where the aircraft had been designed and built. Despite some harsh words of encouragement over the radio from Baker, 'Three incredibly crooked lines of Whirlwinds staggered over Yeovil.'[372] On 5 January, Reg Baker was posted out, the squadron moved to Ibsley to begin training with Typhoons and Geoff Warnes returned to command the unit for a second time. The squadron took six Whirlwinds to Ibsley for possible night operations, but they were never called upon. With improving weather on 12 January, the squadron began a period of intensive flying training and returned to the offensive with its Typhoons on 3 February with an operation to dive bomb a very familiar target: Maupertus airfield.

On 1 January, the Whirlwind was formally declared obsolescent and to be used only for non-operational flying.[373] Work on three aircraft being repaired at Westland was suspended and 263 Squadron's fourteen Whirlwinds were flown to 18MU at Dumfries over the next two months, joining two others that were already there. No non-operational use was ever found for them and in July, the stored aircraft were classed as non-effective airframes. The sixteen aircraft were formally struck off charge in September, but remained in open storage at 18MU's Lennoxlove satellite landing ground where they were joined by the Whirlwind's bigger brother, the unloved Welkin high-altitude fighter. In 1946, Airwork and General Trading were contracted to scrap the aircraft which were then cut up and smelted. One aircraft escaped this fate. P7048 was sent to Westland for repair in May 1943 and retained by the company. It was later purchased by Westland, registered G-AGOI and used as a 'hack' aircraft. At the end of its working life, the engines were removed to drive helicopter rotor test rigs. The airframe was dismantled and buried at Yeovil, but was later exhumed and disposed of properly after concerns were raised that the buried wreckage was polluting ground water.

G-AGOI was used after the war as a company runabout. She had served with No. 137 Squadron as P7048. She was eventually scrapped around 1951 and her remains are said to be buried at the Westland factory in Yeovil. Her Rolls-Royce engines were used in jigs to test helicopter rotor blades. (*Robert Bowater*)

Operational Requirement F.37/35

Amended requirements for Single-Engine,
Single-Seat Day and Night Fighter
Specification F.37/35 – APPENDIX 'B'

General

The Air Staff require a single-engine[374], single-seat, day and night fighter which can fulfil the following conditions:

- Have a speed in excess of the contemporary bomber of at least 40 mph at 15,000 ft.
- Have a sufficient number of forward-firing 20 or 23-mm calibre guns to effect a decisive result in a short space of time and from longer ranges than is possible with machine guns.

It is considered that the practice of mounting one cannon on the engine which is becoming customary in other countries offers insufficient chances of obtaining decisive results in the time and conditions visualised for air fighting, and in order to improve on this it is considered that provision should be made for at least four of these guns.

Performance

- Speed. The maximum possible and not less than 330 mph at 15,000 ft at maximum power with the highest speed possible between 5,000 and 15,000 ft.
- Climb. The best possible to 20,000 ft but secondary to speed and hitting power.

- Service Ceiling. Not less than 30,000 ft is desirable.
- Endurance. Quarter of an hour at maximum power at sea level plus 1 hour at maximum power at which engine can be run continuously at 15,000 ft. This should provide half an hour at maximum power at which the engine can be run continuously (for climb, etc.), plus 1 hour at its most economic speed at 15,000 ft (for patrol), plus quarter of an hour at maximum power at 15,000 ft (for attack). To allow for possible increase in engine power during the life of this aircraft, tankage is to be provided to cover ¼ hour at maximum power at sea level plus 1¼ hours at maximum power at which engine can be run continuously at 15,000 ft.
- Take off and landing. The aircraft to be capable of taking off and landing over a fifty-foot barrier within a distance of 600 yards. An extension to 700 yards might be accepted if the resulting increase of speed justified the extension.

Armament

Four 20 or 23-mm calibre guns to be located outside the airscrew disc. Reloading in the air is not required and the guns should be fired by pneumatic, electrical or means other than Bowden wire. It is important that rigidity of the mountings when firing is given great attention in design. It is contemplated that some or all of these guns should be mounted to permit a degree of elevation of and traverse with some form of control from the pilot's seat. Though it is not at present possible to give details, it is desirable that designers should be aware of the possibility of this development, which should not, however, be allowed to delay matters at this stage.[375] Ammunition: a minimum of sixty rounds per gun.

View

The upper hemisphere must be, so far as possible, unobstructed to the view of the pilot to facilitate search and attack. A good view for formation flying is required, both for formation leader and flank aircraft and for night landing. A field of view of about 10° downwards from the horizontal line of sight over the nose is required for locating the target.[376]

Handling

A high degree of manoeuvrability at high speeds is not required but good control at slow speeds is essential. A minimum alteration of tail trim with variations of throttle settings is required. The aircraft must be a steady firing platform.

Load Factors

- Factors throughout the structure with the centre of pressure in its most backward[377] position in normal flight: 10.0
- Factors throughout the structure with the centre of pressure in its most backward position in horizontal normal flight: 7.5
- Other factors as normally called for in Specifications for Service aircraft and in AP970

Special Features and Equipment

- Enclosed cockpit
- Cockpit heating
- Night-flying equipment
- R/T
- Oxygen for 2½ hours
- Guns to be easily accessible on the ground for loading and maintenance
- Retractable undercarriage and tailwheel permissible
- Wheel brakes
- Engine starting – If an electric starter is provided, a ground accumulator will be used with a plug-in point on the aircraft. An accumulator for this purpose is not required to be carried on the aircraft. The actual starting must be under the control of the pilot. In addition hand-turning gear is required

The Whirlwind Uncovered

Fuselage

The fuselage consisted of two distinct sections: the cockpit section and the rear fuselage with integral fin. The cockpit structure comprised of two longerons and three main frames: the 9-mm armour steel front bulkhead (bolted to the main wing spar), an angled frame supporting the instrument panel and the bulkhead behind the pilot's seat. The base plate carrying the cannon was attached to the front of the cockpit section and a crash pylon consisting of a steel tube tripod topped by a magnesium casting was provided to protect the pilot if the aircraft overturned on the ground. A large removable panel immediately in front of the windscreen provided access to the main electrical terminal blocks, the back of the instrument panel and the fluid reservoir for the windscreen de-icing system.

With just three widely-spaced formers and minimal longitudinal stiffening, the Whirlwind's thickly-skinned rear fuselage more closely approached a true monocoque than its contemporaries. The skinning consisted of ten tapering, hand-rolled strips of 2-mm thick magnesium alloy joined by slender T-section duralumin extrusions. Additional stiffening was provided by longitudinal channel-section stiffeners in the most forward bay where the rear fuselage joined the cockpit section and bending stresses were greatest.

Wing

The Whirlwind's wing was constructed as a single piece centre section and two outer panels. The centre section contained the oil and coolant radiators inboard of the engine nacelles and the fuel tanks (outboard of the nacelles). A single main spar extended the full span of the centre section and two auxiliary spars extended out as far as the nacelles. The portions of all three spars between the nacelles and the fuselage were of open, Warren-truss construction to allow air to flow freely through the radiator duct. The detachable panels allowing access to the radiators were fully stressed (as were some of those on the top surface of the nacelles) and required the engine to be supported with a jack before the panels were removed in order to avoid distorting the structure. Each wing contained three coolant radiators and a single, smaller, oil cooler. The fuel tanks, outboard of the nacelles, were detachable but also formed part of the wing structure and their external surfaces formed the outer skin of the wing.

The construction of the outer wing sections was conventional with a single spar (bolted to the centre section), nine ribs, a false spar or aileron screen at the trailing edge and a detachable wingtip. The nacelles consisted of a framework of steel and duralumin tubes built forwards from the main spar to provide the four mounting points for the engine and attachment points for the undercarriage legs. The engine coolant and oil tanks were mounted behind the engine in the roof of the nacelle.

Flying Controls

All flying control surfaces were alloy-covered, fully-shrouded at their leading edges and operated by single push-pull tubes rather than pairs of cables. The aileron control tubes ran out through the wing along the base of the rear spar via conduits that passed through the rear fuel tanks and were of streamlined cross section where they passed through the radiator duct. These tubes were originally made of aluminium alloy, but the rudder and aileron tubes were replaced with steel ones on aircraft from P7095 onwards and retrofitted to earlier aircraft. Because the rudder was controlled by a single tube, its hinge was not on the centreline, but offset to starboard. Early flight testing revealed not only that the rudder was ineffective at small angles and heavy at larger ones, but also that rudder loads were not symmetrical. To address these problems the rudder was enlarged, a prominent horn balance added and to compensate for the asymmetric loading, and the rudder skin on the port side was given a concave profile. Pilot-controllable trimming tabs were fitted to the rudder and to the starboard elevator, the port elevator tab being fixed at the factory. Balance tabs were fitted to both ailerons with a servo action to reduce control loads. These were not controllable by the pilot, but were ground adjustable to compensate for any tendency for the aircraft to fly with one wing low.

Large, long-travel slats were fitted to the outer wing panels. Aerodynamic forces operated the slats entirely automatically and they would normally be closed when the aircraft was at rest on the ground. The slats were fitted with dampers to ensure that they opened smoothly and were interconnected by a torque tube to ensure symmetrical operation. A series of Whirlwind and Hampden slat failures in early 1941 prompted a review of the safety of fully automatic slats as a result of which Whirlwinds from P7054 onwards were delivered with the outer slats locked shut and earlier aircraft were modified in the field. The large, single piece Fowler flap extended from aileron to aileron giving a flap area of 42.3 square feet or around 17 per cent of the total wing area. The flap was operated by hydraulic jacks mounted in the rear of the engine nacelles and was interconnected with the inner slats and cooling flaps on the upper surface of the trailing edge.

Armament

All operational Whirlwinds were armed with four Hispano Mk 1 cannon with sixty-round drum magazines (although for reliability, the magazines were often not loaded to maximum capacity). To obtain the most compact installation, the guns were slightly inclined outwards to provide clearance for their magazines. The guns were mounted on a light fabricated alloy base plate braced to the front bulkhead by tubular steel braces. A machined alloy casting supported the front mountings of the guns which, in the Hispano's case, took all the recoil loads.

The gun installation was covered by a detachable cowling attached to the fuselage on early aircraft by multiple fasteners at its rear edge. To reduce rearming times, the cowling was redesigned so that it was located at its rear end by pins and fixed at the front by a single large captive nut. At the same time the cowling was stiffened to reduce its susceptibility to blast damage from the guns. The cannons were cocked and fired hydraulically on the first four production Whirlwinds and pneumatically on subsequent aircraft using a compressed air bottle mounted between the cannon. Spent cartridge cases were retained in a streamlined container mounted under the nose and incorporating louvered doors to exhaust explosive gun gases from the nose. A smaller fairing, offset to starboard, contained a G.42B gun camera. The cannons were usually loaded with alternating pairs of ball and high explosive/incendiary (HE/I) shells until late 1942 when semi-armour piercing/incendiary (SAPI) rounds replaced the ball ammunition.

Whirlwinds were fitted with the Barr and Stroud GM2 gunsight, officially referred to as the 'Fixed Gun Reflector Sight, Mk II'. In 1941, these were replaced by the Mk II with a rectangular reflector replacing the circular reflector glass that caused optical distortion. The mechanism was identical and sights were upgraded on squadrons simply by changing the sighting head. Although all operational Whirlwinds were fitted with this sight, P6997 was briefly tested in 1941 with a Mk 1 Gyro gunsight.

Hydraulics

All main systems in the Whirlwind were operated by high-pressure hydraulics powered by a pump on the starboard engine: flaps (which were interconnected with the radiator shutters and the inner slats), wheel brakes and undercarriage. A hydraulic accumulator mounted in the fuselage immediately behind the cockpit provided a reservoir of hydraulic pressure to meet short term demands that could not be supplied immediately by the pump. In the event of hydraulic system failure or if the starboard engine failed, a hand pump was provided to enable the undercarriage and flaps to be operated. A compressed air backup system was provided for use in an emergency to extend the undercarriage and operate the flaps. The engine and propeller controls, fuel cocks and landing lamp pivots were controlled by Exactor hydraulic remote controls.

Fuel System

Two fuel tanks were mounted in each wing outboard of the engines with a nominal total capacity of 134 gallons (609 litres), but the standard fuel load was 118 gallons (536 litres). In each wing, the two tanks fed the engines via a collector box, a remotely-controlled fuel cock and filter. The use of Exactor controls to operate the fuel cocks remotely resulted in very short piping runs for the fuel system, but the fuel systems for each wing were completely independent and there was no provision to transfer fuel from one to the other or to jettison fuel.

Radio

Initially, the Whirlwind was equipped with a TR9D crystal-controlled high-frequency transceiver incorporating a second, direction-finding channel. In early 1941, this was replaced with VHF equipment which gave better reception over greater ranges. At first, this took the form of the hand-built TR1133B four-channel VHF transceiver that was replaced in 1942 with the mass produced TR1143. Whirlwinds also carried the R3003 Identification Friend or Foe (IFF) transponder, a 24-volt version of the R3002 device used by other British fighters. Trials were carried out in late 1943 with the improved IFF Mk III (R3090) using Whirlwind P7100. The installation was approved late in the aircraft's career and highly unlikely that the improved device was fitted to other Whirlwinds.

Dimensions, Weights and Performance

	Whirlwind fighter (*c.* mid-1941)	Fighter-bomber (*c.* late 1942)
Wingspan:	45 feet (13.72 metres)	
Wing area:	250 feet² (23.23 metres²)	
Dihedral:	Centre section – 0°, Outer panels – 2° 13'	
Height (tail down to pitot tube):	10 feet 6 inches (3.20 metres)	
Length (tail up):	32 feet 3 inches (9.83 metres)	
Unloaded weight*:	9,150 lbs (4,150 kg)	9,224 lbs (4,184 kg)
Loaded:	10,337 lbs (4,689 kg)	10,411 lbs (4,722 kg)
With 2 x 250-lb bombs:	N/A	10,911 lbs (4,949 kg)
With 2 x 500-lb bombs:	N/A	11,411 lbs (5,176 kg)
Wing loading (loaded):	41.3 lbs/feet² (202 kg/metres²)	43.6 lbs/feet² (213 kg/metres²) (with 250-lb bombs)
Maximum speed:	338 mph at 15,200 feet (544 kph at 4,633 metres)	318 mph at 15,000 feet (512 kph at 4,572 metres)

* Fully equipped, but no pilot, fuel or ammunition.

The Rolls-Royce Peregrine

Like Petters, carmaker Rolls-Royce was drawn into the aircraft industry during the First World War. Although asked to build Renault aero engines, Rolls-Royce embarked on the design of a range of V12 engines of its own and embodying the same meticulous and thoughtful, if not outstandingly innovative, engineering that was a hallmark of its cars. The Rolls-Royce Eagle and Falcon, joined at the end of the war by the larger Condor, rapidly built a reputation as the finest and most dependable aero engines of the conflict.

With the signing of the armistice in November 1918, demand for military engines evaporated. The market was flooded with surplus engines and there was no substantial civil aero engine market. Accordingly, Rolls-Royce focused its attentions once more on the car business. The company continued to build wartime engines in small numbers, but by the mid-1920s, these un-supercharged V12s with epicyclic reduction gear and separate cylinders, each surrounded by a fabricated water jacket and topped by exposed valve gear, were beginning to look old fashioned and rival Napier overtook Rolls-Royce to become the leading British manufacturer of liquid-cooled aero engines.

In 1925, the company began work on a new engine, initially called F-X, featuring one piece, alloy cylinder blocks with steel wet cylinder liners and enclosed pressure-lubricated valve gear. Although new to Rolls-Royce, many of these features had been incorporated in Hispano-Suiza's advanced V8 of 1915 and the Curtiss D-12 engine that had served as a spur to the development of the F-X. First released in ungeared and unsupercharged form, spur reduction gear and a centrifugal supercharger were soon added. The new engine was such a departure from past Rolls-Royce practice that *Flight* magazine commented: 'External appearances alone are such that ... one would not recognise the engine as a Rolls-Royce.'[378] Within a few years, its layout would be regarded as typically Rolls-Royce. The new engine, later named Kestrel, offered a combination of competitive power output and low frontal area that soon found favour with aircraft designers. Built in larger numbers than any previous Rolls-Royce engine, the Kestrel powered aircraft ranging from Hawker's elegant biplane fighters to heavy bombers and flying boats. Even prototypes of the Messerschmitt Bf 109 fighter and Junkers Ju 87 'Stuka' dive bomber made their first flights under Kestrel power.

Rolls-Royce commenced work on the ultimate Kestrel variant, KV26, in mid-1936. The new variant featured a new supercharger, downdraught carburettor, accessory drives and mountings adapted to suit multi-engine installations and other detail design refinements. Testing began in October 1937 and the new engine completed a 100-hour development type test a few months later. Using 87 octane leaded fuel and at a maximum boost of 6.75 lbs/inches^2, the engine developed 765 bhp at 3,000 rpm, although during 1938, Rolls-Royce also ran a 100-hour test of the engine at 965 bhp. It then underwent flight tests in Rolls-Royce's Heinkel He 70 G-ADZF. The Director of Technical Development (Air Commodore Reynell Verney) reported in April 1937, 'In view of the material increase in output and the many changes in detailed design, it is proposed not to regard it as a further mark of Kestrel, but to revive with its wartime tradition of good service the name Eagle.'[379] In the end, the name Peregrine was chosen.

The Peregrine was a sixty-degree upright V12 with an alloy crankcase and two alloy cylinder blocks/heads with steel wet cylinder liners. Flat-topped, forged aluminium alloy pistons drove H-section, forged steel conrods with forked ends on the left-hand cylinders and plain ones on the right. These drove a hollow, single-piece, forged steel crankshaft running in seven main bearings with the bearing caps cross bolted through the sides of the crankcase in addition to the usual vertical bolts. A single overhead camshaft per cylinder bank operated, via rocker arms, two inlet valves and two sodium-cooled exhaust valves per cylinder. The Peregrine's valve timing was substantially more aggressive than that of earlier Kestrels with no less than forty-five degrees of valve overlap compared with, typically, fourteen degrees for previous engines. If earlier Kestrels had a weakness, it was a proneness to coolant leaks at the top joint of the cylinder liners. On the Peregrine and Merlin, this was addressed by the introduction of additional bolts to clamp the cylinder liners up to the top of the cylinder block. At the rear of the engine was a newly designed, central-entry supercharger with aluminium alloy impeller blades and steel entry vanes. This was driven from the rear end of the crankshaft via three clutch wheels to cushion the drive during rapid changes in engine speed. To minimise frontal area and reduce drag, the drives for the camshafts, pumps and ignition magnetos were at the rear of the engine and a downdraught carburettor was incorporated to allow aircraft designers to use a direct, straight-down carburettor air intake within the 'V' of the engine.

Rolls-Royce engines were designed on the assumption that the coolant radiator would be the lowest point in the cooling system and the header tank the highest with the engine and coolant pump between the two. Accordingly, the cooling system was arranged for the pump to flow coolant out of the radiator and into the engine, and then to the header tank before returning to the radiator. In the Whirlwind installation, the wing-mounted radiators were not located at the lowest point in the system. Therefore, the coolant circuit was rearranged so that the pump forced coolant from the tank into the radiator and engine. The de Havilland Mosquito, Hornet and Westland Welkin later presented similar challenges addressed by the provision of wholly distinct families of 'reverse flow' Merlin engines specifically for those applications.

Originally, the Peregrine was rated at a maximum of 6.75 lbs/inches^2 boost on 87 octane leaded fuel to give a take-off power of 765 hp at 3,000 rpm. After testing at higher boost pressures during the summer of 1940, Rolls-Royce re-rated the engine for short term use at 9 lbs/inches^2 boost with 100 octane fuel. Small modifications were made to the priming system, boost controls and other ancillaries during the Peregrine's life, but otherwise the engines in use at the end of the Whirlwind's career were identical to those with which it entered service over three years earlier. Rolls-Royce built 302 Peregrines including sixteen development units (eleven right-hand rotation Peregrine Is and five left-hand rotation Peregrine IIs). When the Whirlwind programme was curtailed, the original contract for 440 production Peregrine Is (Contract

986561/39) was reduced to 286 units, supplied at a cost of £1,700 each. The final engine was delivered in January 1942.

Peregrine Technical Data

Bore:	5.0 inches (127 mm)
Stroke:	5.5 inches (140 mm)
Swept volume:	1,296 inches³ (21.241)
Compression ratio:	6.0:1
Reduction gear ratio:	0.477:1
Reduction gear ratio:	9.5:1
Dry weight (excluding mountings and exhaust):	1,140 lbs (517 kg)
Rated altitude:	13,500 feet (4,115 metres)
Maximum power:	885 bhp, 3,000 rpm, 6.75 lbs boost (1.46 ata) at 15,000 feet (4,572 metres)
Take-off power using 100 octane fuel (5 mins max):	860 bhp, 3,000 rpm, 9 lbs boost (1.61 ata)
Fuel consumption, maximum climbing conditions:	62.5 gallons/hour (284 litres/hour) per engine
Fuel consumption at maximum cruise (auto-rich):	51 gallons/hour (232 litres/hour) per engine

Summary Individual Histories

Two prototypes ordered under contract 556965/36 issued 6 February 1937.

L6844
05/10/38: Taxiing trials began at Yeovil. Aircraft then dismantled and taken by road to RAF Boscombe Down. 11/10/38: First flight at Boscombe Down. 14/10/38: To Yeovil to continue testing. 10/11/38: Force landed at RAF Warmwell after starboard engine failure. 30/12/38: Brief trials at Boscombe Down by four pilots from A&AEE Martlesham Heath. 31/12/38: To RAE Farnborough for resonance tests. 28/01/39: Returned to Westland. 04/02/40: To RAE by road for wind tunnel tests. Later returned to Westland for armament development. 06/07/40: To A&AEE for trials of Hydran ammunition feed. 09/08/40: Returned to Westland for installation of Châtellerault belt feed. 25/09/40: Allocated to A&AEE for firing trials. 28/05/41: To AGME, Duxford, for further evaluation of gun installation. Tail damaged by ejected belt links during trials. 29/01/42: AGME disbanded and L6844 left (unserviceable) at Duxford with AFDU. 13/04/42: Allocated to No. 4 SoTT, St Athan, as Instructional Airframe 3063 m, but possibly not sent there until 1943.

L6845
29/03/39: First flight at Boscombe Down. 15/04/39: Flown by two A&AEE pilots to compare handling with first prototype. 27/08/39: To A&AEE Martlesham Heath for full armament, maintenance, performance and handling trials. 28/08/39: Moved to Boscombe Down where trials continued. 25/04/40: To Westland to be prepared for issue to RAF. 30/05/40: 25 Sqn. 03/06/40: Canopy collapsed in flight. Sgt Smith unhurt. Repaired on site by Westland. 07/06/40: Tailwheel collapsed, tail casting cracked. Repaired on site. 07/07/40: 263 Sqn. 16/10/40: To Westland to be brought up to current production standard. 30/03/41: 263 Sqn. 11/06/41: Hit tree after single-engine forced landing near Llandenny, Monmouthshire. Sgt Reginald Pascoe killed. Aircraft destroyed.

Production

Two hundred Whirlwinds ordered under contract 980384/39. ITP issued 11/01/39. All cancelled 26/10/39, but 114 reinstated on 06/12/39. The eighty-six aircraft not built were P7123-P7128, P7158-P7177, P7192-P7221 and P7240-P7269.

P6966

22/05/40: First flight. 04/06/40: 25 Sqn. 06/07/40: 263 Sqn. 07/08/40: Tyre burst on take off and jammed undercarriage. PO McDermott parachuted safely and aircraft crashed at Dunmore, Stirlingshire. **October 1979:** Crash site excavated and components recovered. Currently with Airframe Assemblies, Isle of Wight.

P6967

14/06/40: First flight. 17/06/40: 25 Sqn. 26/06/40: Mudguard detached in flight, damaging cowling and propeller. Repaired on site by Westland. 07/07/40: 263 Sqn, delivered by 13/07/40. 23/09/40: Rolls-Royce, Hucknall, for investigation of boost pressure anomalies. 25/08/41: RAE Farnborough. 09/03/42: To Westland to be brought up to current production standard. 17/12/42: 137 Sqn. 09/04/43: Allocated to 6 SoTT as Instructional Airframe 3497M. 04/11/44: SOC.

P6968

30/06/40: First flight. 19/07/40: 263 Sqn. 08/11/40: Taxied into pothole and tail damaged at Drem and Sgt Morton unhurt. Repaired on site by Westland and returned to unit on 15/12/40. 16/02/41: Damaged in take-off accident at St Eval. PO Milligan unhurt. Repaired on site and returned to unit on 24/05/41. 09/10/41: Collided with P6999 and crashed at Saltford, Somerset. PO Ormonde Hoskins killed. Aircraft burned out.

P6969

19/07/40: 263 Sqn. 08/02/41: Believed shot down off Dodman Point, Cornwall, by Arado Ar 196 of Bordfliegerstaffel 5/196. PO Kenneth Graham missing.

P6970

26/07/40: 263 Sqn. 06/11/41: Believed shot down off Cap Barfleur by Bf 109 of JG2. Sgt John Robinson missing.

P6971

31/08/40: 263 Sqn. 04/02/41: Tail damaged in heavy landing at Charmy Down. Sgt Skellon unhurt. Repaired on site by Westland. 15/10/41: Landing incident at Charmy Down and sent to Westland for repair. 12/04/42: 18MU.

04/09/42: 137 Sqn. 13/09/42: 18MU. 27/12/42: 263 Sqn. 11/05/43: Wing hit ground landing in crosswind at Warmwell. Sgt Proctor unhurt. Repaired on site by Westland. 19/10/43: Pilot retracted undercarriage to stop aircraft after overshooting landing at Warmwell. Sgt Blacklock unhurt. Repaired on site by Westland. 11/01/44: To 18MU on re-equipment of squadron. 14/07/44: Declared non-effective when the Whirlwind was classed as obsolete. 30/09/44: SOC and subsequently scrapped by Airwork.

P6972

03/09/40: 263 Sqn. 15/02/41: Sent to Westland for repair 13/03/41: Returned to 263 Sqn. 12/07/41: 39MU. 20/10/41: 51MU. 06/11/41: 137 Sqn. 26/05/42: Damaged and returned to Westland for repair. 31/07/42: 18MU. 14/07/44: Declared non-effective when the Whirlwind was classed as obsolete. 30/09/44: SOC and subsequently scrapped by Airwork.

P6973

17/09/40: 263 Sqn. 04/02/41: Landed at Charmy Down with tailwheel retracted. Sgt Jowitt unhurt. Repaired on site by Westland and returned to unit on 27/02/41. 05/07/41: 51MU. May later have been transferred to 18MU. 25/10/43: To Westland and SOC: cause uncertain, but possibly due to extensive corrosion.

P6974

07/09/40: 263 Sqn. 09/05/41: Slat detached during aerobatics. PO Rudland landed safely. Repaired on site and returned to unit by 22/05/41. 25/02/42: 39MU and later sent to 18MU. 20/02/43: 263 Sqn. 15/06/43: Damaged by flak when attacking shipping off Sark. Flt Sgt Ridley unhurt. Repaired at Westland and returned to unit by 13/07/43. 24/10/43: Damaged by flak during an attack over Cherbourg and landed wheels up at Warmwell. Flt Lt Ross unhurt, but aircraft damaged beyond repair.

P6975

22/10/40: 263 Sqn. 29/12/40: Flew into high ground at Fox Tor Mire, Devon, during transit flight. Flt Lt Wynford Smith killed. See P6978.

P6976

07/11/40: 263 Sqn. 13/02/41: Ran out of fuel during a practice flight and force landed near Cannington, Somerset. Sgt Skellon unhurt. Repaired at Fairwood Common by Westland. 18/08/41: 18MU. 20/02/42: 137 Sqn. 28/08/42: Flown to Westland for repair and returned to unit on 05/09/42. 09/09/42: At Westland for repair and returned to unit on 12/09/42. 15/12/42: Damaged by British flak and Fw 190 near Ramsgate. PO Robert Smith unhurt. Repaired on site at Manston. **01/05/43:** Tyres burst and wing hit ground while landing at Manston. Sgt Aubrey Smith unhurt. Sent to Westland, but recategorised as unrepairable and dismantled.

P6977

08/11/40: 263 Sqn. **05/12/40:** Bounced on landing and collided with P6971. PO Ferdinand unhurt. Repaired on site by Westland. **20/02/41:** Damaged and repaired on site. **17/07/41:** 39MU. **03/10/41:** 263 Sqn. **26/10/41:** Sent to Westland for repair. **01/11/41:** 137 Sqn. **11/11/41:** Damaged at Coltishall in a possible collision with a Blenheim. Sent to Westland, but recategorised as unrepairable and dismantled.

P6978

12/11/40: 263 Sqn. **29/12/40:** Flew into high ground at Fox Tor Mire, Devon, during transit flight. PO Donald Vine killed. See P6975.

P6979

07/11/40: 263 Sqn. Suffered hydraulic failure during delivery flight and eventually delivered 14/11/40. **08/02/41:** Tailwheel collapsed on landing at Exeter. Sgt Rudland unhurt. Repaired on site and returned to unit on 03/05/41. **29/05/41:** Aircraft ground looped after mainwheel tyre burst on landing at Filton. PO Coghlan unhurt. Repaired on site by Westland. **11/11/41:** 48MU. **29/06/42:** 263 Sqn. **09/09/42:** Damaged by flak during a shipping attack off Cap de la Hague. PO Brearley unhurt. Repaired at Westland and returned to unit on 14/09/43. **24/10/43:** Damaged by flak during an attack over Cherbourg and force landed near Digosville. Flt Sgt Len Gray POW.

P6980

16/11/40: To A&AEE for testing with enlarged 'acorn' tail fairing. **07/12/40:** 263 Sqn. **12/12/40:** Crashed into sea off Burnham-on-Sea, Somerset, during firing practice. FO Alan Britton missing.

P6981

07/12/40: 263 Sqn. **05/07/41:** 51MU. **16/02/42:** 137 Sqn. **04/05/42:** 51MU. **08/04/43:** 263 Sqn. **28/04/43:** Damaged by flak attacking shipping off Sept Iles. PO Cotton unhurt. Repaired on site. **01/08/43:** Bounced on landing at Warmwell in crosswind, cartwheeled and caught fire. Sgt Cooper unhurt, but aircraft damaged beyond repair.

P6982

26/11/40: 263 Sqn. **21/05/41:** Swung off runway at Filton and nosed over. PO Norman Freeman unhurt. Repaired on site. **25/08/41:** Ran off runway at Charmy

Down to avoid another aircraft and undercarriage collapsed. Sgt Maddocks unhurt. Repaired on site by Westland. 08/12/41: 51MU. 07/02/42: 137 Sqn. 07/09/42: 18MU. 14/07/44: Declared non-effective when the Whirlwind was classed as obsolete. 30/09/44: SOC and subsequently scrapped by Airwork.

P6983

07/12/40: 263 Sqn. 12/03/41: Slightly damaged at St Eval by enemy bombing. Repaired on site. 06/08/41: Force landed at Hurn after engine failure and hit obstruction. Flt Sgt Brackley unhurt. Repaired on site. 16/09/41: Tyre burst during landing at Charmy Down, aircraft swung and undercarriage collapsed. Sgt Prior unhurt. Repaired at Westland. 28/01/42: 51MU. 16/02/42: 137 Sqn. 22/06/42: Sent to Westland for repair. 03/07/42: 18MU. 18/08/43: 263 Sqn. 11/01/44: 18MU on re-equipment of squadron. 14/07/44: Declared non-effective when the Whirlwind was classed as obsolete. 30/09/44: SOC and subsequently scrapped by Airwork.

P6984

22/12/40: 263 Sqn. 19/01/41: Engines stopped in landing circuit at Exeter due to faulty fire extinguisher system. Flt Lt Pugh parachuted to safety and aircraft crashed at Clyst St Mary, Devon.

P6985

03/01/41: 263 Sqn. 11/03/41: Hit by return fire from Ju 88 and force landed at Mullion. PO Kitchener seriously injured. Aircraft wrecked and burned out.

P6986

04/01/41: 263 Sqn. 15/05/42: 18MU. 13/09/42: 137 Sqn. 31/10/42: 263 Sqn. 16/02/43: 137 Sqn. 25/03/43: Slightly damaged by flak during an attack on Abbeville marshalling yards. 24/06/43: 263 Sqn. 24/10/43: Shot down into the sea by flak at St-Vaast after an attack on Cherbourg. FO Paul Mercer missing.

P6987

04/01/41: 263 Sqn.16/11/41: Collided with stationary Spitfire AD294 while landing at Warmwell. Sgt Dimblebee unhurt. Aircraft returned to Westland for repair. 02/04/42: 51MU. 05/06/42: 263 Sqn. 07/12/42: Shot down by flak during a shipping attack off Jersey. WO Donald McPhail missing.

P6988

04/01/41: 263 Sqn. 14/03/41: Crash landed at Portreath after port engine failed. PO Thornton-Brown seriously injured. Aircraft damaged beyond repair.

A view of P6987 HE-L that was shot down by flak while attacking a convoy off Jersey. (*Robert Bowater*)

P6989

19/01/41: 263 Sqn. 01/04/41: Crashed near Garras, Cornwall, possibly due to return fire from an aircraft identified as a Do 215. Flt Lt David Crooks killed.

P6990

19/01/41: 263 Sqn. 08/11/41: Sent to Westland for repair. 09/04/42: 263 Sqn. 18/12/42: Stn Flt Colerne/39MU. 19/05/43: 263 Sqn. 19/11/43: Sent to Westland, but recategorised on 09/12/43 as unrepairable and dismantled.

P6991

30/12/40: 18MU. 06/02/41: 263 Sqn. 23/03/41: Overshot landing at Portreath. Sgt Lawson unhurt. Repaired on site. 25/09/41: Allotted to 137 Sqn, but aircraft hit flarepath light when taxiing at Charmy Down on 28/09/41. Repaired on site and issued to 263 Sqn. 26/03/42: Damaged and repaired on site by Westland. 09/02/43: Engine failed on take off at Warmwell. Aircraft hit a tree and force landed. Sgt Macaulay unhurt. Sent to Westland, but recategorised on 10/05/43 as unrepairable and dismantled.

P6992

30/12/40: 18MU. 13/02/41: 263 Sqn. 22/02/41: Tail castings fractured at St Eval. Repaired on site by Westland. 20/04/41: Crashed at Burghley Park, Wittering, during low-level aerobatics. FO Bernard Howe killed.

P6993

30/12/40: 18MU. 13/02/41: 263 Sqn. 12/03/41: Slightly damaged at St Eval by enemy bombing. Repaired on site. 05/07/41: 51MU. 28/07/42: 137 Sqn. 20/12/42: Tail damaged when wheel dropped into a pothole while taxiing at Manston. Repaired on site. 22/06/43: Starboard throttle control failed, port engine ran out of fuel and aircraft force landed near Manston. Flt Sgt Barclay unhurt, but aircraft damaged beyond repair.

P6994

24/01/41: 51MU. 13/02/41: 263 Sqn. 30/10/41: Damaged by flak during an attack on Morlaix and overshot landing at Predannack. Sgt Ridley unhurt. Repaired at Westland. 04/02/42: 48MU. 29/03/42: 47MU/Packing Depot, Sealand. 05/06/42: Shipped to USA for evaluation of Hispano cannon installation. Last documented at Eglin Field, Florida, in January 1944. Its final fate is uncertain although it is alleged that its engines were 'acquired' by a naval officer at Pensacola to use in a speedboat.

P6995

25/02/41: 51MU. 18/03/41: 263 Sqn. 24/10/41: Starboard engine overheated in flight due to a loose coolant filler cap and aircraft swung while making a brakeless landing at Colerne. Sgt Brearley unhurt. Repaired at Westland. 24/04/42: 18MU. 06/07/42: 263 Sqn. Briefly returned to Westland for repair on 22/08/42 and 25/10/42. 17/04/43: Declared missing after a night attack on Caen-Mondeville. FO Edgar Brearley's body was later washed ashore at Swanage.

P6996

24/01/41: 51MU. 13/02/41: 263 Sqn. 12/03/41: Slightly damaged at St Eval by enemy bombing. Repaired on site. While with 263 Squadron, a Rolls-Royce working party trialled engine modifications with this aircraft. 15/09/41: Overshot landing at Charmy Down and hit P7039 and a hut. Sgt Meredith slightly injured. Aircraft beyond repair.

P6997

24/01/41: 51MU. 09/04/41: Sent to A&AEE for take-off trials with 9 lbs boost and to determine impact of thickened wing caused by external self-sealing fuel tank covering. 28/05/41: Sent to Westland. 18/06/41: To AFDU for trials with gyro gunsight. Also flown for an Air Ministry aircraft recognition film. 07/08/41: Sent to Westland. 16/08/42: Sent to A&AEE for bombing trials. 14/09/42: Sent to Westland. 03/01/43: 18MU. 26/01/43: 137 Sqn. 24/06/43: Sent to 263 Sqn when 137 Sqn re-equipped. 11/01/44: 18MU on re-equipment of 263 Squadron. 14/07/44: Declared non-effective when the Whirlwind was classed as obsolete. 30/09/44: SOC and subsequently scrapped by Airwork.

P6998

25/02/41: Sent to 263 Sqn, but tailwheel collapsed on landing at Exeter on delivery flight. Repaired on site. 29/09/41: Force landed out of fuel and ran short of the runway at Predannack. FO Coghlan unhurt. Repaired at Westland. 19/03/42: 39MU. 28/03/42: 18MU. 13/04/42: 137 Sqn. 22/12/42: Damaged by flak and force landed at Lympne where it overshot and caught fire. Sgt Sutherland unhurt. Sent to Westland, but recategorised on 20/01/43 as unrepairable and dismantled.

P6999

25/02/41: 48MU. 23/03/41: 263 Sqn. 09/10/41: Collided with P6968. FO Coghlan parachuted safely. Aircraft crashed at Kelston, Somerset, and destroyed.

P7000

25/02/41: 48MU. 01/03/41: 263 Sqn. 12/03/41: Slightly damaged at St Eval by enemy bombing and repaired on site. 31/03/41: Ran off runway taxiing at Portreath and nosed over. PO Stein unhurt. Repaired on site. 15/06/41: Ran off runway at Filton and hit obstacle. Sgt Holmes unhurt. Repaired on site by Westland. 23/10/41: 39MU. 18/03/42: 263 Sqn. 01/04/42: Wingtip hit ground while landing in strong crosswind at Fairwood Common. PO Holmes unhurt. Repaired on site. 29/05/43: Damaged, sent to Westland and returned to unit. 15/06/43: Shot down by flak gunners of 24th Minensuchflotille near Sark. PO Maxwell Cotton missing.

P7001

24/01/41: 48MU. 24/02/41: 51MU. 13/04/41: 263 Sqn. 06/08/41: Damaged by Bf 109s during shipping reconnaissance off Cherbourg. Sqn Ldr Donaldson unhurt. Repaired at Westland and returned to unit by 11/08/41. 10/09/41: Shot down by flak while attacking gun positions near Lestre. PO Dennis Mason killed.

P7002

13/03/41: 263 Sqn. 06/08/41: Damaged by Bf 109s during a shipping reconnaissance off Cherbourg. Flt Lt Rudland unhurt. Repaired at Westland and returned to its unit by 12/08/41. 13/12/41: Undershot landing at Colerne and undercarriage collapsed. PO Currie unhurt. Repaired at Westland. 30/06/42: 18MU. 02/02/43: 137 Sqn. 04/04/43: Propellers hit sea and ditched five miles off Deal. PO Dugdale rescued.

P7003

03/04/41: 39MU. 15/04/41: 263 Sqn. 27/04/42: Fly-in repair at Westland. 21/09/42: Dived into ground near East Stoke, Dorset, on a practice flight. Flt Sgt Jardine killed. Pilot presumed to have lost control flying in cloud.

P7004

02/03/41: 48MU, but delivered to 263 Sqn. 04/05/41: Tailwheel tyre burst taking off at Filton. PO Tooth unhurt. Repaired on site. 08/09/41: Damaged by Bf 109s near Alderney. Sgt King unhurt. Repaired at Ibsley by Westland. 14/03/42: Tyre burst on take off from Pembrey, swung on landing at Fairwood Common and undercarriage collapsed. PO Currie unhurt. Sent to Westland, but recategorised on 05/10/42 as unrepairable and dismantled.

P7005

03/04/41: 39MU. 15/04/41: 263 Sqn. 15/06/41: Hit balloon cable near Weston-super-Mare. PO Holmes landed safely. Repaired on site. 06/01/42: 48MU. 08/03/42: 137 Sqn. 11/04/42: Starboard engine caught fire in flight and landed at East Wretham airfield. FO Furber unhurt. Engine changed on site. 30/05/42: Tailwheel collapsed landing at Matlaske. Flt Sgt Brunet unhurt. Repaired on site. 16/08/42: Port tyre burst in heavy landing at Matlaske and tail unit damaged. Sgt Sutherland unhurt. Repaired on site. 02/03/43: Shot down by flak north of Boulogne. Sgt George Walker, POW.

P7006

04/04/41: 51MU. 16/04/41: 263 Sqn. 29/05/41: Crashed near Woolaston during unauthorised low flying. Sgt Tebbit unhurt. Aircraft damaged beyond repair.

P7007

13/03/41: 18MU. 29/03/41: 263 Sqn. 29/10/41: Hit radio mast attacking Morlaix airfield. Sgt King unhurt. Repaired on site and returned to unit on 10/01/42. 21-22/05/43: Damaged by flak attacking shipping off Pointe de Nacqueville. Flt Lt Coyne unhurt. Repaired at Westland and returned to its unit on 31/05/43. 21/01/44: 18MU on re-equipment of 263 Sqn. 14/07/44: Declared non-effective when the Whirlwind was classed as obsolete. 30/09/44: SOC and subsequently scrapped by Airwork.

P7008

13/03/41: 18MU. 14/04/41: 263 Sqn. 30/04/41: Broke up in midair during a practice attack and crashed near Aldermaston, Berkshire. PO George Milligan killed.

P7009

06/04/41: 18MU. 22/04/41: 263 Sqn. 29/09/41: Ran out of fuel returning from an attack on Lannion airfield. Sgt Thomas Hunter parachuted into the sea, his body being washed ashore later.

P7010

06/04/41: 18MU. 25/01/43: 263 Sqn. 14/04/43: Damaged by flak attacking shipping off Pointe de St-Mathieu and also claimed shot down off Île d'Ouessant by Bf 109 of JG2. Sgt John Macaulay missing.

P7011

10/04/41: 18MU. 13/05/41: 263 Sqn. 04/09/41: Damaged by Bf 109s of JG2 off Cherbourg. Sgt Mason unhurt. Repaired on site. 06/06/42: Under repair at Westland. 23/09/42: 18MU. 07/11/42: 137 Sqn. 24/11/43: 263 Sqn. 08/02/44: 18MU on re-equipment of squadron. 14/07/44: Declared non-effective when the Whirlwind was classed as obsolete. 30/09/44: SOC and subsequently scrapped by Airwork.

P7012

08/04/41: 51MU. 15/11/41: 137 Sqn. 12/02/42: Tail castings cracked at Matlaske. Repaired on site by Westland and returned to its unit on 07/03/42. 09/12/42: Flt Sgt Woodhouse retracted undercarriage after landing at Southend. Repaired at Westland and returned to its unit on 05/02/43. 24/06/43: 263 Sqn. 11/01/44: 18MU on re-equipment of squadron. 14/07/44: Declared non-effective when the Whirlwind was classed as obsolete. 30/09/44: SOC and subsequently scrapped by Airwork.

P7013

10/04/41: 51MU. 04/05/41: 263 Sqn. 12/09/41: Propeller control failed landing at Charmy Down and a wing hit the ground. Sgt Jowitt unhurt.

No. 137 Squadron Whirlwind P7011 SF-U was flown by Flight Sergeant Aubrey Smith. She had the name 'Hazel' inscribed just below the canopy after his girlfriend (later wife). P7011 flew with both Whirlwind squadrons and was scrapped on 14 July 1944. (*Robert Bowater*)

Repaired on site by Westland. 01/10/41: Throttles jammed and aircraft stalled when landing at Charmy Down, its undercarriage collapsing. PO Harvey unhurt. Repaired at Westland. 14/02/42: 48MU. 18/04/42: 263 Sqn. 05/07/42: Collided with P7120 while taxiing at Portreath. Sgt Muirhead unhurt. Repaired on site and returned to its unit on 01/08/42. 24/09/42: Sent to Westland for repair or modification and returned to unit. 20/06/43: Sgt Hughes retracted undercarriage after landing at Zeals. Repaired on site and reissued to its unit on 17/07/43. 09/10/43: Involved in a further incident and aircraft was sent to Westland, but recategorised on 04/11/43 as unrepairable and dismantled.

P7014
10/04/41: 51MU. 15/05/42: 263 Sqn. 08/10/42: Crashed at Warmwell after taking off with propellers in coarse pitch. Flt Lt Johnstone concussed. Sent to Westland but recategorised on 26/10/42 as unrepairable and dismantled.

P7015
23/04/41: 51MU. 15/10/41: 263 Sqn. 30/10/41: Shot down by flak during an attack on Morlaix airfield. FO David Stein killed.

P7035
15/04/41: 39MU. 04/09/41: 51MU. 26/09/41: 137 Sqn. 19/10/41: Sgt Small landed at Charmy Down with tailwheel retracted and damaged tail. Repaired on site and returned to its unit on 28/10/41. 18/01/42: Damaged at Matlaske and repaired on site by Westland. Returned to its unit on 07/02/41. 05/04/42: 263 Sqn. 30/04/42: A wing hit the ground when landing at Fairwood Common. Sgt Meredith unhurt. Repaired on site. 23/07/42: Shot down off Morlaix by Bf 109G of 11/JG2. PO Vivian Currie missing.

P7036
22/02/41: 39MU. 28/09/41: 137 Sqn. 09/03/42: Spun during mock dogfight with a Spitfire and crashed near North Walsham, Norfolk. PO Charles De-Shane killed.

P7037
28/04/41: 39MU. 20/09/41: 263 Sqn, but transferred to 137 Sqn. 09/03/42: Damaged and repaired on site by Westland. Returned to its unit on 16/05/42. 05/10/42: Overshot while landing at Manston and hit a boundary fence. Sgt Barclay unhurt. Repaired at Westland. 08/09/43: 18MU. 10/10/43: 263 Sqn. 08/02/44: 18MU on re-equipment of 263 Squadron. 14/07/44: Declared non-effective when the Whirlwind was classed as obsolete. 30/09/44: SOC and subsequently scrapped by Airwork.

No. 263 Squadron Whirlwind P7035 taxis to take off. She flew with both squadrons between 26 September 1941 and 23 July 1942 when she was shot down by German fighters over the English Channel. Her No. 263 Squadron pilot, twenty-two-year-old Irishman Pilot Officer Les Currie, was killed in action. (*Robert Bowater*)

P7038

28/04/41: 39MU. 04/09/41: 51MU. 26/09/41: 137 Sqn. 01/12/41: 263 Sqn. 03/01/42: Burned out after a cockpit fire at Charmy Down.

P7039

30/04/41: 51MU. 11/06/41: 263 Sqn. 15/09/41: Hit by P6996 while parked at Charmy Down. Repaired on site by Westland. 07/03/42: Tyres burst during a heavy landing at Fairwood Common and aircraft overturned. Sgt Jardine badly injured. Sent to Westland, but recategorised on 21/06/42 as unrepairable and dismantled.

P7040

29/04/41: 18MU. 08/03/43: 263 Sqn. 27/04/43: Tailplane damaged by debris during a shipping attack. PO Lee-White unhurt. Repaired at Westland and returned to its unit on 29/04/43. 24/10/43: Undercarriage damaged by flak over Cherbourg and collapsed on landing. Sgt Cooper unhurt. Repaired on site. Sent for further repair work at Westland and returned to its unit on 22/11/43. 10/02/44: 18MU on re-equipment of 263 Squadron. 14/07/44: Declared non-effective when the Whirlwind was classed as obsolete. 30/09/44: SOC and subsequently scrapped by Airwork.

P7041

07/05/41: 18MU. 27/05/41: 263 Sqn. 28/09/41: Damaged by flak during an attack on Morlaix airfield. Flt Lt Pugh unhurt and aircraft repaired at Predannack by Westland. 02/04/42: Aircraft hit an obstruction at Fairwood Common after its brakes failed while taxiing. Sgt Small unhurt. Sent to Westland, but recategorised on 10/09/42 as unrepairable and dismantled.

P7042

12/05/41: 18MU. The aircraft may have also have spent some time at 27MU. 20/06/41: 263 Sqn. 04/09/41: Shot down by Bf 109 of JG2 off Cherbourg. Sgt Buckwell parachuted, injured and became POW.

P7043

17/05/41: 18MU. 21/05/42: 263 Sqn. 23/05/42: Tailwheel collapsed when landing at Brough as tail castings cracked. Flt Lt Warnes unhurt. Repaired on site and returned to its unit. 07/11/42: Failed to return from an attack on railway targets at Valognes-Montebourg. Believed to have been shot down by flak. FO Donald Gill (RCAF) killed.

P7044

03/05/41: 51MU. 15/06/41: 263 Sqn. 28/09/41: Damaged by flak during an attack on Morlaix airfield. Wg Cdr Donaldson injured. Repaired at Predannack by Westland and returned to its unit. 14/12/41: Crashed near Coleford, Gloucestershire, after losing control in cloud. Sgt Derrick Prior killed.

P7045

14/05/41: 51MU. 08/06/41: 263 Sqn. 12/06/41: Stalled and spun in on approach to Filton. FO Roy Ferdinand killed.

P7046

16/05/41: 51MU. 15/06/41: 263 Sqn. 24/08/41: Overshot when landing at Charmy Down and undercarriage collapsed. Sgt Dimblebee unhurt. Repaired on site by Westland. 09/01/42: 51MU. 16/02/42: 137 Sqn. 27/02/42: Sent to Westland to repair leaking fuel tanks. Returned to its unit on 07/03/42. 30/05/42: Tailwheel oleo collapsed causing damage to tail castings. Repaired on site by Westland. 24/06/43: Sent to 263 Sqn when 137 Sqn re-equipped. 08/07/43: Sent to Westland at Ilchester for repair/modification and returned to its unit. 26/11/43: Damaged by flak during an attack on Martinvast and returned on one engine. FO Mogg unhurt. 08/02/44: Sent to 18MU on re-equipment of 263 Squadron. 14/07/44: Declared non-effective when the Whirlwind was classed as obsolete. 30/09/44: SOC and subsequently scrapped by Airwork.

P7047

22/05/41: 51MU. 15/06/41: Tail castings damaged while being handled on the ground. Repaired on site. 06/04/43: Hydraulic failure at Benson during a ferry flight to 137 Sqn. First Officer Godwin (ATA) landed safely and aircraft repaired on site. 11/04/43: 137 Sqn. 12/07/43: 263 Sqn. 08/10/43: Multiple engine failure returning from a night shipping attack and crashed short of the runway at Tangmere and caught fire. PO James Simpson killed. Aircraft burned out.

P7048

27/05/41: 39MU. 01/12/41: 137 Sqn. 02/04/42: Tailwheel caught in a rut while taxiing at Matlaske and damaged castings in tail. Sgt Roberts unhurt. Repaired on site by Westland and returned to its unit. 31/05/43: Returned to Westland for repair. Retained by and subsequently sold to Westland. 29/03/45: Registered on Civil Register as G-AGOI. 07/05/47: Withdrawn from use and scrapped.

P7049

23/05/41: 39MU. 10/09/41: 51MU. 22/09/41: 137 Sqn. 27/06/42: Landed heavily at Matlaske and propellers hit the ground. PO Furber unhurt. Sent to Westland, but recategorised on 19/10/42 as unrepairable and dismantled.

P7050

24/05/41: 18MU. 28/09/41: 137 Sqn. 12/02/42: Shot down by Bf 109s of JG2 during Operation Fuller. PO John Sandy missing.

P7051

02/06/41: 18MU. 10/06/41: 263 Sqn. 22/11/41: Wingtip hit ground when landing at Colerne. Sgt Reed unhurt. Repaired on site. 29/03/42: Sent to Westland for repair after an unknown incident. 03/08/42: 18MU. 04/09/42: 137 Sqn. 05/10/42: Tailwheel collapsed on landing at Manston and tail castings cracked. Sgt Aubrey Smith unhurt. Repaired on site. 18/01/43: Hit a rut on take off at Manston, crashed, caught fire and bombs exploded. PO Luing unhurt.

P7052

27/05/41: 18MU. 05/11/41: 263 Sqn. 12/02/43: Damaged by flak and ditched off Surtainville. Sgt David Williams missing.

P7053

02/06/41: 18MU. 24/09/41: 137 Sqn. 28/10/41: Collided with P7058 during dogfighting practice and crashed near Englishcombe, Somerset. Sqn Ldr John Sample parachuted too low and was killed.

P7054
17/06/41: 39MU. 11/02/42: 137 Sqn. 15/05/42: Flown to Westland for repair of leaking fuel tanks. 30/05/42: 263 Sqn. 03/06/42: 137 Sqn. 14/09/42: Sent to Westland for repair. 23/01/43: Damaged by flak while searching for railway targets and force landed. WO Doig unhurt and POW.

P7055 *Bellows Argentina No. 1*
17/06/41: 39MU. 01/11/41: 137 Sqn. 12/02/42: Severely damaged by Bf 109s during Operation Fuller. Flt Sgt Charles Mercer unhurt. Repaired at Ipswich airport by Westland. 26/08/42: Taxied over a drain causing damage to undercarriage and nacelles. Repaired at Westland. 11/02/43: 18MU. 13/02/43: 137 Sqn. 24/06/43: 263 Sqn. 19/10/43: Damaged by flak when attacking a train near Flottemanville. Sgt Dunlop unhurt. Repaired on site. 11/01/44: 18MU on re-equipment of 263 Sqn. 14/07/44: Declared non-effective when the Whirlwind was classed as obsolete. 30/09/44: SOC and subsequently scrapped by Airwork.

P7056 *The Pride of Yeovil*
30/06/41: 39MU. 06/10/41: 263 Sqn. 18/12/42: Stn Flt Colerne/39MU. 14/04/43: 137 Sqn. 27/06/43: 263 Sqn on re-equipment of 137 Sqn. 26/08/43: Sent to Westland and cause uncertain, but recategorised on 14/10/43 as unrepairable and dismantled.

P7057
18/06/41: 39MU. Briefly sent to A&AEE as a rogue aircraft as prone to spinning. 28/09/41: 137 Sqn. 28/10/41: Pilot landed wheels up at Colerne. Sgt Brennan unhurt. Repaired on site. 11/01/42: 39MU. 04/04/42: 18MU. 14/07/42: 263 Sqn. 08/08/42: Under repair at Westland. 18/08/42: 263 Sqn. 07/05/43: Undercarriage collapsed after a heavy landing at Warmwell. Sgt Thould unhurt. Sent to Westland, but recategorised on 16/06/43 as unrepairable and dismantled.

P7058
22/06/41: 18MU. 25/09/41: 137 Sqn. 28/10/41: Collided in flight with P7053. Sgt Peskett unhurt. Repaired at Filton. 08/08/42: Tailwheel collapsed taxiing at Drem and repaired on site. 05/10/42: Overshot landing at Manston. PO Samant unhurt. Repaired on site. 25/04/43: Shot down by flak while attacking a train near Roeselare. FO James Rebbetoy killed.

P7059
23/06/41: 18MU. 01/08/42: 263 Sqn. 19/04/43: Sent to Westland for repair and returned to its unit. 22/05/43: Damaged by flak attacking shipping off

Cherbourg and force landed at Warmwell. FO Lee-White unhurt. Sent to Westland, but recategorised on 16/06/43 as unrepairable and dismantled.

P7060
23/06/41: 18MU. 27/09/41: 137 Sqn. 11/12/41: 263 Sqn. 06/06/42: Sent to Westland for repair. Returned to unit. 23/07/42: Shot down into the sea off Morlaix by Bf 109G of 11/JG2. PO John Walker missing.

P7061
25/06/41: 39MU. 19/09/41: 263 Sqn. 05/12/41: Tailwheel collapsed on landing at Charmy Down. Repaired on site. 29/05/42: Sent to Westland for repair. 20/08/42: 18MU. 07/11/42: 137 Sqn. 13/01/43: Collided with P7102 while taxiing at Manston. Sgt Bolster unhurt. Sent to Westland, but recategorised on 23/01/43 as unrepairable and dismantled.

P7062
28/06/41: 39MU. 20/09/41: Allocated to 263 Sqn, but diverted to 137 Sqn. 07/01/42: Overshot when landing at Coltishall. Sgt Maddocks injured. Sent to Westland for repair and then 18MU. 18/07/42: 263 Sqn. 19/02/43: Crashed during practice attacks on army transport near Wroughton, Wiltshire. Flt Sgt Francis Hicks killed.

P7063
30/06/41: 39MU. 20/09/41: Allocated to 263 Sqn, but diverted to 137 Sqn. 03/10/41: Port engine cut out due to a fuel shortage. Aircraft stalled and crashed at Charmy Down. Sgt Peskett unhurt. Sent to Westland for repair. 09/01/42: 18MU. 16/03/42: 137 Sqn. 18/05/43: Failed to return from a night shipping strike off Dunkerque and presumed shot down by flak. FO Eddie Musgrave killed and body later washed ashore in France.

P7064
02/07/41: 51MU. 18/11/41: 137 Sqn. 21/06/42: Flown to Westland for repair and returned to its unit on 24/06/42. 31/10/42: Shot down by flak near Étaples and ditched. Flt Lt van Schaick rescued unhurt by ASR Walrus.

P7089
02/07/41: 51MU. 10/10/41: 263 Sqn. 06/06/42: Flown to Westland for repair and returned to its unit on 13/06/42. 25/01/43: Flown to Westland for repair and returned to its unit on 05/02/43. 23/05/43: Damaged by flak when attacking shipping off Guernsey. FO Cotton unhurt. Sent to Westland, but recategorised on 26/05/43 as unrepairable and dismantled.

P7090

05/07/41: 51MU. 22/09/41: 137 Sqn. 19/02/42: Tail castings fractured. Repaired on site by Westland and returned to unit. 05/04/42: 263 Sqn. 18/11/42: Sent to Westland for repair. 31/12/42: 39MU. 31/12/42: Stn Flt Colerne/39MU. 26/03/43: 263 Sqn. 17/04/43: Missing from a night attack on railway targets in the Bayeux-Caen area and presumed shot down by flak. FO Philip Harvey missing.

P7091

08/07/41: 51MU. 22/09/41: 137 Sqn. 30/10/41: Ran out of fuel and ditched off Lizard Point. Flt Lt Colin Clark rescued, but died of injuries.

P7092

06/07/41: 51MU. 17/10/41: 137 Sqn. 11/01/42: Propeller control failed on take off at Matlaske and a wing hit the ground. PO La Gette unhurt. Repaired at Westland. 25/04/42: 18MU. 04/09/42: 137 Sqn. 14/03/43: Force landed at Lympne. FO Musgrave unhurt. Repaired on site and returned to its unit on 08/04/43. 27/06/43: 263 Sqn when 137 Sqn re-equipped. 08/10/43: Damaged and repaired by Westland. Returned to its unit on 14/10/43. 31/12/43: Damaged and sent to Westland for repair. 22/01/44: Repairs suspended when Whirlwind declared obsolescent and dismantled.

P7093

17/07/41: 51MU. 17/01/42: 137 Sqn. 12/02/42: Shot down into the sea by Bf 109s of JG2 during Operation Fuller. PO Ralph Häggberg missing.

P7094

17/07/41: 51MU. 30/09/41: 137 Sqn. 23/12/41: Engine cut on approach and force landed near Matlaske. Sgt O'Neill slightly injured. Repaired at Westland. 07/09/42: 18MU. 22/09/42: 137 Sqn. 08/10/42: 263 Sqn. 27/04/43: Damaged and sent to Westland for repair. 16/05/43: Returning from a shipping strike and short of fuel, the aircraft crashed near Exeter. Flt Lt Herbert Blackshaw parachuted too low and was killed.

P7095

21/07/41: 51MU. 22/06/42: 137 Sqn. 23/01/43: Damaged by flak during a train attack north of Doullens and force landed near Arras. PO Alfred Brown killed in unclear circumstances.

P7096

24/07/41: 18MU. 30/09/41: 137 Sqn. 14/02/42: Overshot while landing at Horsham St Faith and the starboard undercarriage tore off. Sqn Ldr Coghlan unhurt. Repaired at Westland. 20/11/42: 18MU. 03/01/43: 137 Sqn. 28/04/43: Sent to

Westland for repair. **27/06/43**: 263 Sqn. **12/07/43**: Sent to Westland for repair and returned to its unit on 03/08/43. **14/08/43**: Sent to Westland for repair and returned to its unit on 21/08/43. **27/08/43**: Wingtip hit a tree while taxiing at Warmwell. Sgt Watkins unhurt and aircraft repaired on site. **10/09/43**: Aircraft hit a ridge on landing at Warmwell and the port undercarriage tore off. Sqn Ldr Baker unhurt. Sent to Westland, but recategorised on 29/09/43 as unrepairable and dismantled.

P7097

24/07/41: 18MU. **06/11/41**: 137 Sqn. **08/02/42**: The port engine failed and the starboard engine ran out of fuel, the aircraft force landing near Coltishall. Sgt Rebbetoy unhurt. Repaired at Westland. **21/05/42**: 18MU. **30/05/42**: 263 Sqn. **08/10/43**: Damaged by flak when attacking shipping off Cap de la Hague. PO Heaton unhurt. Aircraft repaired on site. Sent to Westland for further repairs and returned to its unit on 20/10/43. **24/10/43**: Damaged by flak over Cherbourg and repaired on site. Aircraft returned to its unit on 08/11/43. **08/01/44**: 18MU when squadron re-equipped, but swung off the runway at Hawarden on its delivery flight. Repaired and continued to 18MU on 11/01/44. **14/07/44**: Declared non-effective when the Whirlwind was classed as obsolete. **30/09/44**: SOC and later scrapped by Airwork.

P7098

30/07/41: 18MU. **23/01/43**: 137 Sqn. **27/06/43**: 263 Sqn when 137 Sqn re-equipped. **10/01/44**: At Westland for repair. Repairs suspended on 22/01/44 when the Whirlwind was declared obsolescent and dismantled.

P7099

30/07/41: 18MU. **28/07/42**: 263 Sqn. **17-18/04/43**: Failed to return from a night shipping reconnaissance to Houlgate and Saint-Marcouf. FO Basil Abrams missing.

P7100

07/08/41: 18MU. **05/12/41**: 263 Sqn. **14/04/42**: Swung off runway while landing in crosswind at Fairwood Common. PO Harvey unhurt. Repaired at Westland and retained for trials of bomb installation and IFF Mk III. **04/11/43**: 263 Sqn. **27/01/44**: 18MU when squadron re-equipped. **14/07/44**: Declared non-effective when the Whirlwind was classed as obsolete. **30/09/44**: SOC and later scrapped by Airwork.

P7101

07/08/41: 18MU. **18/04/42**: 137 Sqn. **30/06/42**: Collided with a parked Lysander when landing at Matlaske. PO Bartlett unhurt. Sent to Westland, but recategorised on 13/07/42 as unrepairable and dismantled.

Whirlwind P7098 SF-P was delivered to No. 137 Squadron on 23 October 1942 and transferred to No. 263 Squadron at the end of June 1943. Damaged in November of that year, she was not repaired and was eventually struck off charge on 22 January 1944 and scrapped. (*Robert Bowater*)

P7102 *Comrades in Arms*
12/08/41: 18MU. 22/06/42: 137 Sqn. 30/10/42: Damaged by flak when attacking a military camp at Camiers. PO Furber unhurt. Repaired at Westland. 13/01/43: Hit by P7061 while parked at Manston and repaired at Westland. 14/09/43: 263 Sqn. 29/01/44: 18MU when squadron re-equipped. 14/07/44: Declared non-effective when the Whirlwind was classed as obsolete. 30/09/44: SOC and later scrapped by Airwork.

P7103
18/08/41: 18MU. 27/11/41: 137 Sqn. 04/05/42: Broke up in midflight and crashed near Aylsham, Norfolk. PO Robert Wright killed.

P7104
30/08/41: 18MU. 14/04/42: 137 Sqn. 25/07/42: Damaged by return fire from a Ju 88. PO McClure unhurt. Repaired on site. 25/08/42: Flown to Westland for further repair and returned to unit. 30/03/43: Engine failed on approach to Manston and undercarriage collapsed. PO Davidson unhurt. Sent to Westland, but recategorised on 10/05/43 as unrepairable and dismantled.

P7105
30/08/41: 18MU. 25/09/41: 137 Sqn. 05/01/42: Overshot when landing at Matlaske and the undercarriage tore off. Sgt Robert Wright unhurt. Sent

to Westland for repair. **25/07/42:** 18MU. **12/08/42:** 263 Sqn. **03/10/42:** Damaged by flak during a shipping attack at Alderney and returned on one engine. Sqn Ldr Woodward unhurt. **07/12/42:** Shot down by flak during a shipping attack off Jersey. Sqn Ldr Robert Woodward missing.

P7106

30/08/41: 51MU. **20/09/41:** 137 Sqn and delivered by 29/09/41. **25/12/41:** Force landed at Horsham St Faith after engine failure. Sgt Jowitt unhurt. Repaired on site by Westland. **12/02/42:** Shot down by a Bf 109 of JG2 during Operation Fuller. PO George Martin missing.

P7107

30/08/41: 51MU. **20/09/41:** 137 Sqn and delivered by 29/09/41. **12/02/42:** Failed to return from an escort sortie during Operation Fuller. WO Basil Robertson missing.

P7108

10/09/41: 51MU. **13/12/41:** 263 Sqn. **13/02/42:** Swung off runway and overturned at Fairwood Common. Flt Sgt Coyne slightly hurt. Repaired at Westland and sent to 18MU. **27/02/43:** 263 Sqn. **26/03/43:** Damaged by flak during an attack on lock gates at Ouistreham. FO Coyne unhurt. Flown to Westland for repair on 28/03/43 and returned to its unit. **21/05/43:** Damaged by flak during a night shipping attack off Cherbourg. PO Cotton unhurt. Repaired at Westland and returned to its unit on 26/10/43. **08/02/44:** Sent to 18MU when squadron re-equipped. **14/07/44:** Declared non-effective when the Whirlwind was classed as obsolete. **30/09/44:** SOC and later scrapped by Airwork.

P7109

10/09/41: 51MU. **15/11/41:** 137 Sqn. **31/10/42:** Hit by flak when attacking a military camp at Étaples. Sgt Waldron force landed, unhurt and POW.

P7110

26/09/41: 39MU. **15/10/41:** 263 Sqn. **12/01/42:** Tail casting cracked during take off at Charmy Down. Repaired on site and returned to its unit on 14/02/42. **19/02/42:** Engine failed during a convoy patrol. PO Holmes landed safely at Carew Cheriton. Repaired on site. **20/06/42:** Sent to Westland for repair and returned to its unit. **13/04/43:** Sent to Westland for repair and returned to its unit on 17/04/43. **21/06/43:** Hit a tree during an Army Co-operation exercise. Sgt Watkins landed safely at Stoney Cross. Repaired on site by Westland. **13/07/43:** Engine cut out on approach to Warmwell, crash landed and caught fire. Sgt Knott severely burned, but recovered. Aircraft wrecked and burned out.

P7111 *Bellows Uruguay No. 2*

28/09/41: 39MU. 13/03/42: 137 Sqn. 11/04/42: Sent to Westland for repair and later returned to its unit. 15/05/42: Damaged by return fire from a Ju 88. Sgt Brennan unhurt. Repaired on site. 11/02/43: Sent to Westland for repair and returned to its unit on 17/02/42. 17-18/06/43: Damaged by flak during a night attack on a train near Rue. Flt Sgt Barclay unhurt. Repaired on site. 04/07/43: To 263 Sqn when repairs completed. 18/08/43: Damaged and repaired on site. Returned to its unit on 09/09/43. 11/01/44: Repair at Westland CRO suspended when the Whirlwind was declared obsolescent.

P7112

26/09/41: 39MU. 15/10/41: 263 Sqn. 25/11/41: Sent to Westland for repair. Returned to 263 Sqn on 21/12/41. 01/04/42: Overturned after landing at Fairwood Common. PO Harvey bruised. Aircraft damaged beyond repair.

P7113

26/09/41: 39MU. 25/05/42: 18MU. 04/11/42: 263 Sqn. 13/04/43: Repaired at Westland and returned to its unit by 15/04/43. 23/09/43: Shot down by flak over Morlaix. Flt Sgt Wood parachuted, evaded capture and returned to the UK.

P7114

29/09/41: 39MU. 05/11/41: 263 Sqn. 13/05/42: Damaged and sent to Westland for repair and returned to its unit. 09/07/42: Damaged and sent to Westland for repair. 13/09/42: 18MU. 22/09/42: 263 Sqn. 31/10/42:

P7112 served with No. 263 Squadron between 15 October 1941 and 1 April 1942 when she crashed at RAF Fairwood Common. Her pilot, Irishman P/O Philip Harvey, was not injured although P7112 was written off. (*Robert Bowater*)

Damaged and sent to 18MU when repairs were completed. **17/11/42:** 137 Sqn. **19/02/43:** Collided with P7119 during a night take off at Manston. The aircraft caught fire and its bombs exploded. FO Charles Mercer (RCAF) killed.

P7115

13/10/41: 39MU. **04/05/42:** 18MU. **06/09/42:** 137 Sqn. **31/10/42:** Hit by flak when attacking a military camp at Camiers. FO Douglas Jowitt missing.

P7116 *Bellows Argentina No. 2*

27/10/41: 39MU. **03/11/41:** 263 Sqn. **17/06/42:** Flown to Westland for repair and returned to its unit on 23/07/42. **25/07/42:** Hit while parked at Portreath by Beaufort AW274 and repaired on site. **12/12/42:** To Stn Flt Colerne/39MU. **25/03/43:** Damaged and returned to Westland, but recategorised on 22/04/43 as unrepairable. It is believed that extensive corrosion was discovered.

P7117 *Bellows Argentina III*

27/10/41: 39MU. **03/11/41:** 263 Sqn. **16/04/42:** Starboard undercarriage collapsed on landing at Fairwood Common. Sgt Meredith unhurt. Repaired on site by Westland and reissued to its unit on 06/06/42. **09/08/42:** Aircraft hit a lorry during formation take off from Angle. Flt Sgt Reed landed safely. Repaired on site and reissued to its unit on 19/09/42. **03/04/43:** Sent to Westland for repair and returned to its unit on 14/04/43. **18/04/43:** Aircraft failed to return from a night attack on railway targets in Isigny-St Lo area. FO Cecil King, DFM, missing.

Whirlwind P7116 was presentation aircraft *Bellows Argentina No. 2*. She had a long life with No. 263 Squadron between 3 November 1941 and 26 March 1943 when she was struck off charge and scrapped. (*Robert Bowater*)

P7118 *Bellows Argentina No. 4*
11/11/41: 48MU. 20/02/42: 137 Sqn. 29/05/42: PO Jowitt parachuted to safety after an engine glycol leak. Aircraft crashed at Itteringham, Norfolk. Crash site partially excavated in 1981.

P7119 *Bellows Argentina No. 5*
11/11/41: 48MU. 05/02/42: 137 Sqn. 05/06/42: Flown to Westland for repair and returned to its unit on 26/06/42. 23/12/42: Damaged by flak when attacking shipping off Boulogne. FO Furber unhurt. Repaired on site. 19/02/43: Aircraft hit by P7114 while taxiing at Manston, caught fire and its bombs exploded. Lt Neville Freeman (SAAF) killed.

P7120 *Bellows Argentina No. 6*
08/12/41: 48MU. 26/02/42: 263 Sqn. 05/07/42: Aircraft hit while parked at Portreath by P7013. Repaired on site and returned to its unit on 21/07/42. 28/10/42: Pilot landed wheels up at Warmwell. Flt Lt Cooksey unhurt. Sent to Westland, but recategorised on 15/11/42 as unrepairable and dismantled.

P7121 *Bellows Argentina No. 7*
08/12/41: 39MU. 06/02/42: 137 Sqn. 27/02/42: Tailwheel collapsed on landing. PO Bryan unhurt. Repaired on site and returned to its unit on 13/04/42. 16/04/43: Crashed during dive-bombing practice over Manston. FO John Hadow killed.

P7122 *Bellows Uruguay*
16/12/41: 39MU. 13/03/42: 137 Sqn. 09/04/42: Aircraft hit power cables en route to Snailwell. PO Bryan landed safely at Matlaske. Repaired on site and reissued to its unit on 18/04/42. 27/05/42: Pilot shot down a Bristol Blenheim in error and flew on to Netherlands to attack ground targets. Shot down by flak at Velsen. Sgt John Brennan (RCAF) killed.

Second (provisional) order for 200 Whirlwinds under contract 20186./39. All subsequently cancelled: R4243-R4283, R4296-R4325, R4345-R4384, R4400-R4445, R4460-R4479, R4499-R4521.

Endnotes

Chapter 1: Origins

1. TNA: AIR9/37, 'Air Staff Requirements in Aircraft'. Paper by Wg Cdr Welsh of the Directorate of Flying Operations, 01/03/28.
2. The RAF's use of the word 'Interceptor' to describe these aircraft was unfortunate and confusing. All of its single-seat fighters, including the zone fighters, were designed to intercept bombers. The American term 'Pursuit' might have been more appropriate.
3. TNA: AIR2/848, A&AEE Report M/572/Arm.Int2, Gloster F.10/27 gun installation, July 1931. Saro produced the other prototype.
4. TNA: AIR20/169, Newall (DCAS) to Salmond (CAS), May 1930.
5. TNA: AIR2/2741, 'Minutes of a conference on Air Staff Requirements for Fury replacement', 09/08/34.
6. TNA: AIR2/706, 'Minutes of a conference held 16/10/34 to discuss the experimental aircraft programme for 1935'.
7. TNA: AIR2/2821, 'Draft of Air Staff Requirements for a Single Engine, Single-Seat, Day and Night Fighter', 14/03/35.
8. TNA: AIR2/2821, 'Notes on a conference held 29/03/35 to discuss the Operational Requirements for F.10/35 and F.9/35'.
9. TNA: AIR2/605, Hawker brochure 04/09/34, Buchanan to Cave, 10/09/34, Cave to Dowding, 13/09/34, Dowding's agreement, 14/09/34.
10. TNA: AIR2/2850/44A: Supermarine to Buchanan, 27/07/34, 50A, Contracts to Supermarine, 04/09/34 and 59A, ITP, 01/12/34.
11. TNA: AIR20/169 O.R. to Courtney, 01/05/35.
12. TNA: AVIA8/166, High-Speed Monoplane with RR PV12 engine, Verney to Contracts, 28/05/35.
13. TNA: AIR2/2821, Verney to O. R. via Dowding and Courtney, 21/05/35 and Dowding to Courtney, 23/05/35 and AIR2/2741/53A, Corrigenda to Spec. F.5/34.
14. TNA: AIR5/1137 Air Fighting Committee, 15th Mtg. 'Further review by O. R. of the use for air fighting of a gun of larger calibre than machine guns', 26/07/35.
15. TNA: AIR2/2821, Courtney to Ellington, 11/11/35 and reply 13/11/35.
16. TNA: AIR2/2821, Verney to Contracts, 15/01/36 and 'Amended Type Requirements for F.37/35', 01/02/36.

Chapter 2: Contenders and Prototypes

17. TNA: SUPP4/354, Aircraft Contracts Register.
18. TNA: AVIA46/122/2A, Verney (DTD) to Freeman (AMDP), 03/06/36.
19. TNA: AVIA46/122/2A, Freeman to Ellington (CAS), 15/07/36.
20. TNA: AVIA46/122/2A, Verney to Contracts, 27/08/36.
21. TNA: T161/1230, 'Experimental aircraft development expenditure'.
22. TNA: AVIA46/122/2A, Air Ministry Memo No. 46 for the TISC, 19/11/36.
23. TNA: SUPP4/354 Contracts Register, 07/12/36 and AVIA46/122/2A, 48th Meeting of TISC, 26/11/36.
24. TNA: AIR6/28, 65th EPM, 12/01/37.
25. TNA: AIR6/48, Note by Ellington 'B.12/36 Heavy Bomber', 31/12/36 and AIR6/28, Minutes of 64th EPM, 05/01/37.
26. TNA: AIR10/1545, DTD Quarterly Report, 30/04/37 and AVIA46/122/3A, prototype progress report extracts, 10/04/37 and 01/05/37.
27. TNA: AVIA15/2360/20A, Mock-up Examination, 28/05/37.
28. TNA: AIR10/1546, DTD Quarterly Report, 31/07/37.
29. TNA: AVIA18/487, A&AEE Report M/Arm/482, 'Hispano 20 mm Cannon – Type 404 (long) mounted in Dewoitine Type 510' Pt.1, Feb. 37 and Pt. 2, 25/05/37 and AIR2/1318, 'DTD Quarterly Armament Report', 31/01/37.
30. TNA: AIR6/31, 91st EPM, 27/07/37, 95th EPM, 05/10/37 and AIR6/50, EPM, Summary for August 1937.
31. TNA: AIR10/1546, DTD Quarterly Report, 31/07/37 and AVIA15/2360/21A, Mock-up Examination, 06/09/37.
32. TNA: AIR6/31, 97th EPM, 19/10/37 and AIR10/1547, DTD and DAD Quarterly Report, 31/10/37.
33. TNA: AIR10/1548, DTD and DAD Quarterly Report, 31/01/38.
34. TNA: SUPP4/355, Aircraft Contracts Register.
35. TNA: AVIA10/12, Hives (R-R) to Freeman, 27/06/38, AIR10/1549, DTD and DAD Quarterly Progress Report, 30/04/38, AIR10/1640, DGRD Quarterly Report, 31/07/38 and AVIA46/122/3A, Extracts from RTO reports, 1st prototype, 02/03/38 to 25/05/38.
36. TNA: AVIA46/122/3A, RTO weekly reports, extracts, 1st prototype, 06/07/38, 14/07/38 and 20/07/38.
37. TNA: AVIA46/122/3A, RTO weekly reports, extracts 1st prototype, 10/08/38 and 31/08/38.
38. TNA: AIR2/2821, Douglas to Freeman, 12/07/38.
39. TNA: AIR2/2821, Douglas to Freeman, 19/07/38.
40. TNA: AIR2/2821, Lemon (DGP) to Freeman, 24/08/38.
41. Supermarine Specification 460.
42. TNA: AIR2/3514, Douglas to Freeman, 08/08/38.
43. TNA: AIR2/3514, Liptrot (RDA3): Comments on Supermarine submission, 16/09/38.
44. TNA: AIR2/3075/10A, 'Beaufort Fighter', Provisional Specification.
45. TNA: AIR2/3075, Buchanan (DDGP) to Saundby (DDOR), 22/11/38 and Douglas to Newall, 29/11/38.
46. TNA: AIR2/3075, Newall, 01/02/39.
47. TNA: AIR2/3075/1A, 2nd Draft, Air Staff Requirements for a fixed-gun fighter development of the Beaufort.
48. TNA: AVIA15/2360/22A, Preliminary Final Conference, 27/09/37.
49. TNA: AVIA46/122/3A, Weekly letters from RTO.

50. Penrose, Harald, *British Aviation: Ominous Skies 1935-1939*.
51. TNA: AVIA46/122/3A, Weekly letters from RTO.

Chapter 3: Perfecting the Whirlwind

52. TNA: AIR19/2, Aberconway to Sir Kingsley Wood, 10/01/39.
53. TNA: AIR6/55, 146th EPM, 02/12/38. 'Group Schemes for the production of New Type Bombers and Fighters' and AIR2/3044, AM Memo No. 338 to the Treasury Inter-Services Committee (TISC), 20/12/38.
54. TNA: AVIA46/122/8A, Flight and Ground Trials.
55. TNA: AVIA18/663, A&AEE, M/733, Pt. 1 and AVIA1/12, RAE flight log, 1937-39.
56. TNA: AIR19/2, Contracts to Westland, 11/01/39.
57. TNA: AIR6/56, 'Supply Committee, 34th Meeting', 03/01/39 and AIR2/3044, AM Memo No. 350 to the TISC, 17/01/39.
58. TNA: AVIA15/2360/1A, Petter to Air Ministry, 25/11/38, 11D, Petter to Rowe (AD/RDL), 21/12/38, 4A, Petter to Hill, 05/01/39 and AVIA18/1238, RAE Report M.Res.123, 'Tests on a standard Blenheim L6594 and one with opposite handed airscrews K7109'.
59. TNA: AVIA15/2360/11A, Bulman (DD/RDE and DEP) to DAP, DSP, 10/01/39 and 12B, memorandum by Rowe (AD/RDL), 20/01/39.
60. TNA: AVIA10/12, Notes of a meeting with Rolls-Royce, 02/02/39, AIR10/215, Sidgreaves (R-R) to Wood, 31/03/39 and AVIA46/1228A, F.37/35 flight and ground trials.
61. TNA: AVIA15/2360/11E and D, Rowe to Westland, 15/12/38 and Petter's reply, 21/12/38, AVIA46/122/2A, AVIA15/2360/3A, Spurr to Rowe, 04/01/39, AVIA15/2360/9B, Notes on meeting held 13/01/39, AVIA15/2360/10A, Rowe to Petter, 17/01/39.
62. TNA: AVIA15/2360/25A, Minutes of a meeting held to settle outstanding queries affecting production of Westland F.37/35, 23/02/39 and Petter's comments, 25/02/39.
63. TNA: AVIA46/122/8A, flight and ground trials, AVIA15/2360/28B, Petter to Rowe, 10/03/39 and /30A, Notes of Decisions made by AMDP at Informal Conference, 29/03/39.
64. TNA: AVIA2/2821/79A, Minutes: Howat (RDL2(a)), Sorley (DOR) and Woodin (OR1), 16/05/39 and 05/06/39 and AIR2/2821/78A, Specification F.37/35/P.1/WE – Production of Westland F.37/35 aircraft, 05/06/39.
65. TNA: AIR 20/425, 5th DGRD/ACAS Liaison Mtg. 05/05/39 and AVIA15/2360/37A, 'F.37/35 – Maintenance', Rowarth to Rowe, 25/05/39.
66. *Flight*, 01/06/39.
67. TNA: AVIA15/2360/40A, Petter to Davenport, Penrose, Air Ministry et al, 26/05/39.
68. TNA: AVIA15/2360, Rowe to Farren, 13/06/39.
69. TNA: AVIA15/2360/39c, 'Whirlwind Exhaust System', Rowe to Westland, 13/06/39 and reply 20/06/39.
70. TNA: AIR19/1, Private Office Paper, notes on a meeting between Kingsley Wood, Lord Nuffield and Oliver Boden, 15/06/39.
71. TNA: AIR6/57, Supply Committee, 52nd Meeting, 04/07/39.
72. TNA: AVIA10/310, 19th DGP meeting, 'Whirlwind Subcontracting arrangements', 10/07/39.

Chapter 4: Trials, Cancellation and Reprieve

73. RAFML: B214, Hugh Saint, Letter of 12/09/39.
74. TNA: AIR6/39, RAF Expansion Progress Meetings (EPM), 173rd and 178th meetings, 27/06/39 and 01/08/39.
75. TNA: AVIA46/66, 'Meeting to discuss air requirements of the Army' and AIR8/291, 'Composition of the RAF – Long range war programme', Slessor (Director of Plans) to Newall (CAS), 17/11/39.
76. TNA: AIR8/240, 'Progress of Development of Scheme M.', AIR8/291, 'Estimated aircraft requirements to equip and maintain a 32 Division Force', 30/10/39 and AIR20/2022, Intake of aircraft, 03/09/39.
77. TNA: AVIA10/310, 26th meeting of the DDGP, 09/10/39 and AIR6/40, 186th EPM, 10/10/39.
78. TNA: AVIA10/20, Freeman to Bruce-Gardner, 22/09/39.
79. TNA: AIR6/58, Supply Committee, 86th-88th meetings, 12/10/39, 13/10/39 and 14/10/39.
80. TNA: AVIA10/12. 'Note on AMDP meeting with Mr EW Hives', 14/10/39.
81. TNA: AIR19/2, 'Shadow Programme', Kingsley Wood to Aberconway, 26/10/39.
82. TNA: AIR6/40, 187th EPM, 31/10/39.
83. Later variously called The Heston Flight, No. 2 Camouflage Unit, PDU and No. 1 PRU.
84. TNA: AIR41/6, Appendix VIII, 'Photographic Reconnaissance of enemy territory in war', Memorandum by FO M. V Longbottom, August 1939.
85. TNA: AIR20/425, 10th ACAS/DGRD Liaison Meeting, 18/10/39, 'High Speed Photographic Aircraft as an Immediate Requirement'.
86. TNA: AIR6/58, Supply Committee, 89th-93rd meetings, 19-24/10/39, Decision: Contract for Whirlwinds and AIR6/40, 187th EPM, 31/10/39.
87. TNA: AIR6/40, 188th EPM, 14/11/39.
88. TNA: AIR6/58, Supply Committee, 108th-111th meetings, 17-24/11/39.
89. RAFML: B214, Saint, Letter of 27/09/39.
90. Rolls-Royce Archives.
91. RAFML: B236, Saint, Work carried out before 53rd flight and during lay up 19/10/39-22/01/40 and B215, Reports W/E 04/11/39, 02/12/39 and 13/01/40.
92. Rolls-Royce Archives and RAFML: B236, Saint, 'Summary of work carried out before 56th flight and during lay up 07-31/03/40'.
93. TNA: AVIA18/691, A&AEE/733, Pt. 4, 'Brief performance and handling trials'.
94. TNA: AVIA6/13705, 'RAE Large Wind Tunnel Note No. 30', Tests of Whirlwind L6844 in the 24-feet tunnel, May 1940; AVIA6/13709, Note No. 34 and AVIA6/13712, Note No. 38, Estimation of top speed drag from 24-feet tunnel and performance tests.
95. TNA: AVIA6/5444, RAE Note No. E.3750, 'Note on the vibration in flight of the tail unit of the Westland F.37/35 aeroplane No. L6845', November 1939.
96. TNA: AIR20/425, 16th DGRD/ACAS meeting, 07/02/40 and 21st meeting, 17/04/40, 'Aircraft for the PDU'.
97. TNA: AVIA10/40, Prototype Aircraft Progress Report, 29/03/40.
98. TNA: AIR2/7159, 'PDU: Aircraft Requirements', Peck (DOR) to ACAS(T), 30/03/40.
99. TNA: AVIA15/317/1A, Petter to Tedder (DGRD), 15/02/40.
100. TNA: AVIA15/505, 'Belt feed for Hispano 20 mm guns – Hydran', 20A and 34A correspondence between Hydran and Air Ministry.
101. TNA: AVIA15/317, Petter to Tedder, 01/04/40.

102. TNA: AVIA15/317, Petter to Rowe (AD/RDL), 17/04/40 and Petter to Tedder, 02/05/40.
103. TNA: AVIA15/317, Farren (DD/RDA) to Westland, 17/05/40.
104. TNA: AVIA15/317, Rowe to Farren, 30/03/40.
105. TNA: AVIA15/317, Farren to DTD, Tedder, Rowe, DArmD, 04/04/40.
106. TNA: AVIA15/317 Bulman (DDRDE and DEP) to McEntegart (DD/RDQ), 05/05/40 and 19A, Bulman to Freeman (AMDP), 08/05/40.
107. TNA: AVIA15/317/19A, Freeman to Bulman. Undated, but written between 08-11/05/40.
108. TNA: AIR16/326, Mensforth to Beardsworth (CTO, Fighter Command), 15/06/40.
109. TNA: AVIA15/505/25A, 'Report on Ground Firing Trials of M-type feed at Hydran Products' and 35B, A&AEE, 'Type M Servo feed for 20 mm guns', 20/07/40.
110. TNA: AVIA15/505/38A, A&AEE to DArmD, 'Type M Feed: 20 mm Gun in Whirlwind Aircraft', 15/10/40.
111. TNA: AIR29/768, AGME Report No. 15 'Trials of 20 mm guns with Mk 1 feed in Whirlwind L6844', Pt. 1, 21/07/41, Pt. 2 19/08/41 and RAFML: MFC 77/15/124, Movement Card, L6844.
112. TNA: AIR16/326, Mensforth to Sholto Douglas (C-in-C, Fighter Command), 21/01/41 and Westland Archives.
113. TNA: AVIA46/66, 1st Wartime Programme, 'Gross weights of materials for one airframe'.
114. TNA: AVIA46/122, Minutes of 1st Meeting of the Joint Development and Production Committee, 03/02/41.
115. TNA: AVIA15/536, 'Question of fitting 20 mm guns into Aircraft for low anti-tank attack', AD/DTD to DTD, 17/06/40.
116. TNA: AIR8/658, 'Use of Aircraft Against Tanks', Sholto Douglas to Portal (CAS), 26/04/41.
117. TNA: AIR8/658, Sorley (ACAS(T)) to Freeman (VCAS), 30/04/41.
118. TNA: AVIA15/1571/14A, Linnell (CRD) to DTD and DArmD, 15/12/41.
119. TNA: AVIA15/1571/11A, 'Installation of Rolls-Royce cannon in Whirlwind' and 12A, 'Notes on a visit to Westland', both 18/12/41.
120. TNA: AVIA15/1571/17A, Minutes of meeting held at MAP.
121. TNA: AVIA15/1571/20A and B, Serby (DD/RDA) to Frazer Nash and Petter, 26/01/42.
122. TNA: AVIA15/1571, Sorley to Linnell, 30/01/42.

Chapter 5: 'An infinity of trouble' – Early Days with Fighter Command

123. TNA: AIR16/326, 'Report on a visit to Westland', Beardsworth (CTO, Fighter Command) to Dowding, Evill, Nicholl, 24/05/40, AIR 27/305, ORB, 25 Sqn, RAFML: B215, Hugh Saint (Westland technical representative), Report, W/E 01/06/40 and RAFML: AC 94/36, Flying Logbook, Wg Cdr FV Beamish.
124. RAFML: B215, Saint, Report, W/E 08/06/40.
125. TNA: AIR28/525, ORB, Martlesham Heath.
126. RAFML: B215, Saint, Report, W/E 29/06/40 and Rolls-Royce archive.
127. TNA: AIR16/326, Beaverbrook to Dowding, 28/06/40.
128. TNA: AIR16/326, Dowding to Beaverbrook, 01/07/40.
129. TNA: AIR16/326, Nicholl (AOA) to Dowding, 14/06/40 and reply 16/06/40, AIR16/944, Daily state, 18:00 hrs, 05/07/40 and AIR2/4239, 'Introduction of the Beaufighter Aircraft to the Service', Postagrams, 07/07/40 and 10/07/40.

130. TNA: AIR2/4244/99A, 'Fighter Squadron Formation – Policy', PDDO Telegram 15/06/40 and AIR16/943, Daily state, 18:00 hrs, 18/06/40.
131. TNA: AIR27/1547, ORB, 263 Sqn and RAFML: B215, Saint to Westland, 26/07/40.
132. RAFML: B215, Saint to Westland, 26/07/40.
133. RAFML: B216, Saint to Westland, 14/08/40 and 20/08/40.
134. Modifications 56 and 49 respectively.
135. TNA: AIR16/326, 'Report on a conference held at Drem on 25/09/40, on the defects occurring to Whirlwind aircraft' and 'Defects – Whirlwind aircraft', HQ 13 Group to HQ Fighter Command, 24/09/40.
136. TNA: AIR27/1547, ORB, 263 Sqn and AIR16/326, Petter (Westland) to Beardsworth, 15/10/40.
137. TNA: AIR 16/635, Min 102, Dowding to Evill for Stevenson (Director Home Operations) 13/11/40.
138. TNA: AIR 16/326/59A, Dowding to Beaverbrook (MAP), 17/10/40.
139. TNA: AIR16/326/62A, Dowding to Beaverbrook, 27/10/40.
140. TNA: AIR16/326/98A, Andrews (ACAS(T)) to Harris (DCAS), 27/11/40 and reply 29/11/40.
141. RAFML: B216, Saint to Westland, 08/11/40 and Flying Log Book, Peter Wyatt-Smith.
142. TNA: AIR16/326, Petter to Douglas (C-in-C, Fighter Command), 26/11/40.
143. TNA: AIR28/220, ORB, Drem, Ref. Auth HQ FC 0905, 26/11/40.
144. TNA: AIR16/326, Douglas to Petter, 27/11/40.
145. TNA: AIR27/1547, ORB, 263 Sqn.
146. RAFML: B216, Saint, Report of 01/12/40.
147. RAFML: B216, Saint, letter of 05/12/40.
148. TNA: AIR16/365, Fighter Command Order of Battle, 09:00 hrs, 22/12/40.

Chapter 6: Operational at Last

149. RAFML: B216, Saint to Westland, 12/12/40 and TNA: AIR27/1547, ORB, 263 Sqn.
150. RAFML: B216, Saint, Report, 27/12/40.
151. TNA: AIR27/1547, ORB, 263 Sqn and RAFML: B216, Saint, Letter of, 29/12/40.
152. TNA: AIR27/1547, ORB, 263 Sqn.
153. TNA: AIR25/184, 10 Gp Ops Order No. 3, 'Operations against enemy "E" Boats (Rescue Craft)', 07/01/41.
154. RAFML: B216, Saint, Letter of 13/01/41, TNA: AIR27/1547, ORB, 263 Sqn and AIR27/1550, Intelligence Combat Report, 12/01/41.
155. TNA: AIR27/1550, Intelligence Combat Report, 13/01/41.
156. TNA: AVIA5/19, Accident Investigation Report W955, AIR28/261, ORB, Exeter and RAFML: B216, Saint, Letter to Westland, 19/01/41.
157. TNA: AIR25/184, 10 Group Ops Order No. 5, 'Interception of Focke-Wulf Condor 200', 21/01/41.
158. RAFML: B217, Saint papers, MFC 77/16/33 Accident record cards for P6973 and P6971 and TNA: AIR27/1547, ORB, 263 Sqn.
159. TNA: AIR27/1550, Interception Report, (Crooks) and Combat Report (Hughes and Rudland), 08/02/41.
160. TNA: AIR27/1550, Combat Reports, (Kitchener and Thornton-Brown), 01/03/41.
161. TNA: AIR27/1551, Combat Report, (Kitchener), 05/03/41.

162. TNA: AIR27/1551, Combat Report, (Kitchener) and Intelligence Combat Report, 11/03/41.

163. TNA: AIR27/1551/18, Combat Report, (Donaldson), 01/04/41.

164. TNA: AIR27/1550, Combat Report, 06/04/41.

165. TNA: AIR27/1550, Combat Report, (Ferdinand and King), 07/04/41.

166. TNA: AVIA5/20, Accident Investigation Reports W1004 (Hampden P2115) and W1014 (Whirlwind P7008).

167. TNA: AVIA18/691, 6th Part of A&AEE/733 'Handling trials with outboard slats locked', 28/05/41 and AIR2/2821, RDL1 to DOR, 25/05/41.

168. TNA: AIR27/1547, ORB, 263 Sqn and RAFML, MFC 77/16/33 Accident record card, P7006.

169. TNA: AVIA5/20, Accident Investigation Report W1039.

170. TNA: AIR25/184, 10 Gp Monthly Ops Report, June 1941 and AIR27/1551, 'Report on Warhead No. 1'.

171. TNA: AIR16/440, Attack on tanks by fighters; Exercises and Trials, Sholto Douglas to SASO, 15/04/41 and AIR8/568, 'Use of aircraft against tanks', Min. 4, Sinclair to Portal, 30/07/41.

172. TNA: AIR8/568/12B, 'Report of fighter aircraft vs. tanks trials', 04/08/41.

173. TNA: AIR8/568, Brotherhood (OR6) to DDOR, 08/08/41.

Chapter 7: The Turning Point

174. TNA: AIR 25/184, 10 Gp Ops Report, Aug 1941 and AIR27/1551/24-25, 'Warhead No. 2', 02/08/41.

175. TNA: AIR25/184, 10 Gp Ops Report, Aug 1941 and AIR27/1551/26, 'Warhead Operation No. 3', 05/08/41.

176. TNA: AIR27/1551/27, 'Warhead No. 4', 06/08/41 and AIR27/1547, ORB, 263 Sqn.

177. TNA: AIR27/1551/35, Combat Report (Rudland), 06/08/41.

178. TNA: AIR27/1551/30, Intelligence Report, 06/08/41/32-34 Reports, (Brackley, Rudland and Donaldson) and AIR27/907, ORB, 118 Sqn.

179. TNA: AIR25/184, 10 Gp Operational Instruction No. 54, 'MANDOLIN', 08/08/41.

180. TNA: AIR25/184, Amendment 2 to 10 Gp Operational Instruction No. 54, 02/08/41.

181. TNA: AIR25/184, 10 Gp Ops Report, Aug 1941 and AIR27/1551/36-7, 'Report on Operation No. 77', 12/08/41.

182. TNA: AIR25/184, 10 Gp Ops Report, Aug 1941, AIR28/395, ORB, Ibsley and AIR27/1551/38, 'Report on Offensive Operation', 17/08/41.

183. TNA: AIR27/1551/39, Report on Offensive Operation, 24/08/41 and AIR27/598, ORB, 66 Sqn.

184. TNA: AIR25/184, 10 Gp Ops Report, Aug 1941 and AIR27/1551/41-2, 'Report on Offensive Operation', 26/08/41.

185. TNA: AIR27/1551/43, 'Report on Offensive Operation', 26/08/41 and AIR27/1431, ORB, 234 Sqn.

186. TNA: AIR 27/1551/44, 'Report – Colerne Mandolin No. 3', 29/08/41 and AIR25/184, 10 Gp Ops Report, Aug 1941.

187. TNA: AIR27/1547, ORB, 263 Sqn.

188. TNA: AIR25/184, 10 Gp Ops Report, Aug 1941.

189. TNA: AIR27/1547, ORB, 263 Sqn, AIR27/1551/46, FC Combat Report, 04/09/41 and AIR25/184, 10 Gp Ops Report, 'Gudgeon VI', 07/09/41.

190. TNA: AIR27/1551/47, Combat Report, 08/09/41, AIR25/184, 10 Gp Ops Report, 10/09/41 and RAFML: B217, Saint papers.

191. TNA: AIR25/184, 10 Gp Ops Report, Sept 1941 and AIR27/1551/48, Summary of Operation.
192. RAFML: B217, Saint to Westland, 15/09/41.
193. TNA: AIR27/1547, ORB, 263 Sqn, AIR25/184, 10 Gp Ops Report, Sept 1941, AIR27/1551/50-51, Mandolin Operation, 28/09/41, AIR28/649, ORB, Portreath and RAFML: B218, Saint to Westland 29/09/41.
194. TNA: AIR27/1547, ORB, 263 Sqn, AIR27/1551/53-54, Offensive Operation, Mandolin 7, 30/09/41, AIR27/1551/52, Addendum to Report, 01/10/41, AIR28/649, ORB, Portreath and AIR25/184, 10 Gp Ops Report, Sept 1941.

Chapter 8: Two from One

195. TNA: AIR 20/1862, 'Aircraft stored at Maintenance Units at Home', Return of 29/08/41.
196. TNA: AIR 27/954, ORB, 137 Sqn.
197. TNA: AIR 27/954, ORB, 137 Sqn.
198. TNA: AIR 28/651, ORB, RAF Predannack and AIR 27/954, ORB, 137 Sqn.
199. TNA: AIR 27/954, ORB, 137 Sqn and RAFML: B218, Saint papers, Letter to Westland, 29/10/41.
200. TNA: AIR 27/954, ORB, 137 Sqn and AIR 28/651, ORB, Predannack.
201. TNA: AIR 28/651, ORB, Predannack, AIR 27/1547, ORB, 263 Sqn and AIR 27/1551/55, Report on Rhubarb No. 33, 29/10/41.
202. TNA: AIR 28/651, ORB, Predannack, AIR 27/1547, ORB, 263 Sqn and AIR 27/1551/56, Report on Rhubarb No. 35, 30/10/41.
203. TNA: AIR 27/1547, ORB, 263 Sqn.
204. TNA: AIR 28/888, ORB, Warmwell and AIR 27/1547, ORB, 263 Sqn.
205. TNA: AIR 27/1547, ORB, 263 Sqn.
206. RAFML: MFC 77/16/33, Accident Record Card, P6987 and TNA: AIR 27/1547, ORB, 263 Sqn.
207. RAFML: MFC 77/16/33, Accident Record Card, P7038.

Chapter 9: 263 Squadron Feb-Sept 1942

208. TNA: AIR27/1550/98-99, 'Continuation of Squadron History' and AIR27/2060, ORB, 600 Sqn.
209. RAFML: MFC 77/1/56A, F.1180, P7108, 13/02/42.
210. TNA: AIR27/1548, ORB, 263 Sqn.
211. TNA: AIR27/1548, ORB, 263 Sqn and AP1761A Vol. 1, Mod. No. 24.
212. RAFML: MFC77/1/56A, F.1180s, P7039, 07/03/42 and P7004, 14/03/42.
213. TNA: AIR27/1548, ORB, 263 Sqn and RAFML: MFC77/1/56A, F.1180s, P7112, 01/04/42 and P7041, 02/04/42. The squadron ORB identifies the pilot as Small and the obstruction as a fuel bowser. The accident record identifies the pilot as Basil Abrams and the obstacle as a dispersal bay.
214. TNA: AIR25/185, 10 Gp Ops Order, 'Ramrod No. 8', 22/04/42.
215. TNA: AIR27/1548, ORB, 263 Sqn and AIR 27/1551/65, Report, Ramrod No. 18, 30/04/42.
216. TNA: AIR27/1551/68-69, Form F, Ramrod No. 19, AIR27/1551/70, Ops Report, Circus No. 7 and Ramrod No. 19, 05/06/42, AIR 28/649, ORB, Portreath, AIR27/1548, ORB, 263 Sqn and AIR27/936, ORB, 130 Sqn.
217. TNA: AIR27/1439, ORB, 234 Sqn, AIR27/1548, ORB, 263 Sqn and AIR27/1551/74, Composite Report, 10 Gp Rhubarb No. 85.

Chapter 10: The Narrow Sea – 137 Squadron at Matlaske

218. RAFML: B218, Saint, letter of 24/12/41, TNA: AIR28/168, ORB, RAF Coltishall and AIR27/954, ORB, 137 Sqn.
219. TNA: AIR28/168, ORB, Coltishall, AIR50/59/37, Combat Report (Martin and McClure) 01/02/42 and AIR27/954, ORB, 137 Sqn.
220. TNA: AIR28/168, ORB, Coltishall, AIR50/59/38-39, Combat Report, (Robertson), 06/02/42 and AIR27/954, ORB, 137 Sqn.
221. RAFML: B218, Saint, letter of 11/02/42 and TNA: AIR28/168, ORB, Coltishall.
222. TNA: AIR27/954, ORB, 137 Sqn; AIR50/59/40, Combat Report (Mercer and De Houx), 14/02/42; ADM116/458, Board of Enquiry, Evidence given by de Houx and Mercer; AIR41/47, AHB Narrative, The RAF in Maritime War; AIR28/168, ORB, RAF Coltishall; AIR28/897 ORB, Wattisham and RAFML: B218, Saint, report of 16/02/42.
223. TNA: AIR28/168, ORB, Coltishall, AIR27/954, ORB, 137 Sqn and AIR27/1805, ORB, 412 Sqn.
224. TNA: AVIA5/21, Accident Report W1229, AIR28/168, ORB, Coltishall and RAFML: B219, Saint, letter of 08/05/42.
225. TNA: AIR50/59/41, Combat Report, 15/05/42 and AIR28/168, ORB, Coltishall.
226. TNA: AIR28/168, ORB, Coltishall and AIR27/954, ORB, 137 Sqn.
227. TNA: AIR28/168, ORB, Coltishall, AIR27/954, ORB, 137 Sqn and AIR29/866, ORB, 1401 (Met.) Flight.
228. TNA: AIR28/168, ORB, Coltishall and AIR27/954 ORB, 137 Sqn.
229. TNA: AIR28/168, ORB, Coltishall.
230. TNA: AIR28/168, ORB, Coltishall and AIR50/59/42, Form 'F', 27/06/42.
231. RAFML: MF10084, Flying Logbook, L. H. Bartlett and MFC 77/16/56A, Accident Record Card, P7101.
232. TNA: AIR28/168, ORB, Coltishall, AIR 50/59/2, Combat Report (Bartlett) 06/07/42 and RAFML: MF10084, Logbook, Bartlett.
233. TNA: AIR50/59/26 and 34, Combat Reports, R. L. Smith and Waldron, 23/07/42.
234. TNA: AIR28/168, ORB, Coltishall and AIR50/59/17 and 29, Combat Reports, McClure and R. L. Smith, 25/07/42.
235. TNA: AIR50/59/43, Intelligence Combat Report, 29/07/42 and AIR28/168, ORB, Coltishall.
236. TNA: AIR27/954, ORB, 137 Sqn and AIR50/59/46, Combat Report (Luing and O'Neill), 18/08/42.
237. TNA: AIR50/59/48, Combat Report (Brown and van Schaick), 19/08/42.
238. TNA: AIR50/59/47, Combat Report (Bryan and Roberts), 19/08/42, AIR28/168, ORB, Coltishall, AIR27/1605, ORB, 278 Sqn and AIR40/2410, AI(K) Report 239/1942, Oblt Adolf Wolf.

Chapter 11: The Whirlibomber

239. TNA: AIR2/2821/87B, Fighter Command to ACAS(T), 03/07/42.
240. TNA: AVIA18/691, A&AEE/733a, Pt. 2, Handling trials with 2 x 500-lb bombs.
241. TNA: AVIA18/691, A&AEE/733a, Pt. 3, Performance and cooling tests with 2 x 500-lb bombs.
242. TNA: AVIA18/1000, A&AEE, 'Whirlwind Bombing Installation. Report No. 1'.

243. AP.1709/C3-W, Mod. No. 154 and TNA: AVIA 46/122/11A, 06/12/42.

244. TNA: AIR28/166, ORB, Colerne, AIR27/1548, ORB, 263 Sqn and AIR25/182, ORB, 10 Gp.

245. TNA: AIR27/1551/80, Roadstead Report, 08/09/42 and AIR 28/89, ORB, Bolt Head.

246. TNA: AIR27/1551/77-80, Roadstead Report, 09/09/42, AIR27/1548, ORB, 263 Sqn, AIR25/182, ORB, 10 Gp, AIR27/1551/79, Fighter Command, Anti-Shipping Operations, Period 01-15/09/42 and DEFE3/192, Ultra messages ZIP/ZTPG/73898, 73205, 73296 and 73496.

247. *The Times*, 10/09/42, p. 4.

248. TNA: AIR27/1551/97, 'Report on Bombing Activities by 263 Squadron', Woodward, 31/10/42.

249. TNA: AIR27/954, ORB, 137 Sqn and AIR27/2102, ORB, 609 Sqn.

Chapter 12: Rhubarb and Roadstead

250. TNA: AIR27/1550/100, 'Squadron History' and AVIA 5/21, Accident Report W1327.

251. TNA: AIR28/888, ORB, Warmwell and AIR 28/341, ORB, Harrowbeer.

252. TNA: AIR27/1551/85-88, Final Report, 10 Gp Roadstead; AIR27/1551/84, Form 'F', AIR28/888, ORB, Warmwell, AIR27/907, ORB, 118 Sqn and AIR27/1950, ORB, 501 Sqn.

253. TNA: AIR28/888, ORB, Warmwell and AIR27/1551/93, Warmwell Shipping Recco Report.

254. TNA: AIR27/1550/101, 'Squadron History'.

255. TNA: AIR27/1551/95, Composite Report, Warmwell.

256. TNA: AIR27/1551/96, 98-99, Reports, Rhubarb 99.

257. TNA: AIR27/1551/97, Final Report and AIR 27/1551/100, Surfat Report.

258. TNA: AIR27/1551/105, Composite Report, AIR27/907, ORB, 118 Sqn and AIR27/1770, ORB, 400 Sqn.

259. TNA: AIR27/1551/106-109, Surfat Report, AIR28/888, ORB, Warmwell, AIR27/599, ORB, 66 Sqn and DEFE 3/210, Ultra signal ZTPG/91626.

260. TNA: AIR27/1551/112, Final Intelligence Report.

261. TNA: AIR28/651, ORB, Predannack, AIR25/182, ORB, 10 Gp and AIR27/1551/113, Composite Report.

262. TNA: AIR25/182, ORB, 10 Gp and AIR27/1551/114, Composite Report.

263. TNA: AIR27/1548, ORB, 263 Sqn, Warnes to HQ 10 Gp, 'Parachute Containers', 15/01/43.

264. TNA: AIR25/186, 10 Gp Report, Circus 13, AIR27/1597, ORB, 276 Sqn and AIR27/1551/115, ASR Composite Report.

265. TNA: AIR27/1551/116, Composite Report and AIR27/1551/117, Rhubarb Report, Warmwell.

266. TNA: AIR27/253, ORB, 19 Sqn and AIR27/1551/118, Report, Portreath.

267. TNA: AIR27/1551/121, Report, Rhubarb 164, AIR27/1597, ORB 276 Sqn and AIR27/1551/122, ASR Report.

268. TNA: AIR27/1551/125, Report, Warmwell.

269. TNA: AIR27/1551/126, Report, Warmwell.

270. TNA: AIR27/1551/129, Preliminary and composite report, and AIR27/1551/128, Rhubarb Report.

271. TNA: AIR28/341, ORB, Harrowbeer, AIR28/395 ORB, Ibsley, AIR27/1550/103, Final report on operations, AIR25/186, 10 Gp Report, Circus 16 and AIR27/1551/130, Circus 16, Report, Ibsley.

272. TNA: AIR27/1551/136, Op Report, Ramrod 54, AIR28/395 ORB, Ibsley, AIR25/186, 10 Gp Report, Ramrod 54, AIR27/1551/131, Diversion to 10 Gp Ramrod 54, Ibsley and AIR27/1550/103, Final report on operations.

273. TNA: AIR27/1551/134, Composite Report, Circus 17, Warmwell, AIR28/261, ORB, Exeter, AIR27/1551/133, Exeter Wing report, AIR27/1550/103, Final report on operations, AIR28/395 ORB, Ibsley, AIR25/186, 10 Gp Report, Circus 17 and AIR27/1551/138, Ops Report, Circus 17.

274. TNA: AIR27/1551/140, Report, Circus 18, Warmwell and AIR27/1551/141, Composite Report, Ibsley.

275. TNA: AIR25/186, 10 Gp Report, Ramrod 59.

276. TNA: AIR28/395 ORB, Ibsley and AIR27/1551/142, Wing Report, Ibsley.

277. TNA: AIR27/1551/143, Night Rhubarb 23, Portreath and AIR27/1551/144, Further Interrogation, Night Rhubarb 23, Portreath.

278. TNA: AIR27/1551/145 and 147, Night Rhubarb 24, Portreath.

279. TNA: AIR27/1551/146, Night Rhubarb 25, Portreath.

280. TNA: AIR28/888, ORB, Warmwell, AIR27/1551/151-152, Rhubarb Reports, Warmwell and RAFML: B1778, 263 Sqn A Flt Diary.

281. TNA: AIR28/888, ORB, Warmwell, AIR28/395 ORB, Ibsley, AIR25/205, 11 Gp, IB No. 322, AIR27/1551/155, Wing Report, AIR25/205, 11 Gp Report, Ramrod 53 and RAFML: B1778, 263 Sqn A Flt Diary.

282. TNA: AIR28/888, ORB, Warmwell, AIR 28/261, ORB, Exeter and AIR27/1551/156, Wing Report, Roadstead 55, Exeter.

283. TNA: AIR28/888, ORB, Warmwell, AIR27/1551/158, Report, Circus 22, Portreath, AIR27/1551/160, Report, Predannack, AIR28/651, ORB, Predannack and RAFML: B1778, 263 Sqn A Flt Diary.

284. TNA: AIR28/261, ORB, Exeter, AIR27/1548, ORB 263 Sqn, AIR27/1551/159, Composite Report, *Portreath* and *London Gazette* No. 36017, 18/05/43, p. 2199.

285. TNA: AIR28/888, ORB, Warmwell, AIR28/651, ORB, Predannack, AIR28/261, ORB, Exeter, AIR27/1551/162, Roadstead 57, Portreath, AIR27/1551/163-164, Surfat Report, Roadstead 57 and RAFML: B1778, 263 Sqn A Flt Diary.

286. RAFML: B1778, 263 Sqn A Flt Diary and TNA: AIR27/1551/168-169, Composite Report.

287. RAFML: B1778, 263 Sqn A Flight Diary and TNA: AIR27/1551/172-173, Final Report and AIR27/1551/170-171, Report, Warmwell.

288. TNA: AIR 8/888, ORB, Warmwell, AIR27/1551/177 and 178, Shipping Reconnaissance reports, Coyne and Lee-White, AIR27/1551/181, Night Roadstead Report and AIR27/1551/179-180, Surfat Report.

289. TNA: AIR28/888, ORB, Warmwell, AIR28/395 ORB, Ibsley, AIR28/261, ORB, Exeter, AIR27/1551/182-186, Composite and Surfat Reports, Roadstead 59 and RAFML: B1778, 263 Sqn A Flt Diary.

290. TNA: AIR27/1551/185-188, Surfat Reports, Roadstead 60, AIR27/1682, ORB, 310 Sqn and AIR28/261, ORB, Exeter.

291. TNA: AIR28/888, ORB, Warmwell, AIR28/395 ORB, Ibsley, AIR27/1551/190, Surfat Report and RAFML: B1778, 263 Sqn A Flt Diary.

292. TNA: AIR28/888, ORB, Warmwell and AIR27/1551/191, Roadstead 63, Portreath.

293. TNA: AIR28/261, ORB, Exeter, AIR28/888, ORB, Warmwell, AIR27/1682, ORB, 310 Sqn and AIR27/1551/193, Composite Report.

294. TNA: AIR28/888, ORB, Warmwell and AIR27/1151/197-199 and 202, Surfat Report, Roadstead 67.

295. RAFML: B1778, 263 Sqn A Flight Diary, TNA: AIR28/888, ORB, Warmwell, AIR27/1551/221-222, Warmwell Reports and AIR27/1551/200-201, Composite Reports.

296. TNA: AIR28/395 ORB, Ibsley, AIR28/888, ORB, Warmwell, AIR27/1551/205, Composite Report, Middle Wallop, AIR27/1967, ORB, 504 Sqn and AIR27/1551/203-204, Personal Combat Reports, Lee-White and Coyne.

297. RAFML: B1778, 263 Sqn A Flt Diary, TNA: AIR28/888, ORB, Warmwell, AIR27/1551/214, Composite Report, AIR27/1551/215, Surfat Report, Night Roadstead No. 2 and AIR2/4974, Recommendations for Honours and Awards.

298. TNA: AIR28/888, ORB, Warmwell, AIR28/395 ORB, Ibsley, AIR27/1551/216-7, Surfat and Roadstead Reports, Roadstead 70.

299. TNA: AIR28/395 ORB, Ibsley, AIR27/1551/224 and 226-227 Armed Shipping Reconnaissance and Surfat Reports, and KTB, 24th Minensuchflottille.

Chapter 13: 137 Squadron – Manston Months

300. TNA: AIR50/59/33, Personal Report, van Schaick, AIR40/1664, Rhubarb Ops, Appendix VIII, Hutted Camps, AIR27/739, ORB 91 Sqn, AIR27/1600, ORB, 277 Sqn and WO344/329/2, Liberation Questionnaire, Waldron.

301. TNA: AIR50/59/15, Combat Report, McClure and Freeman, 07/11/42.

302. TNA: AIR50/59/49, Intruder Report, 21-22/11/42.

303. TNA: AIR50/59/51, Rhubarb Report, 10/12/42.

304. TNA: AIR50/59/30, Combat Report, R. L. Smith, 15/12/42, AIR27/2105/136, Combat Report, 609 Sqn and AIR27/2102, ORB 609 Sqn.

305. TNA: AIR50/59/10 and 23, Combat Reports, Bryan and Rebbetoy, 19/12/42.

306. TNA: AIR27/2106/125, Beamont to OC RAF Biggin Hill, OC Manston and AIR27/2105/128, HQ 11 Gp to OC, Biggin Hill, 08/12/42.

307. TNA: AIR50/59/52, Rhubarb Report, 21/12/42.

308. TNA: AIR50/59/53, Rhubarb Report, 22/12/42.

309. TNA: AIR27/2102, ORB, 609 Sqn.

310. TNA: AIR25/205, 11 Gp Intelligence Bulletin No. 307, 8-14/01/43.

311. TNA: AIR50/59/54, Rhubarb Report, 11/01/43.

312. TNA: AIR25/205, 11 Gp Intruder Report, 15-16/01/43 and AIR27/2102 ORB, 609 Sqn.

313. TNA: AIR25/205, 11 Gp Intruder Report, 19-20/01/43.

314. TNA: AIR25/205, 11 Gp IB No. 309.

315. TNA: AIR25/205, 11 Gp IB No. 310.

316. TNA: AIR25/205, 11 Gp IB No. 310 and AIR50/59/19, Final Rhubarb Report, Musgrave, 28/01/43.

317. TNA: AIR50/59/20-21, Surfat Report, Musgrave, 10/02/43, AIR41/47, Draft AHB Narrative, 'The RAF in Maritime War' and AIR25/205, 11 Gp IB No. 312.

318. TNA: AIR25/205, 11 Gp IB No. 312.

319. TNA: WO344/330/1, Liberation Questionnaire, Walker.

320. TNA: AIR25/205, 11 Gp IB No. 317.

321. TNA: AIR25/205, 11 Gp Report, Ramrod 44 and IB No. 318.

322. TNA: AIR25/205, 11 Gp Report, Ramrod 46 and IB No. 320.

323. TNA: AIR24/578, 'Casualties on operational flights not due to enemy action'. April 1943.

324. TNA: AIR25/205, 11 Gp IB No. 321 and AIR27/2103, ORB 609 Sqn.

325. TNA: AIR25/205, 11 Gp Report, Ramrod 50 and IBs 322 and 323, and AIR28/385, ORB, Hornchurch.

326. RAFML, MFC 77/16/80, Accident Record Card, P7121, 16/04/43.
327. TNA: AIR25/205, 11 Gp IB No. 325 and AIR28/385, ORB, Hornchurch.
328. TNA: AIR25/206, 11 Gp IB No. 331.
329. TNA: AIR25/206, 11 Gp IB No. 331 and AIR27/2103, ORB, 609 Sqn.
330. TNA: AIR28/692, ORB, Southend and AIR25/206, 11 Gp IB No. 332.
331. TNA: AIR25/206, 11 Gp IB No. 332 and AIR28/692, ORB, Southend.
332. TNA: AIR28/692, ORB, Southend, AIR25/206, 11 Gp IB No. 333 and AIR50/59/36, Combat Report, Wray, 16/06/43.
333. TNA: AIR28/692, ORB, Southend and AIR25/206, 11 Gp IB No. 333.
334. TNA: AIR28/692, ORB, Southend and AIR25/206, 11 Gp IB No. 333.
335. TNA: AIR28/692, ORB, Southend and AIR25/206, 11 Gp IB No. 334.
336. TNA: AIR28/692, ORB, *Southend* and *London Gazette* of 27/07/43 and 24/08/43.

Chapter 14: Then There Was One

337. TNA: AIR28/261, ORB, Exeter, AIR28/395 ORB, Ibsley, AIR28/888 ORB, Warmwell, AIR25/186, 10 Gp, Circus 49 and RAFML: B1778, 263 Sqn A Flt Diary.
338. TNA: AIR28/888 ORB, Warmwell, AIR27/1708, ORB, 317 Sqn, AIR27/1661, ORB, 302 Sqn, AIR25/182, Appendices to ORB, 10 Gp, AIR27/1551/238-239, Surfat Report, DEFE3/298, Ultra signals ZTPG 154690 and 154908 and NHB, KTB, 5 Schnellbootflotille.
339. TNA: AIR28/261, ORB, Exeter, AIR28/888 ORB, Warmwell, AIR27/1551/240, Circus from Predannack, AIR27/1551/241, Composite Report, Warmwell and RAFML: B1778, A Flt Diary.
340. TNA: AIR28/888 ORB, Warmwell and AIR27/1551/243, Surfat Report and Personal Combat Report (Baker).
341. TNA: AIR28/261, ORB, Exeter, AIR25/186, 10 Gp Circus 51 and AIR27/1551/244, Circus from Predannack.
342. TNA: AIR27/1551/246 and 247, Composite Night Shipping Reconnaissance Reports.
343. TNA: AIR28/261, ORB, Exeter, AIR28/888 ORB, Warmwell, AIR27/1551/250, Report, Ramrod 74 and RAFML: B1778, A Flt Diary.
344. RAFML: B1778, A Flt Diary, TNA: AIR28/888 ORB, Warmwell and AIR27/1551/253, Surfat Report.
345. TNA: AIR8/1202, Harris (C-in-C, Bomber Command) to Evill (VCAS), 25/08/43.
346. TNA: AIR 28/514, ORB, Manston, AIR27/2103, ORB 609 Sqn, AIR27/1551/255, Report on Ops from Manston, AIR25/206, 11 Gp IB No 346, AIR25/206, 11 Gp Synopsis and RAFML: B1778, A Flt Diary.
347. TNA: AIR28/888 ORB, Warmwell, AIR28/514, ORB, Manston and RAFML: B1778, A Flt Diary.
348. TNA: AIR28/888 ORB, Warmwell, AIR27/1551/257 and 259, Surfat Reports and AIR27/1551/256, Warmwell Composite Report.
349. TNA: AIR27/1551/262, Composite Night Intruder Report, AIR27/1551/263-265, Final Report, Night Ranger Operations, AIR28/261, ORB, Exeter, AIR27/1553, ORB, 264 Sqn and AIR25/182, ORB, 10 Gp.
350. TNA: AIR27/1551/267, Composite Ramrod 85, AIR28/261, ORB, Exeter, AIR28/888 ORB, Warmwell and RAFML: B1778, A Flt Diary.
351. TNA: AIR28/888 ORB, Warmwell, AIR27/1551/269, Ramrod from Predannack and RAFML: B1778, A Flt Diary.
352. TNA: AIR27/1551/272-278, Composite/Surfat Reports. RAFML: B1778, A Flt

Diary and MFC77/16/80, Accident Record Card, P7047.

353. TNA: AIR28/888 ORB, Warmwell, AIR27/1551/285-290, Composite/Surfat Reports, Night Ranger and RAFML: B1778, A Flt Diary.

354. TNA: AIR28/888 ORB, Warmwell, AIR27/1551/292-293, Composite Rhubarb Reports and RAFML: B1778, A Flt Diary.

355. TNA: AIR28/888 ORB, Warmwell.

356. TNA: AIR28/888 ORB, Warmwell.

357. TNA: AIR28/261, ORB, Exeter, AIR28/888, ORB, Warmwell, AIR25/186, 10 Gp 'Attacks on the Münsterland moving up Channel from Brest to Cherbourg', AIR27/1551/297-301, Draft Report, Roadstead 77 and RAFML: B1778, A Flt Diary.

358. TNA: AIR28/261, ORB, Exeter, AIR28/888 ORB, Warmwell, AIR25/186, 10 Gp Report, Ramrod 96, AIR2/1551/302, Composite Report and RAFML: B1778, A Flt Diary.

359. TNA: AIR28/261, ORB, Exeter, AIR28/888 ORB, Warmwell, AIR27/1551/303, Report Ramrod 99 and RAFML: B1778, A Flt Diary.

360. TNA: WO208/3316 and WO208/5582, MI9 Debrief Statement and Appendix C, Flt Sgt G. A. Wood.

361. TNA: AIR27/1551/314, Report No. 2, Warmwell.

362. RAFML: B1778, A Flt Diary and TNA: AIR27/1551/315, Surfat Report, Roadstead 78.

363. TNA: AIR28/888 ORB, Warmwell, AIR27/1551/318, Surfat Report, Warmwell (Sturgeon), AIR27/1551/320, Shipping Reconnaissance Report, Hurn and AIR27/1551/321, Surfat Report (Baker).

364. TNA: AIR28/888 ORB, Warmwell and AIR27/1551/327, Night Surfat Report, Warmwell.

365. RAFML: B1778, A Flt Diary.

366. TNA: AIR25/182, ORB, 10 Gp Organisation Circular No. 86/Org/1943.

367. TNA: AIR28/888 ORB, Warmwell, AIR27/1551/333, Report Ramrod 106 Pt. 2 and RAFML: B1778, A Flt Diary.

368. TNA: AIR27/1551/335, Report Ramrod 108.

369. TNA: AIR28/888 ORB, Warmwell, AIR27/1551/337, Report Ramrod 109 and RAFML: B1778, A Flt Diary.

370. TNA: AIR28/888 ORB, Warmwell and AIR25/182, ORB 10 Gp.

371. RAFML: B1778, A Flt Diary.

372. RAFML: B1778, A Flt Diary.

373. TNA: AIR2/2821, DDO(A) Obsolescence Notice, 01/01/44.

Appendix 1: Operational Requirement F.37/35

374. Deleted in the final specification.

375. Included in error and deleted in a correction issued 04/04/36.

376. Relaxed to 'not less than 5°' in the final specification.

377. Typo. Given correctly as 'most forward' in the final specification.

Appendix 2: The Whirlwind Uncovered

378. *Flight*, 03/05/28.

379. TNA: AIR 10/1545, DTD Progress Report, Qtr. Ending April 1937.